# Peasants, Landlords and Merchant Capitalists

## Europe and the World Economy, 1500–1800

D0023651

# Peasants, Landlords and Merchant Capitalists

Europe and the World Economy, 1500–1800

PETER KRIEDTE

CAMBRIDGE UNIVERSITY PRESS

Cambridge

London   New York   New Rochelle

Melbourne   Sydney

Published by the Press Syndicate of the University of Cambridge
32 East 57th Street, New York, NY 10022, USA
296 Beaconsfield Parade, Middle Park, Melbourne 3206, Australia

Originally published in German as *Spätfeudalismus und Handelskapital.
Grundlinien der europäischen Wirtschaftsgeschichte vom 16. bis zum
Ausgang des 18. Jahrhunderts* by Vandenhoeck & Ruprecht, Göttingen, 1980
and © Vandenhoeck & Ruprecht, 1980
Translated into English by V. R. Berghahn
First published in English 1983
English translation © Berg Publishers Ltd 1983

Printed in Great Britain by Billing & Sons, Ltd, Worcester

Library of Congress catalogue card number: 83-5141

ISBN 0 521 25755 7 hard covers
ISBN 0 521 27681 0 paperback

# Contents

Introduction

1     THE AGE OF THE PRICE REVOLUTION

1.1   The Growth of the Population
1.2   The Expansion of Agriculture
1.3   Crafts, Commerce and Finance
1.4   The Price Revolution and Socio-Economic Change

2     THE CRISIS OF THE 17TH CENTURY

2.1   Stagnation and the Demographic Crisis
2.2   Agriculture: Crisis and Resurgence
2.3   Proto-Industrialization and Merchant Capitalism
2.4   The Crisis of the 17th Century in its Socio-Economic Context

3     THE UPSWING OF THE 18TH CENTURY

3.1   Population: From Crisis to Renewed Growth
3.2   Agriculture: Expansion or Revolution?
3.3   On the Road to Industrial Capitalism
3.4   Population Growth, Economic Growth and Society

Conclusion

Annotated Bibliography

Sources for Tables and Graphs

Index

# Introduction

The development of the European economy entered a new phase around the turn of the 15th to the 16th century. The crisis of the late middle ages had come to pass; the price revolution of the 16th century appeared on the horizon. The discovery of America and the exploration of the sea route to India created the preconditions of European overseas expansion and of the emergence of a capitalist world-system whose structures were characterized by unequal exchange relations and their maintenance by the open or covert use of force. Notwithstanding these developments which pointed to the future, the economic system as a whole continued to be dominated by the feudal mode of production. The dynamism of merchant capital, to be sure, was not exclusively determined by the feudal system; but it did remain within a framework which was defined by it; it operated in the 'skin' of feudal society without being able to challenge it.

To speak of the 'feudal mode of production' around 1500 implies a dominance of a peasant economy organized on a family basis; it also means that the class of feudal lords appropriated to itself large parts of the agricultural wealth which the peasant economy was generating.

The peasant family was the basic unit of production. It tended to be composed of the two parents and their children. The nuclear family was the general rule. Families which united the father and/or mother of the peasant under the same roof with his own family (three-generation families) remained relatively rare. The labour potential of the nuclear family would occasionally be supplemented by non-familial labour, depending on the family's generational cycle as well as on whether it was able to produce above subsistence level. If a peasant couple had children who were too small to work, they often had no choice but to employ outside labour. The land which had passed into their hands by inheritance constituted the production factor which determined the entire existence of the peasant family. The crop grown on this land tended to be grain which imposed its own specific seasonal rhythm. Stock-farming formed an important supplement to agriculture. Animals were not only used for ploughing, but also provided valuable fertilizer.

1

The purposes of this type of peasant-family production were quite limited. The peasant tried to strike a balance between the labour potential of his family on the one hand, and on the other its own culturally determined needs as well as obligations towards other persons and institutions. If this balance became upset, he had to attempt to redress it by increasing the family's labour input; this could reach the dimensions of 'self-exploitation' (A.V. Chayanov). In short, the objective of the peasant's economic activity was to produce not the exchange value but the utility value (*Gebrauchswert*) of what he was producing.

Until the high middle ages the estates of the landlord, worked with the help of serf labour, had been the central unit of the agrarian economy. It had subsequently become replaced by the peasant community which functioned as a coordinating centre between the peasant households within the individual village. The community also acted as a bulwark against outside intervention, above all by the feudal lord; it was finally a framework which enabled its members to keep control over internal differentiations and to maintain the existing social equilibrium. Of course, the community could fulfil these functions only if it was endowed with strong coercive powers.

The landlords had largely retreated from the production process from the high middle ages onwards. Wherever they managed their own estates, they did so with the help of wage labour. There were two reasons for this development: the large units of the lords were less productive than the peasant holdings—a direct result of the contemporary level of agricultural technology and of social mechanisms which forced the peasant to make more strenuous efforts. This weakness of the demesnes was exacerbated by a shift in the balance of class forces which forced the feudal lords to abandon the system of serf labour. In other words, they had to give up the system of labour on which their own agricultural production had once been based. Thenceforth the landlord appropriated the surplus of peasant production to himself primarily in the form of dues in money and kind, whereas feudal services rendered in the form of labour declined in importance. The peasant was now fully in control of his own labour. The economic relationship between him and the landlord was limited to 'transfer payments'. All three types of feudal dues were characterized by what E. Balibar has called the 'non-coincidence' of production and appropriation; the two processes had become separated from one another. In view of this, the feudal lord had to resort to means of violence of a non-economic nature in order to enforce his claims upon the peasant's surplus production.

The dynamics of the feudal mode of production—initially less concerned with modification and transformation than with mere reproduction as they were—can be traced through the long-term ups and downs of the agricultural economy of Europe. The available series of grain prices and other data, above all the figures relating to demographic change, demonstrate that the upswing of the high middle ages, which was accompanied by a migration movement and the emergence of the towns, ended in the crisis of the 14th and 15th centuries. There followed the price revolution of the 16th century which in turn led to the crisis of the 17th century. It was only the upswing of the 18th century which ushered in a new age (see Table 1 and Figure 1, the latter from 1500 only). The causes of this sequence of booms and depressions in the European economy may be explained in three ways.

(1) First of all there tended to exist a positive interaction between population growth and economic growth during a long-term

*Table 1:*

Population change in Europe, 1500-1800 (mill.)

| | 1500 abs. | Index | 1600 abs. | Index | 1700 abs. | Index | 1800 abs. | Index |
|---|---|---|---|---|---|---|---|---|
| Northern Europe[1] | 1.6 | 100 | 2.6 | 163 | 3.1 | 194 | 5.0 | 313 |
| Northwestern Europe[2] | 6.3 | 100 | 9.7 | 154 | 12.7 | 202 | 21.2 | 337 |
| Western Europe[3] | 17.0 | 100 | 17.9 | 105 | 20.8 | 122 | 27.9 | 164 |
| Southern Europe[4] | 16.4 | 100 | 21.7 | 132 | 21.7 | 132 | 31.3 | 191 |
| Central Europe[5] | 18.5 | 100 | 24.0 | 130 | 24.5 | 132 | 33.5 | 181 |
| Total | 59.8 | 100 | 75.9 | 127 | 82.8 | 138 | 118.9 | 199 |
| Eastern Europe[6] | 12 | 100 | 15 | 125 | 20 | 167 | 36 | 300 |
| Southeastern Europe[7] | 9.1 | 100 | 11.2 | 123 | 12.2 | 134 | 20.8 | 229 |
| Total | 21.1 | 100 | 26.2 | 124 | 32.2 | 153 | 56.8 | 269 |
| European total | 80.9 | 100 | 102.1 | 126 | 115.0 | 142 | 175.7 | 217 |

[1]Denmark, Norway, Sweden, Finland; [2]British Isles, Netherlands, Belgium; [3]France; [4]Portugal, Spain, Italy; [5]Germany, Switzerland, Austria, Poland, Czech parts of Czechoslovakia; [6]Russia (European parts); [7]Slovakia, Hungary, Rumania, Balkan countries (respective present-day frontiers).

*Figure 1:*
Grain prices in England, France and Germany, 1501–1810,
in grams of silver per Doppelzentner (ca. two hundredweight;
moving ten-year averages)

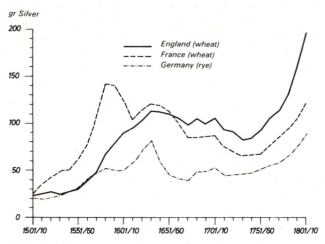

upswing which stimulated the development of the productive potential of the economy. But sooner or later this linkage turned into a boomerang. If population growth and economic growth had mutually accelerated each other, the latter began to lag in comparison to demographic change. Population growth made its adjustment to economic growth too late, if at all. There were more people than agricultural production could sustain. The peasants began to plough up land of inferior quality which had hitherto been used for grazing Livestock declined and manure became scarcer. The balance between grain-growing and stock-rearing, which had been of crucial importance to soil fertility, was being destroyed. The law of diminishing agricultural returns came into force. Productivity per head decreased. There were innumerable small-holdings, whose owners lived on the starvation line. If the harvest was poor, they would actually starve in large numbers.

(2) The above-mentioned changes in the sphere of production forces were bound to affect production relations in general. This separation of the production process from the appropriation process which had now become typical of the feudal mode of production implied that the share of the feudal lords in the agricultural product tended to decline in the course of this long-term historical

development. And the sharper the tensions within the productive system of the economy, the higher the rise in agricultural prices. At the same time the rent which the peasants were obliged to pay in cash remained unchanged. Hitherto the decline in feudal income had been more or less compensated for by an extension of the land which was subject to rent. Yet this compensatory mechanism disappeared, once land development had begun to slow down. Wherever possible the feudal lords tried to prevent a fall in their income by raising the level of rents. They did this through a manipulation of the basis on which it was calculated. They would demand entry fines; they might retake land in order to re-lease it; they would expand their demesnes and work them with the help of serf labour; or, finally, they would exploit their monopoly rights.

The peasants thus found themselves in a double squeeze. Their margin of subsistence was shrinking, while the pressure exerted by the lords mounted. The potentialities for a crisis accumulated until they finally exploded in a series of food crises. In a narrow sense such food crises were the result of crop failure, and these were in turn manifestations of metereological conditions during the harvest cycle (see, e.g. Figure 2). What made the weather factor so serious was the underdeveloped state of agricultural production. This is why Pierre Vilar has called the harvest cycle the 'original cycle of the feudal mode of production'. If one now considers its repercussions as reflected in mortality rates, it becomes clear that the long-term cycle was more important than the short-term one. One harvest failure at the beginning of a long-term cycle was not yet the last straw. But a

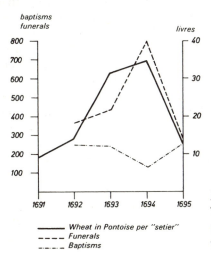

*Figure 2:*
The famine of 1693/94 in the Meulan region (north-west of Paris)

——— Wheat in Pontoise per "setier"
– – – – Funerals
–·–·– Baptisms

subsistence crisis was the more serious, the more the long-term impoverishment of the peasants had progressed and the pressure of feudal charges had increased. Thus the long-term cycle tended to dominate the short-term one without being able to determine its course completely. What ultimately caused a reversal of the long-term trend was a series of major subsistence crises, often in quick succession, which were in themselves the result of that trend.

The population decline which set in with the above-mentioned food crises exacerbated the already difficult income situation of the feudal nobility. The death of every rent-paying peasant was tantamount to a further reduction in rents. This was true not only in terms of absolute figures, but also in terms of the proportions exacted as feudal dues. As the demand for peasant holdings declined, those peasants that were left were able to negotiate better terms; the feudal lords saw the slices which they were accustomed to taking shrink relatively as well as absolutely. They were under pressure to look for alternative ways of maintaining their economic position.

Among these alternatives there was war as a means of bringing about a redistribution of incomes by military force; there was also the acquisition of offices. This implies that the state, whose autonomy *vis-à-vis* the feudal lords was but limited, began to appear as a factor on the historical stage. The crisis had undermined the old system of appropriation of which the state had been a beneficiary. Yet the attempt not merely to maintain the income of the feudal lords, but to increase it, dealt a fatal blow to the peasant economy. The immediate drain resulting from wars and the intolerable fiscal burdens destroyed the peasant's reproductive capacity. These developments exacerbated the crisis which finally culminated in a contraction of the economy which could not be halted. If an end to the downhill slide at last came into sight, it was because its impact began to mobilise forces which made it possible for the peasant economy to regain a new equilibrium: once the population had declined, the size of the holdings increased again; marginal land of poor quality ceased to be cultivated. Both developments contributed to a marked increase in productivity. A new growth cycle could set in.

(3) Population change occupied a key position in this model which we have derived from our analysis of the feudal mode of production. The factor at the root of this change—i.e. the shifting ratio between population and resources on the one hand and the mechanisms of feudal exploitation on the other—cannot always provide a satisfactory explanation, however. Population growth was also blocked and reversed by developments which were extraneous to the

feudal mode of production. Among these factors three are of particular importance: epidemics, wars and the role of the state of the early modern period. All three have already been alluded to in sections (1) and (2) above; yet it would be wrong to assume that they can always or wholly be related to the prevailing system of production. True, the demographic catastrophe which was unleashed by the plague of 1348 could probably not be fully explained without the impoverishment which affected large parts of Europe's population. On the other hand, the plague was also an exogeneous phenomenon, a product of that *'unification microbienne du monde'* (E. Le Roy Ladurie) resulting from the Oriental trade through which the disease was carried to Europe.

The same applies to the wars which the emergent national states conducted and to the pressures which they imposed on the peasants to finance them. Neither was always inseparably connected with the decline in feudal income. On the contrary, there is some reason to assume that the interconnections which have been made in this chapter became less strong, and the more so since the state machineries succeeded in increasing their autonomy *vis-à-vis* the feudal lords. In short, it would be wrong to underestimate the impact of forces upon the historical process which, if at all, can be derived from the feudal economy only in a very general sense.

If the long-term upswings of the European economy were twice interrupted by extended crises, this was due to the causes set out above. They were responsible that the dynamics of feudalism never went beyond the long waves of upswings and crises, which acted to perpetuate the feudal mode of production. These ups and downs ultimately generated a new balance between population and available resources; they also redefined the relationships between divergent social groups.

Side by side with the agricultural economy there arose in the towns which had grown up in the high middle ages a specialized sector engaged in the manufacture of goods on an artisanal basis. The 'autarkic division of labour' (K. Modzelewski) which had hitherto existed in feudal agriculture gradually gave way to a division of labour between town and country. Agricultural production continued in the countryside; the production of manufactured goods moved to the towns. Of course, this division was by no means universal. The peasants continued to manufacture goods for their own consumption. Nor was it possible to dispense altogether with certain craftsmen such as blacksmiths. Mining and iron production were likewise tied to the countryside. The demographic and agricultural surplus of the surrounding countryside was crucial for the emergence and growth of the towns as well as for the division of labour between town and country. Only if there was a demographic surplus on which they could feed were towns able to grow. This is also true of later urban development, even if it is erroneous to assume that the towns could not have maintained their size without an influx of people from the countryside. The agricultural surplus was even more vital. It would have been impossible for the towns to develop into a dense network without an agricultural revolution which improved agriculture's productivity. The surplus of dozens of villages was required in order to secure the food supply of even smaller towns. Thus the growth of the towns and of the artisanal economy were directly dependent upon the contributions by the agricultural sector of the economy.

The basic unit of production in the urban centres was again the family. However, women and children were as a rule not engaged in the production process. The wife's role tended to be limited to the household; the husband was in charge of the workshop. In addition, there were the journeymen and apprentices. With a few exceptions like the building trade, they lived under the master's roof and were also maintained by him. They were fully integrated into the household and were under the master's disciplinary authority. It was this relationship rather than a labour-capital tie which defined the position of these dependants.

The small urban craftsmen manufactured utility values, not exchange values. He aimed to produce enough to be able to acquire foodstuffs and other things commensurate with his social rank; he did not aim to generate a surplus in order to produce larger quantities of goods for a subsequent cycle.

What he produced was highly labour-intensive and not capital-intensive. The tools were simple and tailored to the needs of a craftsman who had acquired the skill of using them through an apprenticeship under the guidance of another worker. In this sense there existed a close link between the worker and the means of production. Accordingly there was no division of labour in the workshops. Only one craftsman handled a product from start to finish. But there was a professional division which often reached extreme forms. As early as 1300, there existed in Paris more than 300 handicrafts. More than 200 different handicrafts have been found to have been practised in Frankfurt in the 14th and 15th centuries. Thus the carpenters were divided into joiner, turners, tub-makers, coopers, mill-wrights and wheel-wrights. This professional fragmentation was a result of the lack of a division of labour in the workshop. Rarely was an individual craftsman so skilled as to be able to produce different goods of consistently high quality.

The individual craftsmen were organized in guilds. As compulsory associations, they fulfilled two roles: they were concerned with 'the internal regulation of labour and external monopoly' (Max Weber). Both functions were intimately intertwined and were designed to secure the livelihood of the guild members. For this reason, the guilds fixed production quotas and supply; they restricted price and quality competition among the members; they delayed the introduction of new products and technologies; they limited access to the market and tried to operate as monopolists in the raw materials and finished goods markets. The idea was to safeguard equality of the terms of production among the associates, to block differentiation and to prevent the formation of what Weber has called 'capital leverage' *(Kapitalsmacht)*. The economic policies of the guilds were not totally inimical to growth. Yet whenever economic growth and social equilibrium came into conflict, the guilds would opt in favour of the latter principle.

The towns were both centres of the production of manufactured goods and market places. They hence formed not merely the one of the two pillars of a town-and-country division of labour that had developed since the high middle ages; they were also the point where economic transactions took place. The town was therefore charged with the task to coordinate and organize a trading economy based on the division of labour. Merchants assumed these functions with the exception of those cases where the producer was able to sell directly to the consumer. The merchants mediated between those two sides and tried to make a profit by selling goods at a higher price than they had purchased them. Once this cycle of exchange had been completed, it made sense to continue it on a larger scale and thus to accumulate capital. This kind of economic behaviour was all the more attractive to the merchant as an expansion of his business promised economies of scale, thanks to reduced overheads per unit. The utility value, the creation of which had guided the producers' economic activity, lost its earlier significance. As A. Genovesi observed in 1765, 'although the merchant likes the profits already made, his sights are nevertheless invariably fixed on future profits'. Thus the sphere of the circulation of goods rather than the sphere of production came to gain supremacy. The deployment and accumulation of commercial capital became the decisive stimuli in the development of the non-agricultural economy until the onset of industrialization.

There are a number of reasons for this. For one, the productivity of the craft shops was too low and lacking a potential for development to enable the artisans to make larger profits. The guilds also did their best to prevent an evolution towards capitalism. If there were any potentialities for increased production and hence increased profits, they existed at the level of the inter-regional and international division of labour. So long as these markets lacked transparency and there were no generally accepted standards of value, it was in this field that large profits could be reaped.

The ways in which the merchants accumulated capital did display capitalist features quite early on. But they were even more deeply moulded by the conditions which were set by the prevailing feudal system. Towns and merchant capital found themselves in a relationship of 'internal externality' *vis-à-vis* the feudal mode of production, as J. Merrington has put it. However dynamic the merchants may have been, there was no denying the fact that their activities were based, directly or indirectly, on the rents which the landlords—the 'productive class' in F. Quesnay's words—were able to raise. In this sense the relationship which the merchant capitalist established with production was similar to that of the feudal lords. The merchants established fields of activity for which they obtained sanction from the feudal authorities in the form of monopolies and privileges. The frequently observed tendency of merchant capital to 'refeudalize' itself neatly conforms with this development. One merchant family after the other turned its back on trade and commerce and acquired an estate in the countryside. Merchant capital became landed capital. Capitalist ground rent and the system of feudal rents became inextricably intermeshed.

The dynamics of craft production and commerce tended, more or less, to follow the movements of the agricultural sector; but it was not an identical development. Except for the trade in agricultural produce, the non-agricultural sector of the European economy was less affected by the long-term upswings and crises which have been discussed above. The price movement of manufactured goods tended to undulate with that of basic foodstuffs; but the vacillations were far less marked. By and large the former lagged behind the latter in periods of boom. On the other hand, non-agricultural prices were liable to drop less sharply than agricultural ones in times of depression. There were two reasons for this: (1) Unlike food production and exceptions apart, the production of manufactured goods is not subject to the law of diminishing returns. (2) Demand for manufactured goods is, again unlike that for basic foodstuffs, dependent on disposable incomes and hence elastic.

At first glance the short-term cycle appears to be more important for the development of the non-agricultural economy than the long-term waves. As soon as grain prices were pushed up in the wake of a bad harvest, demand inevitably focused on the agricultural sector in order to provide for basic needs. Demand for manufactured products declined. Thus an 'agricultural underproduction crisis' (E. Labrousse) unleashed an underconsumption crisis in the manu-facturing sector. What made short-term crises of the traditional type so significant for this sector was that all long-term calculations involved a considerable risk. This in turn reinforced the merchants in their proclivity to keep away from the production sphere altogether. However, the question of short-term or long-term cycles quickly turns out to be a fallacious one. As we have seen above, both were closely related. And finally the repercussions of the agricultural crises upon the manufacturing and commercial sector add force to the argument that it was, its relative autonomy notwithstanding, still tied to the feudal system as a whole (see Figure 3).

It was only around 1500 that the capacity for change inherent in the feudal system and its manufacturing and commercial appendices became visible to some small degree. But before this potential is examined, it is important to be aware of the obstacles which socio-economic change was likely to encounter. The peasant community

*Figure 3:*
### Index of the underproduction crisis in manufacturing at Lille in 1662/63
(1666/70 = 100)

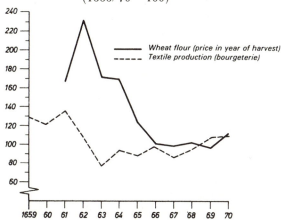

and the guilds were centres of this resistence. Both were forms of organizations which the small agricultural producers and artisans had created in order to arm themselves against outside intervention, especially on the part of the feudal lords and the merchants. The two organizations were also designed to prevent a destruction of the existing internal socio-economic equilibrium as a result of the infiltration of capitalist modes of production; this is why the members had subjected themselves to firm regulations and had allowed their freedom of movement to be curtailed. The impact of the feudal system was ambivalent. It left the peasant in control of the labour process; but the path of agricultural progress was blocked as long as the landlords appropriated to themselves a large part of the production and as long as the community insisted on the maintenance of existing collectivist ties to the soil. On the other hand, it is true that feudal dues and state taxes pushed the peasant into producing for the market and thus increased the economic contribution of the agricultural sector. In this way the pressures of exploitation could equally well act as a stimulus to the commercialization of agriculture.

It is not possible to explain the crisis of the' urban export trade purely in terms of the economic depression and external factors, like wars. Rather it must be seen in connection with the promotion, by the merchant capitalists, of manufacturing in the countryside and the mobilization of the underemployed rural labour force for this purpose. Two factors, above all, induced the merchants to adopt this strategy: Firstly, at a time when wages in the towns were, broadly speaking, moving upwards, it seemed logical to shift production to the countryside where wages were considerably lower. In the vicinity of Amiens, for example, they are supposed to have been 50% to 73% below the rates paid in the town itself. This discrepancy was due to the fact that the small rural producers were without protection against the *diktat* of the merchants. They did not have the backing of a guild, and sheer desperation forced them to accept the terms imposed upon them. Up to a point, families engaged in the rural cottage industries were able to survive on relatively low wages because many of them owned a plot of land, at least during the early phase, and were able to grow some food for self-provision. Moreover, unlike the artisans who belonged to a guild, they could rely on all members of the family to collaborate. Thus the Town Clerk of Bielefeld by the name of Consbruch wrote about the linen weavers of the Ravensberg region in 1794 that 'most of them live on their own produce and this enables them, in view of the lower cost of living in the countryside, to make more attractive goods and to sell them at a lower price than the weavers in the towns. This is why few people in the towns can be persuaded to take up weaving and why the location and expansion of the craft in the countryside is, in all respects, extremely advantageous.' The merchant capitalist who put out this work was therefore able to pocket a differential profit, at least for as long as the new system had not yet generally established itself.

The second reason for the move of manufacturing to the countryside was the insufficient flexibility with which the urban economies responded to demand. Indeed in many cases it was a deliberate policy of the guilds to keep supplies limited. The result was that the urban manufacturers were unable to keep pace with rising demand. This demand expanded particularly rapidly in the international markets and above all those of the colonial world which, in the age of a 'new colonialism' (E. J. Hobsbawm), assumed increasing importance for European manufactured goods. In regions where urban production had been badly affected by the ravages of war, merchant capitalists felt an even greater compulsion to exploit the industrial potential of the countryside. In Silesia, for example, where in 1618 there existed in all probability more looms in the countryside than in the towns, urban weavers, with a few exceptions, had their trade ruined by the Thirty Years' War. By 1648 some 81% of all Silesian looms were located in the countryside. The rise of rural linen production was steep also along the West coast of France. In 1686, the town of Cadiz received linen worth 3,750,000 livres; it was known as *bretañas* produced to the south-west of St. Malo in Brittany. About 90% of this linen was for the American market.

The reproductive behaviour specific to those engaged in these cottage industries and the supra-regional character of the markets for their products, often reaching out far into the colonial world, determined the growth of these 'proto-industrial' areas, as they are now being called. The families were able to guarantee the elastic supply of labour which proto-industrialization as a dynamically expansionist system required. The world market which was slowly coming into existence acted as the engine of proto-industrial growth. Given the conditions of the time there was only one way of transcending the limitations of the domestic markets and to increase demand: through the 'appropriation of foreign purchasing power' (W. Hoffmann). One of the key features of the proto-industrial system was that labour costs were being 'externalized', i.e. the merchant capitalists took over no more than a fraction of the labour costs and off-loaded most of them on to the rural sector. A pre-capitalist peasant society was thus incorporated into the reproduction and accumulation machinery of merchant capitalism.

What kind of tremendous opportunities lay dormant in the expansion of rural manufacturing, may be discovered if the development of England is compared with that of the northern parts of the Netherlands. The countryside had been the preferred location of English textile manufacturing since the late middle ages. Consequently there was little room here for a conflict between town and country to become a factor in urban crisis in the 17th century. However, the concentration of rural industries in regions which had specialized in stock-rearing and dairy farming as well as the decline of the old draperies and the rise of the new draperies constituted crisis elements; for a number of regions failed to make the transition from heavy cloths to new draperies.

As far as the manufacturing and commercial sphere is concerned, everything hinged on how the merchant capitalists responded to varying demand and what attitude they took *vis-à-vis* the production sphere. If they were content to market those goods which were produced by the artisans in the towns, no great changes were to be expected. The production sphere and the circulation of goods remained separate. The circulation sphere was preponderant only in a formal way. Changes occurred, however, once the merchants were no longer prepared to acquiesce in the production monopoly established by the guilds and tried to break or circumvent it. It was difficult to break it because any attempt to build up production associations which were independent of the guilds encountered the fierce resistance of the established associations. Notwithstanding the successes which the merchant capitalists had, for example, in the Italian cities of the late middle ages, often there was no alternative but to move production to the countryside or to small village-type towns where there were no guilds.

Two developments favoured this solution. We have seen how accumulation and population growth created a stratum of agricultural producers with little or no land who were dependent on a subsidiary source of income. It was on these people that the merchants were able to rely, if they opted for building up production centres in the countryside. Especially in linen and cloth manufacture they were able to link up with the traditional rural production of goods for home consumption. These small rural artisans continued to produce utility values, but, unlike their counterparts in the urban guilds, they were now subject to the whims of the merchants. It was the latter (rather than the guild) who dictated the terms. And once merchant capital had freed the production of goods from the shackles of the guild system, there were few obstacles to further expansion, at least for the time being.

These developments, which took place in the fold of the feudal system and were to undermine it in the long run, were barely discernible at the turn of the 15th to the 16th century. Nevertheless, with the benefit of hindsight, it seems clear that the two trends which affected the agricultural sector, on the one hand, and the manufacturing-commercial sector on the other, were intimately connected. Areas of concentrated rural manufacture could develop and grow only if the surrounding region supplied them with foodstuffs. These regions generated an essential part of the demand for the manufactured goods produced in such zones. Specialization in one region was predicated on the specialization of the other region. It was only in the course of this process that the markets expanded geographically. Households which hitherto had been involved in both agricultural and non-agricultural production, concentrated on the one or the other, and by doing so they generated a demand for goods which they had stopped producing.

Specialization increased agricultural productivity. The vagaries of the seasonal harvest cycle diminished. A growing economic inter-dependence made it possible to balance harvest failures in one region by using the surpluses of another. Short-term crises of the traditional type lost much of their devastating impact. Demand on the domestic market did not only grow, but it also became less volatile. And finally there was growing demand from overseas. This became an important factor once the metropolitan countries of Europe had established their formal or informal domination over the extra-European world and had integrated it into their economies. The stimulus which was provided by both domestic and overseas demand furthered manufacturing in early modern Europe.

More important than the sheer quantitative growth were the social changes that resulted from these developments. In the regions with concentrated manufacture traditional feudal dependencies became overlain by new relationships, which were, in embryo, capitalist; the structures of a society beyond feudalism began to assume shape.

The emergent state machines were to play an extremely important role in this process of socio-economic transformation. Taxes supplemented, but also competed against feudal dues. Above all, taxes increased so drastically over time that they began to outpace the latter, thereby restricting the landlords' freedom of manoeuvre. At first there emerged a 'centralized feudalism' (G. Bois) which did not replace, but supplemented the original type of feudalism. Its essential feature was that it redistributed to the feudal lords the revenue which had flowed into the state's coffers. But soon the state developed a more ambiguous role, trying, as it were, to satisfy two claims upon it at once, i.e. the maintenance of feudal domination and the stimulation of economic growth. Ultimately the state became a mirror of several modes of production which existed side-by-side. Its relative autonomy was strengthened, and the discrepancy between its own fiscal system and that of feudalism became more marked. Its role as the steering centre of a 'centralized feudalism' receded into the background.

The state alone, owing to its monopoly of violence which it claimed and slowly succeeded in asserting, was in a position to impose wage labour conditions upon the production sphere, institutionally to guarantee the freedom of exchange of goods in the commercial sphere and, finally, to formalize the legal framework without which the nascent capitalist society would not have been able to exist. Also, by expanding the transport infrastructure, it promoted the general conditions required in an economy which produced goods for the market.

Generally speaking, particularist forces remained strong enough, however, to prevent centralization from becoming overpowering and to keep the state bureaucracies from arresting the socio-economic change which had begun. The decentralized and fragmented structures of exploitation typical of European feudalism exerted such a lasting influence on the fibre of European society that it provided a new and secure basis for the rapidly expanding non-agricultural sector. In this decentralized nature, European feudalism differed fundamentally from the Asiatic mode of production and laid the decisive structural foundations for the rise of Europe.

There is no doubt that this process which finally ended in the Industrial Revolution was a violent one. The burden of dues, which the peasants had to pay to the landlords and to the state, forced them to seek access to the market and to reinforce their production for the market. If the land which they had at their disposal became too small, they would try either to work as wage labourers for wealthier peasants or on the estates of the landlords; or they would try to supplement their income in the rural cottage industries. If they opted for the latter alternative, they would throw themselves into the arms of the merchant capitalists. This 'enfored commercialization' (W. Kula) was not infrequently followed by the disintegration of the rural community as a local point of reference. The socio-economic process assumed its most violent forms in the serf labour of the peasants on the *Vorwerke* of Eastern and East-Central Europe, on the one hand, and on the slave labour plantations of Central and South America, on the other. Elsewhere the fragmented structures of exploitation left possibilities of resistance open to the dependent sections of the population. Here they were able to prevent the economic pressures on them from becoming intolerable.

# 1. The Age of the Price Revolution

In the second half of the 15th century the long-drawn-out crisis of the late middle ages was followed by a period of long-term growth. The population grew, agriculture and manufacturing expanded; markets stretched far into overseas territories; the volume of trade and the circulation of money increased. At the same time prices saw a rise, in particular those for basic foodstuffs. Contemporaries were struck by this change. In his dispute with de Malestroit, Jean Bodin in 1568 traced the origins of the inflation to the silver imports from the Americas. Many scholars have been inclined to agree with him to this day. But the causes of the inflationary development are more likely to have deeper roots.

## 1.1 The Growth of the Population

The population of Europe increased slowly, though not un-interruptedly, from the second half of the 15th century. Its index rose from 100 to 127 in the western parts of Europe, with the figures for Eastern and South-Eastern Europe being too unreliable for quotation (see Table 1, p. 3). If, by using J.C. Russell's calculations, one takes 1450 as the starting point, the index figures would be 100 (1450), 155 (1500) and 195 (1700).

This would seem to indicate that population growth in the 16th century slowed down appreciably by comparison with the second half of the 15th century. And indeed, once the losses which had been inflicted by the plagues of the 14th and early 15th centuries had been made good, the tempo of demographic change decelerated. However, the global figures quoted above conceal the fact that the population grew more rapidly in some regions than in others. A slow growth occurred in Central, Western and Southern Europe with the index rising to 123; Northern and North-western Europe, on the other hand, saw a rapid expansion, with the index climbing as high as 156. The population of the Province of Holland grew particularly fast, reaching 328 index points in 1650, with 197 for the northern Low Countries as a whole. The discrepancies in growth between Southern Europe, on the one hand, and Northern and Northwestern Europe on the other, may be taken as one piece of indirect evidence that the former region was losing its leading economic position to the latter.

But what were the reasons for the overall growth? It is probable that control mechanisms existed in European society as early as the high middle ages which were designed to prevent the tensions between the rise of the population and the scarce resources of agriculture from becoming acute. The most important mechanisms which were at the disposal of both the landlords and the communities were: (1) To tie the permission to marry to the availability of a full-time occupation either in the form of a farm or a craftshop and, closely related to this, (2) to force those who did not meet this qualification (e.g. farm hands, maids, journeymen) to remain single.

The inevitable result of such policies were a late marriage age and a high percentage of bachelors and spinsters. As P. Chaunu has put it, the increased marriage age was in effect the 'contraceptive weapon of classical Europe'. For it is the marriage age of the women which decides whether her reproductive potential is fully available. Fertility in pre-industrial Europe was hence controlled via the marriage age and, in the second place, by the frequency of marriage. Birth control within marriage was initially without major importance and became a factor in various places only in the 17th century. Nobility and bourgeoisie appear to have led the way in this respect, even if exceptions have been found to exist among these groups, too.

Since there was plenty of unused land available around the middle of the 15th century, the above-mentioned checks on marriage could be relaxed. It appears that the marriage age was correspondingly lower. Thus, if the few references that have been found for France are reliable, it was by then between 21 and 22 years of age. It was slightly higher in England. The marriage age for women was also low among the English nobility and the bourgeoisie of Geneva (see Table 2). In view of this, the birth rate was also correspondingly higher, sometimes reaching a level which is to be found in the Third World today.

Population growth in the late 15th and 16th centuries does appear, however, to have been less a result of higher fertility than of a lower mortality rate. 'Positive checks', as Malthus was to call them in contradistinction to 'preventive checks', lost some of their efficacy once the economy picked up and the supply of the population with food improved. The link between the harvest cycle and the death rate became more tenuous. With the plague being on the retreat, 'autonomous' mortality which was purely biologically conditioned (J.D. Chambers) and unconnected with socio-economic factors appears to have changed. Still, the death toll among the population continued to be very high by present day standards. Of 1,000 newborn babies 200 would die before their first birthday, and in years of crisis this figure would rise to 300. Only two-thirds would live up to the age of 15. In 1561–1600, average life expectancy in Geneva was 23 years and less than 29 years among the city's bourgeoisie; around 1600 it was 26.6 years in the Venetian Terra Ferma, but about 43 years in Colyton in Southwest England (1538–1624; see also Table 2).

*Table 2:*

Selected demographic indicators for 16th-century Europe

|  | Colyton[1] 1538/99 | Terling[2] 1550/1624 | Bourgeoisie of Geneva 1550/99 | English High Aristocracy 1550/99 |
|---|---|---|---|---|
| Av. marriage age of women | 27.0 | 24.5 | 21.4 | 22.8 |
| Infant mortality per 1,000 (0-1 year) | 120–140 | 128 | – | 190 |
| Child mortality per 1,000 (1-14 years) | 124 | 149 | – | 94 |
| Child mortality per 1,000 (1-19 years) | – | – | 519 | – |
| Av. life expectancy | 40.6–45.8[3] | – | 28.5/9 | 37.0 |

[1]Village in Devon/England;   [2]Village in Essex/England;   [3]1538-1624

The population growth slowed down in the second half of the 16th century and in particular since the famine of the early 1570's. 'Preventive' as well as 'positive' checks now reduced the growth rate. People were forced to change their reproductive life. The marriage age rose again. But the adaptation to the deteriorating economic situation did not occur fast enough. The size of the population and available resources were still too far apart. Thus famines, epidemics and wars once again assumed the role of establishing a new equilibrium.

## 1.2 The Expansion of Agriculture

Extension and intensification of production had marked the agricultural crisis of the late middle ages which had succeeded the growth period of the high middle ages. This meant that, on the one hand, land which had been used for grain-growing was transformed into meadows and pastures. Grain production was restricted in favour of stock-farming; on the other hand, land was also taken into intensive cultivation for the production of wine, fruit and other marketable produce. The population decline of the late middle ages lay at the heart of both processes; for it was this decline which stimulated the production of foodstuffs that were not directly exposed to demographic change. The 16th century then saw a reversal of this earlier development under the pressure of a growing population: fields and pastures were again taken under the plough for grain production. If a rising number of people was to be fed, cereals offered a more economical way of mobilizing potential than livestock-rearing.

But this proved insufficient. New land had to be developed and, as the Zimmern Chronicle, dated ca. 1550, reports, forests were cleared and land claimed even in remote and mountainous regions. New regulations tried to stop the destruction of trees and shrubs. The reclaiming of land in swampy areas and the building of dykes were also widespread, most successfully on the North Sea coast. The average index for land reclamation per annum in the northern Low Countries rose from 100 in 1515–39 to 346 in 1540–64; it dropped to 75 in 1565–89 during the Wars of Independence, but moved back to 340 in 1590–1614 and even to a high 419 in the period 1615–39. Along the German North Sea coast it proved impossible to recover the enormous land losses of the late middle ages. Nevertheless, through the building of dykes some 48,000 hectares of land were reclaimed in the 16th century up to the beginning of the 1600s.

All in all the trend was towards extensive agriculture, and there was little intensive cultivation. This basic pattern did not prevail around towns or in areas of widespread urbanization as in the Po Valley in Italy and in the Netherlands. Nor did it apply to countries such as England where there existed favourable conditions for a commercialization of agriculture (for the development of seed-yield ratios see Table 3).

This was also the time when patterns of production developed in opposite directions in Western Europe, on the one hand, and Eastern and East-Central Europe, on the other. What in economic terms had long been a sliding scale, now became a contrast which was to be a distinguishing feature between East and West in subsequent centuries, with the River Elbe acting as the dividing line. At the one end of the scale, in England, we witness the beginning of a commercialized agriculture; at the other end, in the East, there

*Table 3:*

Average yield ratios of wheat, rye and barley in different parts
of Europe, 1500–1820 (multiples of seed)

| | England/ Netherlands | France/Spain Italy | Germany/ Switzerland/ Scandinavia | Russia/Poland Czechosl./ Hungary |
|---|---|---|---|---|
| 1500–49 | 7.4 | 6.7 | 4.0 | 3.9 |
| 1550–99 | 7.3 | – | 4.4 | 4.3 |
| 1600–49 | 6.7 | – | 4.5 | 4.0 |
| 1650–99 | 9.3 | 6.2 | 4.1 | 3.8 |
| 1700–49 | – | 6.3 | 4.1 | 3.5 |
| 1750–99 | 10.1 | 7.0 | 5.1 | 4.7 |
| 1800–20 | 11.1 | 6.2 | 5.4 | – |

occurred the refeudalization of agriculture with the transition to *Gutswirtschaft*. The River Elbe thus became the most significant socio-economic divide in Europe. East-Central Europe, as an exporter of grain and timber became economically dependent on Western Europe in a way that was not dissimilar to the more recent dependency of the suppliers of raw materials in the developing world on the industrial countries of the West.

The transformation of fields into pastures for sheep farming slowly came to a halt in England in the first half of the 16th century and under pressure from a growing and land-hungry population which protested against sheep that 'eat up and swallow down the very men themselves' (Th. More). This did not imply a return to a grain-growing monoculture, though. Rather grain production and stock-farming began mutually to complement each other. This was known as 'up-and-down husbandry', i.e. land was turned into pasture, to be ploughed up again at some later date. This technique improved the quality of the grassland; no less importantly, manure which would otherwise be lost on the common was absorbed to fertilize what would one day be taken under the plough again.

The introduction of 'up-and-down husbandry' was related to changes which were to affect the social structure of the village very profoundly. The technique could be established only if the land had either been 'enclosed' or 'put in severalty'. Wherever enclosure took place, the rights of other villagers to use this land, and grazing rights in particular, were abolished. The joint use which had been typical of the 'open field' economy came to an end. Enclosure was frequently preceded by a consolidation of farm-holdings which was to safeguard a more efficient use of the land. Thus hedges and fences became symbols of a new age, for everyone to see. They reflected the victory of 'agrarian individualism' (M. Bloch) over the collectivism which had been the key feature of the village economy. This traditional system with its joint land use had become an obstacle to the evolution of agriculture's productive forces and was hence destroyed. However, it would be wrong to exaggerate the extent of the enclosure movement of the 16th and early 17th century. Leicestershire, for example, which was relatively widely affected by it, saw no more than 10% of its agricultural land enclosed (see Table 4).

*Table 4:*
Enclosures in Leicestershire, 1450–1850

| Period | % of Cultivated land |
|---|---|
| 1450–1607 | 10 |
| 1608–1729 | 52 |
| 1730–1850 | 38 |
| | 100 |

Nor would it be correct to reduce the socio-economic pressures behind the enclosure movement simply to a discrepancy between production forces and production relations. The growth of the population had unleashed a wave of claims on common land and wasteland. There was a threat that this land might be withdrawn from common use, and landlords as well as yeomen tried to block this possibility by resorting to enclosure. Moreover, the population growth pushed up prices; increased demand created the pre-conditions for greater productivity and for establishing property titles which excluded the rights of other parties. A further decisive factor was that demand rose not only for cereals and vegetables, but also for wool which was required by the textile industry. This demand declined somewhat in the second half of the 16th century, when wheat prices trebled, but the price of wool no more than doubled between 1541–50 and 1601–10. In many ways it was less the demand for grain and—to a lesser extent—meat than the demand of the textile industry for wool which accelerated the pace of the commercialization of English agriculture. The wool trade became the pace-maker of capitalism in the countryside.

The landlords were the early protagonists of the enclosure movement. The price revolution had put them into a difficult

position: while prices were rising, their rent income remained
stagnant. A redistribution of agricultural income in favour of the
peasants was hence almost inevitable. The property rights of the
latter made an adjustment of feudal dues to the rising price levels in
many cases impossible. Wherever the landlords had a free hand, two
options were available to them: they could either try to increase rents
or resort to enclosure in order to lease the land again at a higher rent.
The advantage of the second option was that it was possible to
demand a larger sum for enclosed property. In the first half of the 16th
century the initiative for enclosure in Leicestershire came in about
70% of the cases from the landlords. But after the middle of the
century, the peasants themselves became active, once they had come to
see the benefits of enclosure. Thus market considerations began to
affect the behaviour of the hardcore of agrarian society in England.

On the European Continent, the tensions generated by population
growth tended to be sharper than in England, with the exception of
the Netherlands. The return to grain production assumed more
extreme proportions. On the other hand, the beginnings of
commercialization of agriculture were more modest. In France stock-
farming and intensive agriculture lost out. In the Languedoc in the
South pastures were ploughed up and grazing rights were restricted.
Livestock gave way to the production of cereals and vegetables.
Vineyards fell victim to this process in the Languedoc and Maine.
There were, to be sure, marked differences in the development of the
economic system in various regions. But there was a general trend
towards a leasing of land. In the Hurepoix region south of Paris, the
expropriation of the peasants had progressed so far by 1547–64 that
they had no more than about 40% of the land (see Table 5, based on
seven *seigneuries* only). The remaining 60% was shared between the
nobility and the bourgeoisie. The strong position of the latter was a

*Table 5:*

Distribution of landed property in 7 seigneurial districts in
the French Hurepoix region, 1547–64

|  | Hectares | % |
|---|---|---|
| Peasants | 2048.51 | 33.8 |
| Seigneurs (self-managing) | 1938.65 | 31.9 |
| Parisian bourgeoisie | 1416.27 | 23.3 |
| Local bourgeoisie | 355.71 | 5.9 |
| Others | 310.39 | 5.1 |
| Total | 6069,53 | 100,0 |

peculiarity which could be found in particular in the vicinity of cities. Generally speaking, it was the landlords who initiated the expropriation of the peasants, and for the same motives as their English counterparts. But it is typical of the relative backwardness of France *vis-à-vis* England that the landlords in the West and the South of the country resorted to '*métayage*', a system which generally left them with half the value of the net production. In this way, feudal and capitalist elements became inextricably intertwined.

Sixteenth-century Spain saw the growth of an opposition movement by agricultural interest groups against the *Mesta*, the national organization of sheep farmers whose flocks moved across the Iberian peninsula with the changing seasons. The *Mesta* had enjoyed the support of the monarchy for fiscal reasons, above all during the reign of Ferdinand II, Isabella and Charles V. But it had some difficulty in maintaining its priviledged position under Philip II. The rapid rise in demand for basic foodstuffs made it increasingly difficult to continue a policy which clearly favoured sheep farming against agriculture. The number of sheep held by the *Mesta*, which had reached a maximum of three million around 1520, declined after 1556 to about two million. But this reduction was still insufficient so that by the end of the century it was virtually impossible to supply the population of Spain with enough food.

Agriculture made great strides in Northern and Central Italy. It also expanded in the South and in Sicily, but growth was not of the intensive kind. The 'return of the Italians to agriculture' (R. Romano) had begun in the 15th century. Francesco Guicciardini relates with some pride that Italy was being cultivated up to her mountain tops. Considerable sums of capital reached the countryside from the towns. Land purchases of the Venetian oligarchy in the Terra Ferma region became so extensive that the income drawn from these investments rose four-fold between 1510 and 1588. But, like in Spain, the position of the peasants was liable to deteriorate, and quasi-feudal elements began to reappear in the highly commercialized Italian agricultural system.

In Germany west of the River Elbe agriculture once more became the dominant activity. Stock-farming experienced a marked decline and became a supplier of draught animals and fertiliser. Wine-growing expanded in the south-west; but it declined in other regions, especially in the north and east, where it had spread in the late middle ages. Although more land was made available for grain growing, productivity improved but marginally. There were exceptions to this rule, mainly in the vicinity of some towns, in the lower Rhine region and in Schleswig-Holstein. The latter area in North Germany saw the proliferation of a variant of up-and-down husbandry, known as *Koppelwirtschaft.*

The slow change in productivity was accompanied by an equally slow change of the production system. It was only in the Rhineland that short-term leases replaced the older forms of feudal rent on a larger scale. Generally speaking, the landlords did not extend the land which they kept under their own management. The system by which they extracted their income from the peasants remained feudal. The growth of territorial states in Central Europe meant that the landlords faced fresh competition for the allocation of their main source of revenue. The state was interested in preserving a dues-paying peasantry and hence resisted attempts by the landlords to extend their holdings. These tensions gave the peasants more breathing space which increased their chances of survival.

Agriculture reached its highest degree of intensification in the Netherlands in the 16th century. The old three-field system was replaced by new forms of agricultural production. One of these was not to allow land to lie fallow until the fourth, fifth or even sixth year. There was also a system of up-and-down husbandry as well as a 'system with cultivation of fodder crops', as Slicher van Bath put it, on the fallow or in connection with crop rotation. The production of commercial crops was expanded. These developments must be seen against the background of the high level of urbanization and a well-established manufacturing economy, both of which increased demand for the produce of intensive agriculture. Moreover, there were the grain imports from the Baltic Sea region, which filled the gaps left by the trend towards specialization in agricultural production. Grain imports amounted to at least 13—14% of the total requirement between 1562 and 1569. Specialization and commercialization in the northern parts of the country were also furthered by the fact that there were but few landlords. Consequently the peasants were not subject to any major restrictions in their economic activity. Whereas small-scale, but intensive agriculture predominated in the southern parts of the Netherlands, the north became a region with wealthy farmers who formed the nucleus of an agricultural capitalism.

Wilhelm Abel has spoken of the 'Thünen Circles' which began to emerge around the Netherlands and Western Europe in general, in the 16th century. By this he means a zone of intensive agriculture which also included the dairy farming in the marshes along the German North Sea coast and the *Koppelwirtschaft* of Holstein; and this zone was in turn surrounded by a 'grain belt' in which the three-field system predominated. Beyond this belt was a grassland zone stretching from Jutland, the Danish Isles and Russia across to the Ukraine and Hungary which supplied Western Europe with livestock. The emergence of these belts was less a result of natural conditions than of those of the market and of relative location and cost advantages. As a rule production methods became less intensive with growing distance from the central zone of consumption around the densely populated Low Countries. This relationship is neatly reflected in the price differentials between East and West. Thus during the years 1551–1600 average grain prices in Danzig were only 53% of those paid in the Netherlands; prices for oxen ex Danzig were a mere 27% of the levels at Antwerp. The Netherlands were able to impose production structures on their suppliers which were tailored to the requirements of the market in that Northwestern corner of Europe. Indeed, trade relations between the Low Countries and the Baltic regions assumed a quasi-colonial character.

Concentration on grain export inevitably also left a deep mark on the economic system in large parts of East-Central Europe. However, there were other preconditions which facilitated a restructuring of the economy in those countries. The agricultural crisis of the late middle ages undermined the earlier gains by the peasants in terms of feudal rights and obligations and prepared the way for a reversal in two ways. Firstly, the decimation of the population created the material prerequisites of the expansion of the demesnes. The scarcity of labour to which the landlords responded by tying their peasants more firmly to the land generated the social conditions for what Friedrich Engels called the 'second [wave of] serfdom'. Nor were there many institutional obstacles to seigneurial actions because the state had lost the means of influencing this development once colonization had taken place and German law had been established. It was partly preceded, partly accompanied by the 'immunity movement' which granted privileges to the nobility. Thus the state became an instrument in the hands of the feudal lords and was in no position to counteract the growing pressures exerted by the landlords on the peasants.

It was left to the export boom of the 16th century to set free forces which transformed the old system based on feudal payments to one relying on the serf labour to work the *Vorwerke* of East-Central Europe. Searching for a solution to the decline of their incomes and keen to participate in the expansion of the economy, the landlords expanded the land under their own management and increased the

*Table 6:*

Some structural features of the 'Vorwerk' in Poland, 1500-1655

|  | 1500/50 | 1551/80 | 1580/1605[1] | 1606/30[1] | 1631/55[1] |
|---|---|---|---|---|---|
| Size of Vorwerk (in *Hufen*) | 3.1 | 3.6 | 4.0 | 4.4 | 6.2 |
| Size of peasant holdings (in *Hufen*) | 6.5 | 4.5 | – | – | – |
| Ratio of peasant *Hufe* to Vorwerk-*Hufe* | 2.1 | 1.3 | | 0.9 | |
| Weekly serf labour per *Hufe* (in days) | 1.7 | 3 | 3[2] | 4[2] | 5[2] |
| Percentage of serf labour used for cultivation of *Vorwerk* area | 57 | 63 | 52 | 68 | 60 |

[1]Greater Poland;  [2]Eastern parts of Greater Poland; 1580-1612, 1613-26, 1627-55; Western parts of Greater Poland; 1580-94, 1695-1615, 1616-55.

labour services (see Table 6). Thus the *Vorwerk* of a Polish aristocrat grew from an average of 3.1 *Hufen* 1500-50 to 3.6 *Hufen* in 1551-80. By 1631-55 it had reached the size of 6.2 *Hufen* for the whole of Greater Poland. In 1551-80 the ratio between land held by peasants and that managed by the landlords was about 1.3:1. The labour services which had been limited to a few days in the year during the high middle ages rose to two days per week between 1500 and 1550 and to three in 1551-80. By this time no less than 63% of the labour on the demesnes was provided by serfs, with the remaining 32% coming from wage labourers employed by the landlords. In 1551-80 some 93.9% of the landlords' income was raised through the *Vorwerk* economy. Dues and other payments from the peasants dropped to a mere 6.1%. Andrzej Wyczański has done a calculation which shows the high profitability of this economic system: in 1551-80 the income of a nobleman in the western parts of Greater Poland would have dropped by about one third, if the mixed system of serf labour and wage labour had been replaced by one relying exclusively on wage labour.

In the decade of the 1560s Poland exported about 6% of its net grain production and about 15-20% of the grain which was sent to the market; the figures for rye, the main crop, were 12% and 40% respectively. The Brandenburg Mark which, together with the rest of East Elbia, experienced a development similar to that of Poland was equally closely tied into the East-Central European grain trade. Danzig rose to the position of the most important port for grain exports in the Baltic region. Between the end of the 15th century and the 1710s, exports increased ten-fold from 10,000 *Last* per annum to 100,000 *Last*. In 1619 some 175,000 *Last* are assumed to have reached Danzig (see Figure 4). The Polish estate-owners transported their

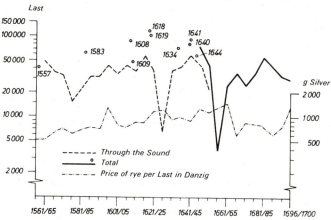

*Figure 4:*
Volume of grain exports from Danzig
1557–1700 (quinquennial averages in *Last*)

grain down the River Vistula on rafts to sell in Danzig. Some of these noble families shipped up to 800 *Last* per annum. While Danzig saw a period of great prosperity, other Polish towns declined. Internal trade contracted. The peasants, pushed to the margins of the economy, were cut off from the market and hence also disappeared as buyers of basic manufactured goods. Those elements of the *szlachta* (middle nobility), who benefited from the export boom, tended to buy foreign luxury goods. Shrinking demand and foreign competition put the screws on the artisans in the towns. At the same time Polish merchants suffered from the policies adopted by the nobility which aimed to establish a direct link between the large-scale grain producers and foreign merchants.

The introduction of a *Vorwerk* economy and the labour policies adopted by it amounted to a retrograde step away from the simple market economy which had emerged elsewhere. East-Central Europe returned to forms of appropriation which had existed in the past. In this sense the refeudalization of agriculture in these parts of Europe represented the most extreme contrast to the rise of a commercialized system in England. And yet it was not a mere reversal of earlier

historical trends. What was new was that the world market rather
than the seigneurial estate provided the central reference point; new
was also the division of labour which, although it remained
unchanged on the estates, came to be based at a higher level on the
above-mentioned regional differentiations and was dictated by the
highly developed commercial zone in the northwestern corner of
Europe. Feudal ties had been loosened in the high middle ages which
saw the emergence of a simple market economy. In the 16th century
this process became reversed under the impact of a world market
which thrived on unequal terms of exchange. The world market was
not always the point of reference of the *Vorwerk* economy, though.
This economy also developed, albeit more slowly and hesitatingly, in
regions which were outside the Baltic sphere. According to J.
Topolski there appear to have been two types of *Vorwerk* systems.
The first one was linked to the export market; the other one was part
of the domestic economy. Export demand and domestic demand
therefore combined to effect the transition to a *Vorwerk* economy.
The first impetus for the change came from the regions which
exported grain to Western-Europe; but the success of these exports
acted as a stimulus to other regions which were not part of the export
network.

There was furthermore the export of livestock from Eastern Europe
and Denmark which assumed enormous proportions in the 16th
century. Hungarian traders sold more than 180,000 oxen in Vienna
between 1549 and 1551. In the 1560s and 1570s annual exports from
Hungary were about 150,000 head. The share of livestock in terms of
total Hungarian exports (excluding copper and precious metals) rose
from about 55% at the beginning of the 16th century to 93.6% in 1542.
The trade in Denmark and Schleswig was no less significant. It
grew from 20,000 head per annum between 1480 and 1500 to 55-60,000
in the period 1660–1620. The customs post at Gottorp in Holstein
handled 12,813 head in 1485; by 1612 this figure had reached its
absolute maximum of 52,350 head (see Figure 5). In good years an
estimated 40,000 oxen were exported from Western Russia and the
Ukraine. As Duke Johann Friedrich the Elder of Saxony claimed, the
cattle market at Buttstadt near Weimar often received '15[,000],
16[,000] and even 20,000 oxen'. One prerequisite of such huge
livestock exports was, of course, the existence of large concentrations
of consumers, e.g. in the Netherlands; but there is also the expansion
of grain production at the expense of livestock farming to be
considered which occurred in Western and Central Europe. Its
volume notwithstanding, the livestock trade did not have

repercussions on the system of production which were in any way comparable to the impact of the grain exports on Eastern Europe agriculture.

*Figure 5:*

Volume of oxen drift over land to Frisia and the Netherlands, 1491–1700 (ten-year averages of animals registered by Gottorf customs post)

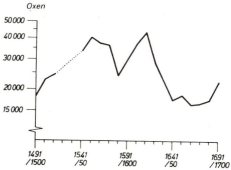

Turning farther east, Russia was still outside the 'Thünen Circles' in the 16th century. Nevertheless, her agriculture was exposed to developments which were very similar to those in East-Central Europe. In both regions a decimation of the labour force as a result of epidemics, famines and wars in the late middle ages created the preconditions of change. The policy of tying the peasants to the land reached its first climax in 1497 when the possibility of opting out of feudal services was limited to the period around St. George's Day (26 November). Thenceforth the landlords extended their estates, and the transition to the *Vorwerk* economy set in. The great crisis of 1560-1620 proved to be the turning point. The pressure of serfdom became so intolerable that the peasant economy began to crack. Many peaants opted out of the system by escaping to the fertile Black Soil regions of the Southeast. The only solution which the Tsarist autocracy and the feudal lords could think of when faced with this depopulation was to tie the peasants even more firmly to the land and to expand their demesnes. However, the point of reference of this economy was not the world market, but the domestic market.

## 1.3 Crafts, Commerce and Finance

The crisis of the late middle ages had been less damaging to manufacturing than to agriculture. Manufactured goods were less sensitive to income fluctuations. One response by the artisans to the crisis was to form cartels. What ended the crisis in the 16th century was an increased demand for goods by a growing population and new opportunities resulting from the opening up of markets overseas.

However, the end of the century saw a gradual decline in the effective growth rate for manufactured products where the demand was generated by population growth; by then inflation had begun to undermine the spending power of the consumer; declining real income also caused demand to concentrate increasingly on basic foodstuffs. Although the colonial system of the 16th century, as will be seen later, (pp. 42ff.), was based primarily on plunder and exploitation, the non-European world, and the American colonies in particular, nevertheless assumed an increasing importance as markets for finished goods from Europe, even if this trade was not to be compared with that of the late 17th and 18th centuries. Thus a remarkable correlation has been found to exist between the fluctuations in the production of textiles at Lille and the trans-Atlantic trade of Seville which seems to indicate that exports to the Americas were far from insignificant. Overall the growth of the European economy brought about a number of marked shifts in the regional distribution of craft production. In the late middle ages Nuremberg and Augsburg became centres of the Upper German region which emerged as a major area of manufacturing next to those in Upper and Central Italy and the Netherlands. Metal goods production provided the main basis of Nuremberg's economic position. Augsburg's steep rise, on the other hand, was due to the production of a cloth based on a mixture of linen and cotton, known as fustian.

The Fuggers, Augsburg's most important and famous merchant family, started in this trade. Nuremberg and Augsburg also became trade centres with a vast hinterland. In the case of Nuremberg it included large parts of Eastern Europe. Augsburg, on the other hand, succeeded in establishing itself in silver and copper mining in the Eastern Alps and in Upper Hungary. Ultimately, the city more or less came to dominate these industries. These activities enabled the Upper German merchant capitalists to gain control of the Portuguese spice trade whose main centre after 1501 was Antwerp. The Portuguese needed copper, silver and metal goods for their African and East Indian trade. The Fuggers directed their copper and silver exports towards Antwerp and away from Venice which had monopolized the spice trade until then (see Table 7). Antwerp became a stronghold of the Upper German merchants. At the beginning of the 16th century, the

*Table 7:*

Size of the Hungarian copper trade of the Fuggers, 1497–1539
(annual averages in tons and percentages)

| Period | Tonnage of total exports | Exports to Antwerp via Danzig and Stettin (in %) | Exports to Venice and Trieste (in %)[2] |
|--------|------|------|------|
| 1497–1503 | 1390.4 | 12.3[1] | 32.1 |
| 1507–09 | 1476.8 | 49.3 | 13.3 |
| 1510–18 | 1625.2 | 55.8 | 2.6 |
| 1519–26 | 1367.3 | 35.2 | 4.5 |
| 1527–39 | 1099.1 | 53.9 | 10.2 |

[1] 1497/99: 0,48 %    [2]The remaining exports went to Nuremberg, Leipzig, Hamburg, Frankfurt and Lüneburg; but the final destination of large parts of these exports was probably again Antwerp.

Upper German region, Northern and Central Italy and the southern parts of the Netherlands still held their uncontested leadership position in manufacturing. But in subsequent decades the northern parts of the Netherlands as well as England and France moved to the forefront. The older commercial countries declined. Spain and Poland became importers of goods.

A few regional exceptions apart, textiles were the leading sector both in terms of national income and of the number of people it employed. There was little change in this respect up to the first phase of the Industrial Revolution. The industry's dominant role was due to the fact that, next to food, textiles satisfied a basic human need. Initially the share of textile production for self-provision continued to be high; but there was a growing number of people who were dependent on the market. Fashion transformed traditional clothing habits. The market grew not only in size, but also experienced a change in quality standards.

England which had risen from an exporter of wool to one of textiles succeeded in securing for itself an important position in the heavy cloths market. Exports rose by 96% in the first half of the 16th century (1499/1500–1549/50). In the peak year of 1549–50 the country exported 147,161 'shortcloths' (the unit of calculation then in use). There was a recession in the 1560s before exports regained a fairly stable level in the last quarter of the century (see Figure 6). Between 1606 and 1614 exports averaged about 179,000 'shortcloths' per annum. A structural change occurred in the sense that the cheaper and lighter kerseys gained ground *vis-à-vis* the traditional heavy

*Figure 6:*
Quinquennial averages of English
shortcloth exports, 1501- 1640[1]

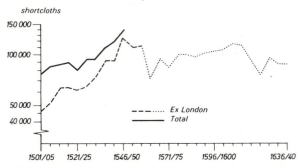

[1]From 1606/10 excl. of cloths exported by foreign merchants.

cloths. Kerseys still belonged to the category of 'old draperies'; but their emergence points to a trend which ultimately led to the so-called 'new draperies' taking the lead on a broad front.

The 'new draperies' were relatively cheap and light textiles which, like linen, were an outgrowth of the 'commercialization of rural techniques' (D.C. Coleman). These fabrics gained their popularity first in the southern parts of the Netherlands. Their success is closely related to the decline of the textile industry of the Flemish towns. Indeed, the 'new draperies' made a major contribution to the collapse of the 'old draperies', with Hondschoote becoming the most important centre of the new industry. This town exported an average of 86,956 pieces per annum in the 1560s and 1570s. After its destruction in 1582, Lille took over as the metropolis of the Flemish *'nouvelles draperies'*. Other refugees from the southern Netherlands re-established the industry further north and in England. Thus some 58,627 pieces were produced in Leiden by the beginning of the 17th century. In England, where the 'new draperies' first gained a foothold in the 1560s, they made up about a quarter of total textile exports in 1606-14, rising to 42% by about 1640 (see Table 8).

Towards the end of the 16th century, the Württemberg town of Calw became the centre of the industry in Germany. The textile manufacturers in Italy, on the other hand, who had occupied first place at the beginning of the 16th century, failed to adapt to changing demand and, as we shall see, this proved to be a major cause of their decline in the 17th century. What made the 'new draperies' so successful was that they were cheaper, lighter and more attractive to wear. They appealed to a larger group of consumers and were able to respond to changes in fashions. It was also of vital importance to their success that the Italian colony of merchants in Antwerp opened up the Mediterranean markets which were to become the most important for these fabrics.

*Table 8:*

Cloth exports of London and provincial ports in the first half of the 17th century (000s)

| | London | | Provincial ports | | Total | | |
|---|---|---|---|---|---|---|---|
| | No. of pieces | £ | No. of pieces | £ | No. of pieces | £ | % |
| 1606/14: Shortcloths | 132 | 880 | 47 | 313 | 179 | 1193 | 77 |
| New draperies | – | 267 | – | 80 | – | 347 | 23 |
| Total | – | 1147 | – | 393 | – | 1540 | 100 |
| ca. 1640: Shortcloths | 87 | 580 | 40 | 267 | 127 | 847 | 58 |
| New draperies | – | 515 | – | 90 | – | 605 | 42 |
| Total | – | 1095 | – | 357 | – | 1452 | 100 |

It was not only the 'new draperies', but also linen which benefited from the structural changes in demand that spelled the end of the manufacturers of 'aristocratic' cloths. The linen industry spread above all throughout Western and Northwestern France, Flanders and Germany, i.e. regions in which climatic conditions were favourable for the growing of flax. In the German-speaking lands, East-Central Europe and Silesia gained increasing importance beside the traditional regions of Upper Swabia and Westphalia. It was merchant capitalists from Upper Germany and from Nuremberg in particular, who moved into these new regions. They secured the production for themselves by concluding collective agreements with local guilds. Around 1610–20 some 4,400 masters were covered by such agreements. Dutch and English merchants emerged as rivals of the Upper German firms around the turn of the century. These men brought the rural production under their control with the help of local landlords and by circumventing the towns. It was a development which, as Herbert Kisch has observed, resembled the 'classic pattern of colonial penetration'. Slowly the Upper German cloths began to lose out. As late as 1595, it is true, some 410,000 pieces of fustian were taken to the Augsburg *Schau*, an institution which controlled the quality of products. But in the long run these materials could not compete against the cheaper linen, on the one hand, and on the other, the more expensive high-quality textiles of the time.

Except for the production of yarns, towns tended to remain the centres of textile manufacture and trade. It was only in the second half of the 16th century that the industry spread into the countryside, following a trend which had set in in England and Flanders long ago. There, wool manufacture had shifted from the town to the country since the late middle ages and had established itself as a 'cottage industry' among small-holders and landless rural producers. This 'industry' was organized as a putting-out system: whereas production was on a family basis, both marketing of the finished goods and the acquisition of the necessary raw materials was taken over by merchant capitalists. The small producers became dependent on this type of entrepreneur *(Verleger)* who provided them with raw materials, offered credit facilities and sold the goods, taking advantage of his knowledge of the markets. Only where the acquisition of raw materials, as in the case of linen manufacturers, did not present any difficulties and production required no supervision, did a system of direct purchasing *(Kaufsystem)* survive which left the producer with a modicum of formal independence *vis-à-vis* the merchant. However, these putters-out were not always merchant capitalists in terms of their backgrounds. In some cases, producers succeeded in establishing themselves as *Verleger* of their co-producers. It also happened that those artisans were able to work their way up to this position who were the last in the production and finishing process. In Calw, for example, the dyers became the *Verleger* of the weavers.

Mining, metal production and the iron trade were far less significant than textiles in the 16th century. This did not prevent modes of production to emerge much earlier in these industries which were clearly capitalist. Next to timber, iron was the most important industrial raw material. However, at the beginning of the 16th century its production was still quite limited. It is estimated that it amounted to some 70,000 tons of wrought iron, half of which was produced in Central Europe. Output probably doubled in the course of the century. Furnaces and the related indirect techniques of iron-making, which had spread from Northern Italy in the late middle ages, slowly established themselves. Although production in the Upper Palatinate around the mining towns of Amberg and Sulzbach declined in the course of the 16th century, this region continued to be the most important in Europe in terms of output. In 1609 some 178 forge hammers were in operation there. The total number of workers was around 10,550 of whom 40% were engaged in charcoal production. More than 20% of the population of the Upper Palatinate in the 16th century earned their livelihood in the iron industry.

Silver and copper mining expanded from the middle of the 15th century. The growth of the former was due to the demand for silver coins in a growing economy. Production was concentrated in Thuringia, the *Erzgebirge* south of Dresden, the Carpathian Mountains and in the eastern Alps. It reached its peak in 1526–35, with an annual output of about 96 tons. This was five times of what it had been in 1450. Up to the eve of the Thirty Years' War, production slipped back to around 24 tons. This decline was due to the competition of silver from the Americas which began to appear on the European markets.

*Figure 7:*
Volume of Central European copper
production, 1501–1620 (ten-year
averages in tons)

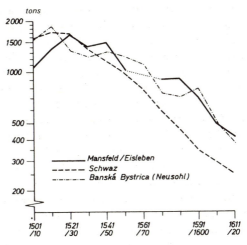

Production of copper rose until the second decade of the 16th century, before it began to stagnate; it fell markedly after the middle of the century (see Figure 7). It is possible that the declining per capita income of the European population led to a shrinking of the demand for manufactured goods based on copper. The most important regions with an 80–90% share of total European output were Schwaz, Taufers, Rattenberg, Röhrer Bühel and Radmer-on-Hasel in Tyrol; of Neusohl in Upper Hungary (known as Banská Bystrica in Czechoslovakia today) and of Mansfeld and Eisleben in Thuringia; Sweden emerged as the fourth major producer only towards the end of the 16th century. The copper market developed into something like an oligopoly after the beginning of the century. Between 1500 and 1546 the Fuggers held a partial monopoly together with the Thurzos, a family of mining engineers from Cracow. They controlled copper production in Upper Hungary and dominated the marketing of Tyrolean copper. The Fuggers determined pricing policies within the oligopoly. According to the Fuggers' balance sheet of 31 December 1546, their stocks of copper amounted to one million guldens out of total holdings worth 1.25 million guldens (see Table 10, p. 00). After the Fuggers had dropped out, none of the other Upper German firms which continued to dominate the market succeeded in gaining a comparable position in the copper trade for a similarly long time. Also the vertical concentration achieved by the Fuggers in linking copper mining with copper manufacture remained more or less an exception.

If traditional co-operative structures were destroyed in the mining and smelting industries, it was less due to the demand for working capital, as had been the case in the urban crafts system, than the need for fixed capital to finance technological innovations. The co-operative which held a share in the mines and mined the ore themselves were in no position to raise larger sums of money for investments. They had to rely on merchant capitalists or to give way to other associations which came from the outside and had the necessary funds at their disposal. The masters of small furnaces or forges often found themselves in a similar predicament. Thus the putting-out system became the dominant form of organization in the mining and metal industries. Yet time and again, the merchant capitalists were forced to take production into their own hands. This is true, for example, of the copper mines at Neusohl which were jointly exploited by the Fuggers and Thurzos. Consequently there emerged at Neusohl a centralized mining company the likes of which did not exist elsewhere in the 16th century. By 1527 the Fuggers had invested some 210,000 guldens in this venture, rising to 368,000 guldens by 1536. But the putting-out system also required large, in some cases even enormous, sums, in particular in areas where a sovereign had taken mines and furnaces into his own possession. The Augsburg firm of Manlich, for example, made an agreement with one branch of the family of the Count of Mansfeld for the purchase of 300,000 guldens worth of copper.

The emergence of large firms was accompanied by a concentration of labour which had not been seen so far. In the middle of the 16th century some 11,500 miners were employed in the Tyrolean mining district of Schwaz, of whom 7,460 worked in the Falkenstein pits alone. A trucking system and other exploitative practices· were widespread. The labourers in turn developed forms of collective resistance. The Mansfeld miners repeatedly went on strike to protest against unpaid wages. There are reports of similar protests from other regions. The conflict between capital and labour began to manifest itself.

As far as metal manufacture was concerned, Nuremberg was able to maintain its pre-eminent position, based as it was on the adjacent mining area of Upper Palatinate. Other regions, like the English Midlands and those around Aachen, Liège and the *Bergisches Land* east of Cologne, did not reach a similar importance. Iron and brass goods as well as precision instruments from Nuremberg were exported throughout the world. The city's metal brooches, pots, bowls and kettles were much in demand in Africa. As the arms manufacturers of the Holy Roman Empire, the Nurembergers were at times inundated with orders, especially during the wars against the Turks. In 1557, the city's blade-smiths are said to have produced between 90,000 and 100,000 blades a week. This was possible only because the merchant capitalists and the masters dependent upon them were able to rely on a veritable industrial 'reserve army' (H. Aubin) in the shape of labourers engaged in piece-work. According to some estimates, they comprised one third of the population working. in crafts and trades.

The sources of energy on which the manufacturing economy could grow, continued to be very limited. Human and domestic animal labour, water-power and wind-power apart, there existed only organic substances, above all, wood. Owing to the great demand for wood in the iron industry, supplies were insufficient. If the industry therefore wished to expand beyond the confines set by existing sources of energy, coal had to be brought in to substitute wood. England appears to have made most progress along this route. For technical reasons, it was not yet possible to use coal for iron-smelting, but it came to be utilized for other purposes, leading to a relaxation of demand for wood. Coal mining quickly assumed capitalist features. There was barely another branch in which the share of fixed capital was as high as in this industry. Soon the sums invested surpassed the £1,000 mark. The Newcastle mines employed some 5,800 people in 1637–38, of whom some 3,000 were face-workers. The Liège region gained in some respects a comparable position on the European Continent. About 50,000 tons of coal were mined there around the middle of the 16th century.

Nevertheless, despite these activities, the age was shaped not by manufacturing capitalists, but by the merchants. They appeared to instil it with a dynamic which knew no bounds. As K. Marx put it, 'commerce dominated industry'; yet, a few exceptions apart, the merchant capitalists did not penetrate into the production sphere and organized it to manufacture goods for their account. The putting-out system turned out to be the appropriate form for controlling production without a direct involvement in it. But only the merchants were able to accumulate funds of the size required as working or, occasionally, as fixed capital for the manufacture of goods. Their role was therefore not merely to organize production and the exchange of goods on an interregional and international level, but also to engage in capital formation.

Commerce expanded throughout Europe in the 16th century, be it on land or on water; be it in the Mediterranean, the Baltic, along the Atlantic coast or in Central Europe. To it must be added the trade with the Americas and Asia. The European market widened to form the world market. In 1497, 795 ships passed through the Sound; by 1557–58 this figure had risen to 2,251 ships, to reach an annual average of 5,554 ships in 1591–1600. In 1607–8 some 1,407 ships docked in Livorno, the port of the city of Florence; a year later the number was 2,454. In the last quarter of the previous century, the figure had been rarely more than 500 ships per annum. Sailings to the Far East rose from an annual average of 21 in the decade 1491/2–1501/2 to 114 between 1591–2 and 1600–1. At the same time the share of Portuguese ships was eclipsed (see Figure 16, p. 86), when the Dutch and the English successfully undermined the monopoly which the Portuguese had been holding in the Far Eastern trade. The Spanish trade with the Americas experienced an enormous development. Between the years 1506–10 and 1591–1600 the number of sailings between Seville and Spanish-America increased 45 to 186, with total tonnage growing from 4,480 to 36,140 tons (see Figure 8, p. 41). This, to be sure, was no more than approximately 6–7% of the tonnage passing through the Sound at this time! This picture is totally changed, however, if one calculates the silver value of the goods imported from overseas as against that of the grain shipped from the Baltic region, as can be seen from Table 9.

In other words, the value of the grain imports from the Baltic region was a mere 64% of the value of the spices from the Far East and 28% of the precious metal imports from the Americas. And yet it was only the trade in Central Europe, in the Baltic and along the Atlantic coast which assumed modern features. As we have seen, it comprised

*Figure 8:*

Volume of sea traffic in quinquennial averages between
Seville and Spanish-America, 1506–1650 (both ways)

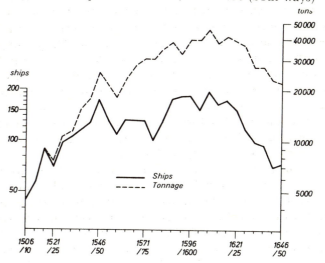

mass consumption goods, above all cereals, livestock and copper
from Eastern Europe and textiles and metal goods from the Western
parts of the Continent. There was also salt from Southwestern
Europe. Some 90% of Polish exports were in grain, livestock and furs.
Hungary's exports of livestock and copper were probably even
higher. Textiles led the list of imports, comprising 48% of the goods
imported to Poland by sea in 1565–85 .and 68.7% of Hungarian
imports in 1542.

*Table 9:*

Imports into Europe, 1591–1600 (annual averages)

| Region of origin | Type of goods | Weight (in tons) | Value (in tons of silver) |
|---|---|---|---|
| Baltic | Grain | ca. 126 109.4 | ca.  87.5[1] |
| Asia[2] | Spices | ca.  2 712.0 | ca. 136.8[3] |
| America | Precious metals | ca.   287.7 | ca. 309.4 |

[1]Based on grain prices on Amsterdam market in 1591/1600.  [2]Ca. 1600.
[3]Based on prices on Antwerp market and, where source not indicated, on
German prices for spices.

The intercontinental trade, on the other hand, continued to follow the traditional pattern, with a heavy emphasis on spices and precious metals. Some 95.6% of the goods reaching Spain from the Americas in 1594 were precious metals; by 1609 the figure was 84%. Spices had a similarly high share of Portuguese imports from East India.

The trade with the Americas differed from that with the Far East in that it began to depart from the traditional one-way pattern. A growing volume of goods—wine, oil, linen, cloths—flooded into America from Spain. The Spanish mother-country achieved a high trade surplus through its link with its American colonies. By the beginning of the 1570s, almost half of the silver shipped to Spain was used in payment of imports to America. All in all, however, European overseas trade remained dominated by precious metals and spices. At the end of the 16th century pepper fetched six or seven times the original purchase price, and profits amounted to as much as one third of the final retail price. The speculative character of the spices and precious metals markets promoted the accumulation of merchant capital, but it also kept the merchants away from the production sphere and hence contributed to a conservation of the existing system of production.

This leads us to consider the stimuli behind the overseas expansion of the Spaniards and Portuguese. It was the search for gold which caused the latter to venture into Africa; their desire to undermine the Venetian monopoly in the profitable spice trade pushed them beyond Africa towards East India. Gold was also the lure in the conquest of America, as the log-book of Christopher Columbus demonstrates. The discovery of America was not, to quote Pierre Vilar, 'a coincidence unrelated to economic factors', but rather the 'culmination of an internal evolution of the Western economy'. This economy had grown since the middle of the 15th century. Yet this growth would only continue if metal coins were available in sufficient quantities. And thus the re-emergence of the occidental economy unleashed a further process which ended in the subjugation of the non-European world to the metropolitan centres of Europe. This connection arose in the case of the Iberian peninsula under specific conditions. There overseas expansion offered a solution to the problem of declining incomes which the nobility, impoverished by the crisis of the late middle ages as it was, had experienced. The landlords 'externalized' the crisis, and they combined with mercantile interests which had their base in the Mediterranean. At first the feudal element continued to be the determining one; for the methods adopted in the conquest of America were no more than an extension of the medieval *reconquista*. Pierre Vilar has quite aptly spoken of 'Spanish imperialism' as 'the highest stage of feudalism'.

Looting, plunder and naked exploitation were the main features of the colonial system of the 16th century. The feverish search for precious metals overruled all moral scruples. Faced with the *conquistadores* and the excessive demands which they made on native labour, the demographic and economic equilibrium of the old American culture collapsed. The population of the Antilles was exterminated within a few decades. The population of Mexico which had numbered 25.3 million in 1519 slumped to one million by 1600. The inhabitants of Peru were in all probability similarly decimated. The plantation economy whose origins go back to the first half of the 16th century pointed to a later era of colonial exploitation. Towards the end of the century these plantations were not yet of major importance, however. Silver mining in Mexico and Peru dominated the field. Its productivity was so low that it could be continued only because native labour cost next to nothing. The Potosí mines in Peru were so high in the mountains that work there was way above what was physiologically endurable. In short, the silver mines of Central and South America cost millions of lives.

Although Europe's overseas trade continued to be structured along traditional lines, the first contours of an asymmetrically organized world market began to emerge in the 16th century. It was at this time that the metropolitan centres in Western Europe started to integrate regions which were more or less dependent on them into a system of an unequal division of labour. Whereas the centres reserved the manufacture of finished goods for themselves, the peripheral regions were restricted either to the production of basic foodstuffs (as in the case of East-Central Europe) or of precious metals and expensive foods (as in the case of the Americas though, with regard to the latter, only in embryonic fashion). Fundamentally different forms of work organization were characteristic of this new system: formally free labour, on the one hand, and serf or slave labour, on the other.

One consequence of this was that the division of labour between metropoles and peripheries assumed the form of an unequal exchange between the two spheres. To begin with, there was the direct one-way transfer resulting from plunder, but also from the sending back of profits to Europe; it came to be complemented by indirect transfers because the labour that went into products from the periphery was less well paid than that contained in metropolitan goods. The metropolitan centres stood to benefit from the difference, provided it was not wiped out by lower productivity on the periphery.

The Far East was not yet included in this system of an unequal division of labour. No attempts at colonization took place there comparable to those in the Americas. Portugal, it is true, succeeded in bringing the trade inside the Asian continent under her control; but she failed when she tried to cut off Venice from the spice trade which went through the sea ports of the Levant. The share of the European pepper trade along the South African route rose to 55% between 1505 and 1549. But it dropped back to 45% in the second half of the 16th century. The Portuguese *Estado da India* began to operate independently from Portugal and transformed itself into an institution which lived on the tributes which it imposed on the inner-Asia trade and on the ships passing through the Red Sea. Two figures may be given to illustrate that Asia's position in the world of the 16th century cannot really be compared to that of the Americas: no more than about 13% of the spices from the Far East were exported to Europe; on the other hand, 75% of America's precious metals were shipped across the Atlantic. And even these figures do not tell the whole truth; for it would surely be quite illegitimate to mention the murderous mining techniques applied in the Americas and the methods of spice cultivation in the same breath.

Europe's expansion overseas led to tangible changes in the economic balance within the European Continent. Antwerp became the most important trade centre. Its power was based on cloths from England, Central European silver and copper and luxuries from overseas; its trade with the colonial dependencies provided the stimulus for Antwerp's dynamic economy. The upswing in the trade on the Continent which was borne by the merchant capitalists of Upper Germany and the overseas trade converged in that city. Its rise in the first two decades of the 16th century was made possible by a 'Portuguese-German commercial alliance' (H. van der Wee) which was based on spices and metals. In the 1520s and 1530s, this alliance weakened in the face of the competition of silver from the Spanish-Americas and because of the failure to establish a Portuguese monopoly in the spice trade. But Antwerp succeeded in building new foundations through its trade with Spain, Italy, France and England and through the expansion of manufacturing in the Netherlands. In 1543-45 some 74% of Dutch exports passed through Antwerp. By 1560 the share of manufactured goods from the Netherlands reached about 72% of total exports. Some 29% of these, to be sure, were re-exports, above all textiles from England. Foodstuffs headed the list of imports to the tune of 44%.

When Antwerp declined from the late 1560s as a result of political and religious troubles, a number of other cities initially benefited from this, among them Genoa, Livorno, London, Amsterdam and Hamburg. But ultimately Antwerp's position was inherited by Amsterdam. Whereas the rise of the former had been due to its role as an intermediary between England, Central Europe and the overseas territories, Amsterdam's commercial strength came to rest on its trade in commodities from the Baltic and from the Atlantic coast. Grain and timber from the countries along the south coast of the Baltic Sea and iron ore and copper from Sweden were exchanged for salt from Portugal and the Bay of Biscay and herrings from the North Sea. Amsterdam became the most important centre of the grain trade in Europe when the Iberian peninsula and Italy were hit by serious shortages. Towards the end of the 16th century, Holland was the main commercial power in Europe. It held a quasi-monopoly over the Baltic trade. The share of ships arriving from the Baltic in Amsterdam (and in other parts of the Northern Netherlands, but excluding local traffic) rose from 56% in 1557–60 to 79% in 1611–20. In terms of tonnage, the share was even as high as 85%. Around 1570 the city's commercial fleet had a capacity of 232,000 tons; the fleet of the Hanseatic League was second with 110,000 tons. Less than a century earlier both the Dutch and the Hanseatic fleets had had roughly the same size of 60,000 tons.

Techniques and organizational forms of this trade were slow to change. In this respect Europe did not see a revolution, but rather the proliferation of the methods developed by the Italians. Private companies dominated the scene, either as pure family enterprises or as firms with outside partners. It was only in the second half of the 16th century that innovations were made when the joint-stock company and the *voor-compagnieen* emerged in England and Holland respectively. Thus the *Russia Company* was founded in 1555. The *Levant Company* was established in 1581, followed by the *East India Company* in 1600. These joint-stock companies differed from the loosely organized 'regulated companies', like the *Company of Merchant Adventurers* or the *Eastland Company* whose members conducted their business on their own account. The joint-stock company had, as indicated by the name, a capital stock which was issued in the form of shares to merchants and investors. A similar system was adopted for the Dutch *voorcompagnieen* which emerged in 1595 and which were given this name because they preceded the *United East India Company*. The joint-stock company was developed because the capital requirements for large-scale and long-term overseas transactions were often beyond the means of family firms; it was also a way of distributing the risk of dangerous ventures on to several shoulders. In short, the vagaries of the market forced the merchants to develop new forms of organization. The establishment of these forms went hand-in-hand with a growing emphasis on calculability and 'rationality' which Max Weber has written about. Double-entry bookkeeping which had been confined to Italy up to the late middle ages now became a widespread practice.

The credit system likewise saw an extraordinary expansion in an attempt to satisfy the growing requirements of the merchants. Bills of exchange came to be used throughout Europe as a means of payment. Towards the end of the 16th century they also became negotiable. In this respect the bill of exchange was preceded in Northwestern Europe by the 'bill obligatory' (*cédule obligatoire; schulderkenning*). The discounting of both types of bill became general practice. Antwerp and Lyons emerged as Europe's leading clearing and financial centres up the second half of the 16th century. The former operated within the Spanish monarchy, the latter within France. But the bankruptcies of the two states in 1557 ushered in the decline of the two cities.

At first the clearing business was conducted in both cities in connection with a fair which took place four times a year. Gradually the fair centres changed into financial centres, a metamorphosis in which Antwerp gained a lead over Lyons. The credit business which was centred around the 'new' exchange established in 1531 continued to coincide with the four annual fairs; the commodities business on the other hand which was taken over by the 'English' exchange came to be transacted on a permanent basis and independently of the fairs.

The financial practices adopted and developed further by Antwerp prepared the way for banking in the centuries to come. They were to reach their ultimate refinement later in the London 'City'. In subsequent decades the Genoese exchanges built their reputation as the main clearing centres on the ruins of Antwerp and Lyons. These exchanges took place at Besançon at first and later in different places until they found a permanent home in Piacenza after 1579. But in 1627 they too went under in the aftermath of the financial crisis of the Spanish estate. The Genoese fairs were pure fairs of exchange. As a Venetian put it in 1604 and without exaggerating, not a single *quatrina* would change hands here. On the other hand, turnover reached astronomical figures. In 1588 it is said to have been over 37 million *écus de marc*, and a few years later even 48 million. To quote Fernand Braudel: 'For a long time, the Mediterranean took control of the wealth of the world through Genoa.'

The rapidly growing credit requirements of the state authorities were at the heart of the expansion of high finance in the 16th century. Spain's public expenditure experienced a growth in real terms by some 80% between 1520 and 1600, and state revenue could not possibly keep up with this. In certain years the Castilian monarchy spent twice the amount of what it received. Loans became the only solution. Other monarchies were in a similar predicament, and the rise of the Fuggers to the position of one of the major financial powers of the 16th century is therefore intimately connected with the inadequate financial base of the early modern state. After the Fuggers had laid the foundations of their empire as merchant capitalists they made credits available to the Habsburgs, and this in turn gave them access to the silver and copper mines of the eastern Alps. These mines and the Fuggers' commitments in Upper Hungary helped them to gain control of the European copper market. Beside the trade in ores, the loan business became their main activity. In 1546 Emperor Charles V alone owed two million guldens of a total of 3.9 million guldens which the Fuggers had given in loans (see Table 10).

*Table 10:*
**Balance-sheet of the Fugger firm for year ended 31.12.1546**
**(000s gulden)**

| a) Assets | | b) Liabilities | |
|---|---|---|---|
| Landed estates and | | Short-term debts | 1300 |
| mines | 800 | Long-term debts | 700 |
| Stock | 1250 | Capital stock | 5100 |
| Cash-in-hand | 250 | | |
| Outstanding debts | 3900 | | |
| Partners' private acc. | 400 | | 7100 |
| Misc. | 500 | | |
| | 7100 | | |

The larger a particular state, the more it depended on the credit facilities of the great commercial families. Increasing territorial expansion also meant a growing distance between those parts where revenue was raised and where it was needed. The costs of extracting silver from the Americas could only be covered with the help of international finance capital and could be mobilized only by means of exchanges. As Richard Ehrenberg has correctly observed, 'it was not the Potosí silver mines, but the Genoese fairs of exchange which made it possible for Philip II to conduct his world power policy decade after decade'. Although this capital became increasingly centralized, by the end of the 16th century its earlier close links with merchant capitalism had been loosened and it began to play a role of its own. It was only in a very indirect way, i.e. through the military expenditure of the State, that it was of benefit to the production sphere.

## 1.4 The Price Revolution and Socio-Economic Change

The cumulative effect of inflation on grain prices in the 16th century was on average about 1.4% per annum. By 20th century standards, this might be considered insignificant and the term 'price revolution' hence seem inappropriate. A more definitive verdict will not be possible, however, until we have taken due account of the economic and social context in which inflation occurred. If grain prices were at 100 index points in 1501-10, they rose as follows in the course of the 16th century:

| | |
|---|---|
| England (see Figure 9) | 425 |
| Northern Netherlands | 318 |
| Southern Netherlands | 380 |
| France | 651 |
| Spain (New Castille and Valencia) | 376 |
| Germany | 255 |
| Austria | 271 |
| Poland | 403 |

Prices for manufactured goods did not rise quite so steeply and merely doubled. The price rises which deserve to be called a 'price revolution', it is true, hit most countries only in the second half of the 16th century; but price levels generally began to move up from the beginning of the century at the latest. If one does not include the Central European production of silver, it is therefore problematical to reduce the cause of the so-called price revolution to the imports of gold and silver from the Americas. These imports did not reach Europe on a larger scale until the second half of the 16th century. They amounted to 236.3 tons in 1531-40, rising to 755.5 tons in the decade 1551-60 and finally to 3093.9 tons in 1591-1600. After this they levelled off in the subsequent four decades at a figure which was one-fifth below the earlier maximum (see Figure 9). All in all some 20.664 tons of silver and gold (gold = ca. 10.8% of this total) were imported between 1503 and 1650. According to estimates by F. Braudel and F. Spooner, these imports increased the amount of precious metals circulating in coins in Europe by less than 50% at best. In order to salvage their hypothesis that these imports fuelled

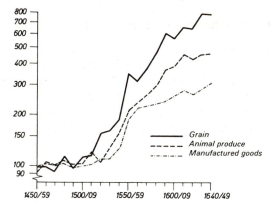

*Figure 9:*
Index of nominal prices in ten-year
averages for England, 1450–1649
(1450/99 = 100)

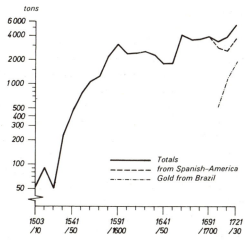

*Figure 10:*
Volume of exports in precious metals
from America to Europe, 1503–1730
(ten-year averages in tons silver)

inflation, both authors had to take recourse to the argument that the increased speed of money circulation was responsible for the price rises. In line with monetary theory, this would mean that prices would rise equally for all products. But as Figure 10 shows, this was not at all the case. In short, the discrepancy between the prices for basic foodstuffs and those for other goods put a question mark behind this theory.

It is therefore safer to assume that the growth of the money in circulation is, in conditions of economic expansion, more probably a reflection of this expansion than its cause. The above-mentioned price discrepancies would, moreover, appear to make it likely that other non-monetary factors unleashed the 'price revolution'; Spanish silver at least played no more than a secondary role. The gap between the prices for basic foodstuffs and those for other products can only be explained in terms of the different elasticities of demand for food, on the one hand, and manufactured goods, on the other, among a growing population. Rising prices for basic foodstuffs do not result in a reduced demand; it is inelastic. The opposite is true of non-essential goods; here rising prices tend to depress demand. In short, in times of a population growth with which supply fails to keep up, food prices are liable to rise more steeply than prices for manufactured goods (see Table 11). Rising demand and insufficient supply also affected production costs in differing ways. It was the same problem of diminishing agricultural returns as in the high middle ages: an expansion of grain production at the expense of stock-farming reduced the quantity of manure and hence the fertility of the soil. Productivity declined. Moreover, poor soil was ploughed up for production and its yield was correspondingly very low. All this was bound to push up prices which were determined by the unit costs of grain produced on the poorest soil. Manufactured goods, on the other hand, were not affected by these mechanisms. Their production and costs could be adjusted more flexibly to changing demand, resulting in the above-mentioned price discrepancies.

Inflation was only one aspect of the price revolution of the 16th

*Table 11:*

**Index of estimated rents and prices in southern England, 1510/19–1650/59**

|         | Rents[1] | Prices for wheat | Prices for wool |
|---------|----------|------------------|-----------------|
| 1510/19 | 100      | 100              | 100             |
| 1550/59 | 308      | 253              | 171             |
| 1600/09 | 672      | 435              | 262             |
| 1650/59 | 845      | 573              | (117)           |

[1]On new takings on the Herbert Estates, Wiltshire.

century. It was paralleled by a rise in ground rents and fall in real wages. The economic mechanisms underlying these developments benefited the peasants in the first instance and increased their income, unless they were marginal producers who sent very little of their produce to the market. And indeed the records speak of well-to-do peasants at this time. Yet rising peasant incomes were bound to call the landlords onto the scene. They saw, especially in areas where they received cash rents, how the price revolution redistributed agricultural income to their disadvantage. Consequently they tried to prevent or reverse a reduction of their percentage. Where rent increases were difficult to achieve, they raised other contributions, such as entry fines. Many landlords did quite well out of this. The Holy Spirit Hospital at Biberach-on-Riss increased these fines so steeply (1500-9 = 100; 1620-29 = 1,085) that the real value of the feudal rent remained unaffected by the inflationary devaluation of the cash payments. Newly rented land on the Herbert Estates in Wiltshire in South England was so expensive that the landlord's total gains in some years rose faster than the price of wheat (see Table 11). On the whole, the landlords fared best where they enlarged their own property in order to lease it as happened in England or Western France or in order to manage their estates themselves with the help of serf labour.

There are many difficulties in producing a balance-sheet from what has been said so far. Thus it was by no means certain from the start which group would gain the larger share of the increased wealth. What was decisive in this respect was the property structure and the economic behaviour of the feudal lords. In general it seems safe to assume that, disregarding exceptional developments, feudal burdens diminished in Western Europe, at least initially. East of the River Elbe, by contrast, the balance tilted clearly towards the nobility.

Meanwhile the fall in real wages assumed catastrophic proportions. In England *nominal* wages rose from 100 index points in 1501-25 to 131 in 1575-1600; the equivalent figures for France and Germany were 126 and 157 respectively; Austria, where nominal wages declined to 95, and the Southern Netherlands, where they rose as high as 282, remained exceptions. But *real* wages fell, i.e. wages lagged behind prices for manufactured goods, not to mention grain prices. Thus the real wage index for building workers dropped by more than 50% between 1476-1500 and 1591-1600 (see Figure 11). Recent research has shown that a building worker in Augsburg was able adequately to maintain his wife and two children from his annual income during the first three decades of the 16th century. Thenceforth

*Figure 11:*

Index of real wages of building workers in relation to a 'basket' of
goods in the age of the Price Revolution (1521/30 = 100)

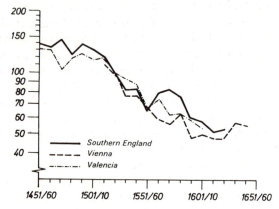

his living standard began to fall. Between 1566 and 1575 and from
1585 up to the outbreak of the Thirty Years' War his wages could no
longer pay for the subsistence minimum of his family. Meat slowly
disappeared from the diet of the poorer sections of the population. In
the late middle ages, annual meat consumption had reached the
figure of 100 kilos per person—an incredible quantity by today's
standards. Up to the beginning of the 19th century, this figure
declined to less than 20 kilos. Sheer need forced people to eat cheaper
and less nutritious food. As Wilhelm Abel put it, the 'meat standard of
the late middle ages' was replaced by the 'grain standard of the early
modern period'.

The reasons for this fall in real wages are not difficult to discern.
Population growth multiplied the supply of labour. But demand for
labour did not increase commensurately. Hence wages did not keep
up with the rising cost of living. Per capita production declined at
the same time and per capita income followed suit. The wage-
earning population like the small-holders' were pushed into a
marginal existence. They precipitated, as Marx, quoting William
Th. Thornton, put it, 'from the golden age straight into the iron one'.

The dynamic development of the 16th century which profoundly
affected all spheres of life ended up in another general crisis.
Conditions of economic growth reversed to usher in a period of
decline. The rapid growth of the population which had been one of
the main triggers of the upswing became a barrier which stifled
growth. The process of expansion did not merely come to a halt;

worse, it deteriorated into what G. Bois has described as a period of 'stagflation'. Thus agricultural output began to stagnate from the middle of the 16th century, if not before, and soon began to fall. In the, Cambrésis in Northern France grain production reached its peak as early as 1520 before it went into a slow decline. Taking 1370-79 as 100, the index had dropped to 70-80 by 1450, moved back to 80-90 around 1520, but fell again to around 75 in 1600-30. A similar situation arose in the eastern parts of Normandy. And Polish agricultural production was on the decline since the end of the century.

But while food production continued to stagnate and even fell, the population did not stop growing. The gap between needs and resources widened. Prices rose. At the same time the conflict between peasants, landlords and the state over the distribution of agricultural income became more acute. We have looked at the different policies which the landlords adopted in Western and Eastern Europe in the previous crisis (see above pp. 20ff.). Now they turned the screw again. But there were also increased tax burdens. In Spain they doubled in nominal terms between 1556 and 1584. The picture for France emerges from Table 28 on p. 93 below. Soon the incipient Malthusian crisis escalated into a major social crisis. The more the new century approached, the more serious and devastating became the supply problems. At the beginning of the 1570s Europe was hit by a famine worse than any of the previous ones. Portugal, Spain and Italy became dependent on grain deliveries from the North. In Italy which had been suffering from bad harvests since 1586, the situation reached crisis point in 1590. The Grand Duke of Tuscany, with Venice following in his footsteps, sent his agents as far as Danzig to buy up grain. Some 16,000 tons of Northern and East-Central European grain reached the port of Livorno in 1593. Between 1590 and 1593 some 78 ships from Amsterdam, 59 ships from Hamburg and 29 ships from Danzig docked in the harbour. The inelasticity of demand for basic foodstuffs and the economic contradictions inherent in the feudal system were beginning to undermine the earlier expansion.

Although, as has been seen (above, p. 49), prices for non-agricultural goods rose less steeply than grain prices, the increased strains within the economy were also having their effect on the manufacturing sector. As real incomes declined in the face of rising grain prices, demand began to focus on basic foodstuffs. Inevitably, the production of other goods was adversely affected by this. Even in Antwerp where real wages fell less sharply than elsewhere from 100 in 1450-59 to 82.7 in 1594-1600, a mason with a family of four had to use 78.5% of his income for the purchase of foodstuffs. Accommodation, heating and light swallowed up another 10.4% so that a mere 10.1% was left for clothing and other needs. However, those industries which were engaged in the production of luxury goods very likely suffered less under the depression. The social groups which would buy such luxuries tended to benefit from the redistribution of wealth which occurred during crisis periods. Other trades were correspondingly worse hit by the slump in mass demand for their cheaper products, and demand in the underdeveloped and colonial world was not yet so important as to be able to fill the breach. In short, the ups and downs in the agricultural sector continued to dominate the overall economic situation without being able to determine the situation of the manufacturing sector completely.

These economic developments and the problems they generated were accompanied by changes in the social structure of the European countries. The crisis sharpened the differentials in income and property. Pauperization and proletarianization were paralleled by an increased accumulation of wealth. Soon contemporaries began to get worried about the growth in the number of beggars and vagrants. The Magistrate of Berlin warned in 1540 that 'many alien beggars are milling about'. Vagrants and bandits posed a threat to the countryside. The beggars were driven from the towns at periodic intervals; but soon they were back again. The English Poor Laws with their draconian penalties go back to this time.

The number of landless peasants and small-holders also increased disproportionately. There were the small-holders, *haricotiers*, 'gardeners' and others who had some land. They must be distinguished from the cottagers, *manouvriers* and *Büdner* who in most cases at least owned a small house and a plot. And finally there were the wage labourers and *Einlieger* (lodgers) who lived on the farms of the landlords and wealthier peasants, sometimes having rented a small piece of land from their employer. In Saxony 25.8% of the population living in the countryside belonged to the first two categories in 1550 (see Table 12). In 1577 some 43.2% wer small-holders and cottagers (see Table 44, p. 149). In the Principality of Schweidnitz-Jauer, the number of peasants declined to 20.5% up to 1619, with the share of small-holders, cottagers and wage labourers rising to 69.6%. In Overijssel in the Low Countries some 61.4% were peasants as against 38.6% small-holders and cottagers in 1602. There is also the example of a French grain-growing village which comprised up to 72 *manouvriers* as against 100 *laboureurs* (peasants). The percentage of the rural poor in terms of the total population in the English countryside is thought to have been between one quarter

*Table 12:*
## Social structure of the population of Saxony, 1550–1843

|  | 1550[1] abs. | % | 1750 abs. | % | 1843 abs. | % |
|---|---|---|---|---|---|---|
| Citizens | 116 000 | 26.7 | 200 000 | 19.7 | 300 000 | 16.2 |
| Urban *Inwohner* | 22 000 | 5.1 | 166 000 | 16.3 | 326 500 | 17.6 |
| Peasants | 215 000 | 49.5 | 250 000 | 24.6 | 250 000 | 13.5 |
| Cottagers | 20 000 | 4.6 | 310 000 | 30.4 | 869 000 | 46.8 |
| Village *Inwohner* | 55 000 | 12.6 | 82 000 | 8.1 | 100 000 | 5.4 |
| Clergy | 3 500 | 0.9 | 4 500 | 0.4 | 4 500 | 0,2 |
| Seigneurs | 2 400 | 0.6 | 5 500 | 0.5 | 6 000 | 0.3 |
| Total | 434 000 | 100.0 | 1018 000 | 100.0 | 1856 000 | 100.0 |

[1]Excl. Upper Lusatia

and one third. In some areas, such as the Languedoc, demographic pressures caused a fragmentation of land ownership. The number of medium-sized farms declined as small-holdings and, to a lesser extent, large units proliferated. As E. Le Roy Ladurie has observed, the property structure became 'crystallized around two extremes' which were functionally interdependent. The small-holders who did not produce enough to feed themselves had to hire themselves out to the large farms which filled their manpower requirements in this way.

However, the population growth was not exclusively reponsible for the emergence of this stratum of small-holders or landless people in the countryside. No less significant was the social polarization which took place within the village community under the impact of economic change. Some peasants succeeded in enlarging their landed property; but the majority were pushed to the margins of the economy. High prices and low wages created favourable conditions for accumulation, and the famines of the late 16th and early 17th century merely accelerated this process. Work on Chippenham in Cambridgeshire has shown that the bad harvests of those years resulted in a decisive shift. Between 1544 and 1712 the medium-sized farms all but disappeared. At the same time the proportion of properties of 90 acres or more rose from 3% to 14%; households without land increased from 32% to 63% (see Table 13). The concentration of land as well as the population explosion was contained only in those cases where the landlord and the village were strong enough to control these developments.

*Table 13:*
### Sizes of peasant holdings in Chippenham
### (Cambridgeshire/England) 1544-1712

| Size of holdings | 1544 | | 1712 | |
|---|---|---|---|---|
| | No. | % | No. | % |
| 90 acres and above | 2 | 3.0 | 7 | 14.3 |
| ca. 60–75 acres[1] | 8 | 12.1 | 2 | 4.1 |
| ca. 30–45 acres[2] | 11 | 16.7 | 0 | 0 |
| ca. 15 acres[3] and less | 10 | 15.2 | 4 | 8.2 |
| Over 2 acres | 31 | 47.0 | 13 | 26.5 |
| 2 acres and less | 14 | 21.2 | 5 | 10.2 |
| Landless households | 21 | 31.8 | 31 | 63.3 |
| Totals | 66 | 100.0 | 49 | 100.0 |

[1] = 2 – 2½ yardland;   [2] = 1 – 1½ yardland;   [3] = ½ yardland

Yet whatever the dividing lines which emerged between poor and wealthier peasants, the feudal relationship with the landlord continued to be the crucial factor. As long as the price revolution was underway, the system of feudal appropriation tended to encounter special difficulties, as we have seen above (p. 24). the upper nobility in particular had problems to maintain its share of income from landed property. In the Hennegau, in the southern Netherlands, for example, it declined from 59% to 47% between 1502 and 1564-73. The French *noblesse d'épée* likewise became impoverished, and more than one of its members was forced to hand his property over to bourgeois money-lenders. Only where they succeeded in adapting the management of their estates to the conditions of an age of rising agricultural prices, were they able to survive. In England, the gentry prospered; together with the yeomen, they had been the promoters of agricultural modernization. In Warwickshire, the gentry's income increased almost four-fold. The aristocracy, on the other hand, was much less successful in adapting to changing economic conditions. A peer's income fell by about 26% between 1559 and 1602, and the average number of manors per family declined from 54 to 39. Judging from such losses, the financial crisis of the English aristocracy reached its climax between 1585 and 1606. And although the real income of the peers started to rise again until it reached its 1559 level in 1641, the number of manors continued to fall. It may be assumed that the aristocracy's share in the national product which had seen an overall rise also experienced a drop (see Table 14).

*Table 14:*

**Estimated net income and number of manors of some aristocratic families in England, 1558/59-1641**

|  | 1558/59 | 1602 | 1641 |
|---|---|---|---|
| No. of peers | 63 | ·58 | 121 |
| Mean net income in pounds | 2 200 | 2 930 | 5 040 |
| Mean net income at 1559 prices | 2 200 | 1 630 | 2 290 |
| Index of net income | 100 | 74 | 104 |
| No. of families | 63 | 57 | 121 |
| No. of manors per family | 54 | 39 | 25 |
| Index of manors per family | 100 | 72 | 46 |

The structure of landed property in Poland changed in the opposite direction from that of England. There the owners of the very large estates strengthened their position *vis-à-vis* the minor nobility by systematically exploiting the opportunities provided by the export of grain. As Witold Kula has been able to demonstrate, the magnates who, unlike the middle nobility, sent their grain to Danzig on their own account were able to offer much better terms of trade than the *szlachta*. More and more, the land became concentrated in the hands of the former. Only West Prussia which was dominated by the minor nobility and regions like Masovia where noblemen populated the area like a 'swarm of locusts' escaped this development. Thus in the administrative district of Cracow the share in the land by the magnates (with ten or more villages) rose from 8.7% in 1581 to 24.8% in 1629. The democracy of nobles which had existed in 16th century Poland thus lost its main supports.

In terms of the total population, the lower strata grew disproportionately faster both in the towns and in the country. In Saxony residents *(Inwohner)* of towns who, though not necessarily belonging to the lower strata, did not possess citizens' rights made up 15.9% in 1550 (see Table 12, p. 55). In Lyons the *menu peuple* numbered between 6% and 8% of the population in normal times. But this figure rose to 15-20% during famines. The percentage of groups which lived on the starvation line in English towns was even higher. In Leicester and Exeter it is deemed to have been one third and in Coventry even one half.

The growth of the lower classes also led to an increased inequality of income and wealth. Whereas the lower orders saw their income eroded under the impact of inflation and a surplus of labour, other groups and above all merchants were able to participate in the growth of the economy and to strengthen their position both in relative and in absolute terms. In Augsburg some 6% of those eligible to pay taxes owned 87.7% of the total taxable wealth in 1618. At Exeter, Nottingham and Leicester roughly two-thirds of the wealth was in the hands of respectively 7.7%, 12.5% and 13.5% of the population. Yet despite these trends, towns began only slowly to develop something like a class structure. Only where a cottage industry emerged and large sections of the population became dependent on a putting-out system or worked in larger manufacturing units did a class dichotomy become a determining feature. Yet time and again this dichotomy was overlain by the older conflicts between rich and poor which exploded over such central questions as food supplies and taxation. Still, there is little doubt that these conflicts also fuelled class divisions. Both, after all, were closely interrelated. The experience to be at the mercy of others who employed them began to imprint itself upon the consciousness of many artisans and wage labourers. The journeymen in the Parisian and Lyonnais printing industry, for example, who carried on a dispute with their employers for over 30 years between 1539 and 1572, charged the latter that they were enriching themselves at the expense of their journeymen's 'sweat, admirable zeal and even their blood'.

The growing tensions within the European social structure exploded in a large number of violent outbursts, uprisings and revolts. The Peasants' War of 1525 in Germany no doubt occupies a special place among these conflicts because it covered a much larger geographical area than any other rising in the 16th century. Several factors both of a structural and conjunctural nature combined to generate the situation which resulted in this war. Serfdom, a product of the crisis of the late middle ages, was the most important bone of contention. The combination of material and personal dependence which was characteristic of serfdom was not only designed to prevent the depopulation of the countryside, but also to secure for the landlords a higher share of the agricultural income in times of crisis. Serfdom, it is true, weakened from the end of the 15th century. But the economic predicament of the peasants did not improve. On the contrary, it worsened as various pressures increased. Once the population had begun to grow again, the ratio between the size of the population and the available land deteriorated. A large number of small-holdings emerged. Farms were divided up. Conflicts over village resources, above all the commons, increased. Here and there the landlords put up feudal rents. They tried to restrict the use of the common and of the woodlands. State taxes merely exacerbated the situation of the peasants. The dynamite which had accumulated over a longer period exploded at the beginning of 1525 in Upper Swabia. From there the revolt spread as far as Thuringia. But by the beginning of June the poorly organized peasant armies had been defeated. The chronicles report that 100,000 people died.

Another consequence of the slowly unfolding socio-economic crisis was that capital was taken out of the commercial sector and invested in landed property. It was a process which can be observed throughout Europe. But its causes were not so much a lack of investment opportunities in manufacturing and trade than the different time-scales along which the ups and downs in the agricultural and commercial sectors evolved. The growing gap in the supply of and demand for agricultural produce not only caused the demand for manufactured goods to peter out, but also favoured the transfer of capital to the agricultural sector. The retreat of the Fuggers, the eminent merchant family, into landownership is one of the most famous cases in point. The size of their landed property increased to 230–250 sq. kilometres by the end of the 16th century and was valued at more than two million guldens. This was almost the same amount as the family lost in the 1607 bankruptcy of the Spanish state. The Fuggers became feudal landlords. They thus integrated themselves into a social order which was opposed to the one from which they had emerged. Fernand Braudel has spoken in this context, not without dramatic effect, of the 'treason of the bourgeoisie'. But the bourgeoisie of the 16th century did not have a consciousness of itself. The nobility, to quote Braudel again, continued to be its 'sun'. As early as 1531, Anton Fugger justified the acquisition of landed estates not in terms of their economic benefits but in terms of the 'honour' attached to them. This raises the question of what was the status system of the 16th century and what were the channels of social mobility at this time.

The system of stratification into feudal estates *(Stände)* which had existed in the middle ages survived well into the modern period. It was vertically structured, like a pyramid, and extended from the landless and propertyless poor all the way up to the upper nobility. In principle it encompassed the whole of society, although there was a town-and-country differentiation at the lower end of the scale. Side-by-side with this stratification into feudal estates there emerged, as Lawrence Stone has shown with reference to England, status hierarchies for which 'profession' was the determinant. Stone included the merchants, judges, clerics and royal officials among these. These groups which were initially regarded as inferior by the nobility succeeded in narrowing the social distance to the latter and to constitute themselves as separate status groups. Ignoring the exceptional situation in the commercial city republics, English society appears to have progressed farthest in the direction of these differentiations in the 16th century. The social mobility which facilitated this development reached unprecedented dimensions during the century which preceded the English Revolution. There was the combined effect of an economic boom which strengthened the forces of the market and of a massive turnover in landed property which resulted from the sale of Church property. Thus, while the total population doubled between 1540 and 1640, the upper classes trebled in size. The gentry's share of land under cultivation almost doubled (see Table 15).

*Table 15:*
Distribution of land by social groups in England and Wales, 1436–1873 (%)

| | 1436[1] | ca. 1690 | ca. 1790 | 1873[1] |
|---|---|---|---|---|
| Great owners | 15–20 | 15–20 | 20–25 | 24 |
| Gentry | 25 | 45–50 | 50 | 55 |
| Yeomen/freeholders | 20 | 25–33 | 15 | 10 |
| Church and Crown | 25–33 | 5–10 | 10 | 10 |

[1] excl. Wales

On the European Continent the traditional system of stratification proved much more durable. While commerce was becoming increasingly attractive to the English gentry, merchants on the Continent were increasingly inclined, towards the end of the century, to see themselves as part of the feudal society and their activities as 'a stage on their way up into the noble estates' (R. Gascon). The acquisition of landed property and, especially in France, of offices was the means towards this end. As *noblesse de robe*, large sections of the French bourgeoisie made their way into the feudal upper stratum. Whereas the crisis of the aristocracy paved the way to revolution in England, the economic difficulties of the *noblesse d'épée* enabled the French monarchy to divest the old nobility of its 'official' functions and to establish an absolutist system with the help of the *noblesse de robe*. At the end of a century of unprecedented economic expansion, everything converged to bring about a renewed strengthening of the traditional structures of European society.

# 2. The Crisis of the 17th Century

The long-term crisis which grew out of the 'price revolution' of the 16th century did not affect all European countries evenly. That revolution ended in Spain, Italy and France between 1590 and 1600; in Germany it lasted until the 1620s and 1630s and in England and the Low Countries even until the 1640s. Yet even those countries where the change was delayed experienced minor crises earlier on. The crisis of the years 1619—1622 may not possess the general importance which Ruggiero Romano had ascribed it; nevertheless, it was not just confined to the European South. The Spanish trade with the Americas was affected by it, but so were English textile exports and the trade with the Baltic region. As early as the beginning of the 17th century Germany was hit by a trade and credit crisis. Grain prices stopped rising. Many farmers and landowners were unable to repay the credits which they had taken up in the earlier days of expansion. Grain yields began to decline on the demesnes in the Brunswick region east of Hanover towards the end of the 16th century; the productivity of the soil had become exhausted. Some countries were more seriously affected by the crisis of the 17th century than others. It spelt the final decline for Spain and Italy. England, on the other hand, was relatively less badly affected. It was in this period that she gained an advantage over France with which the latter was unable to catch up.

## 2.1 Stagnation and the Demographic Crisis

The growth of the population of the 16th century came to a more or less abrupt end in Western and Southern Europe (see Table 1, p. 3). Demographic figures stagnated or declined slightly, as Table 16 demonstrates. But the extent of the crisis is actually hidden by these figures. The Thirty Years' War had catastrophic consequences as far as Germany is concerned. It has been estimated that population losses amounted to 40% in the countryside and to 33% in the towns. Brandenburg, Saxony and Bavaria lost about half of their populations. While North Germany was able to maintain its

*Table 16:*

Indices of population growth in 17th-century Europe

|  | 1600 | 1700 |
|---|---|---|
| Northern and Northwestern Europe | 100 | 128 |
| Central, Western and Southern Europe | 100 | 105 |
| Total | 100 | 109 |

numbers, the losses in Pomerania, Hesse, Palatinate and Württemberg were two-thirds and above. In Bohemia the population declined from 1.7 million in 1618 to 930,000 in 1654. The Swedish-Polish War of 1654-60 wrought similar havoc to Poland. The population of Poland and Masovia fell from 3.83 million in 1655 to 2.5 million in 1660. The Great Northern War of 1700-21 once more reduced the population (which had grown again to 3.25 million by 1700) to 2.85 million in 1720. Italy's population contracted from 13.3 million to 11.5 million between 1600 and 1650, to reach 13.4 million by 1700. The Spanish population declined from 7.68 million in 1587-92 to 5.25 million in 1646-50. It increased slightly thereafter and amounted to seven million by 1712-17. The population of France remained relatively stable in the 17th century, but this facade of stability veils fluctuations of up to 20%. The catastrophes of the late 16th century were followed by a slight increase which was halted in different French provinces between 1630 and 1660-70. Thenceforth figures stagnated or began to decline. The violent crises of the period after 1691-93 depressed the number of people to an absolute low point. In the Languedoc the rural population fell by 18% between 1677 and 1714. Demographic developments in Northern and Northwestern Europe differed considerably from the picture presented so far. There growth continued, albeit at a reduced pace. The population index which had been at 100 in 1600 rose to 128 in 1700 (see Table 16). Stagnation set in only in the second half of the century, after growth rates had continued to be relatively high in the first half. Thus the population of England and Wales which had reached 100 index points in 1603 increased to 141 in 1670. Thereafter the rise was negligible (144 in 1731). A similar trend can be observed for the northern parts of the Netherlands. Starting from a base line of 100 in 1600, the population climbed to 125 in 1650 and to 126 in 1700. Trends varied from province to province. Thus the index fell in Holland and Frisia from 100 in 1650 to 98 and 90 respectively in 1700; on the other hand, there was an increase in other provinces.

The 17th-century reversal of the population growth of the previous century had many causes. Wars, epidemics and famines come to mind most immediately. But they present no more than the surface of events. Disregarding primarily exogenous factors like the Thirty Years' War and other military conflicts, the demographic movement of the 17th century was a reaction to the excessive population growth of the 16th which ended in a deterioration of the overall economic situation and also led the landlords to appropriate a larger portion of the agricultural income to themselves. In this sense demographic decline was a reflection of both a 'Malthusian' and a social crisis. However, it was not clear from the start how the adjustment would take place; or, to use Malthusian terminology, whether it would occur through 'positive' or 'negative' checks. Nevertheless, one thing is certain: given the relatively autonomous way in which demographic factors tended to operate in society, it was bound to take quite a long time before family life and birth patterns would adapt to the new economic situation. Only by bearing this in mind can we explain why food supply problems arose in the first place. Only when these problems became acute, did people change their reproductive behaviour. Thus the average marriage age began to rise again. In France it increased from 21-22 to about 25 years of age; in Colyton in Southwest England, where it had been very high as early as the second

*Table 17:*

Some Indicators of changes in the marriage age of women, 16th-18th century

| | 1550/99 | 1600/49 | 1650/99 | 1700/49 | 1750/99 |
|---|---|---|---|---|---|
| Colyton[1] | 27.0[2] | 27.1 | 29.4 | 28.3 | 26.3 |
| Bottesford[3] | – | 25.7 | 26.4 | 27.5 | 26.5 |
| Shepshed[3] | – | 28.1 | | 27.4 | 24.1[4] |
| Tourouvre-au-Perche[5] | – | – | 24.1[6] | 24.9[6] | 26.2[6] |
| Meulan[7] | – | – | 24.9[8] | | 25.5[8] |
| Heuchelheim[9] | – | – | 24.1[10] | 25.8[10] | 23.8[10] |
| Giessen[11] | – | 25.4[12] | 24.3[12] | 24.3[12] | – |
| Bourgeoisie of Geneva | 21.4 | 24.6 | 25.7 | 26.3 | 24.0 |
| English High Aristocracy | 22.8 | 23.4 | 23.6 | 24.6 | 25.0 |

[1]Village in Devon/England; [2]Figure for 1538/99; [3]Village in Leicestershire/England; [4]Figure for 1750/1824; [5]Village northwest of Chartres/France; [6]Figures for 1665/99, 1700/34, 1735/70 respectively; [7]Small town northwest of Paris; [8]Figures for 1660/1739 respectively; [9]Village west of Giessen/Hesse; [10]Figures for 1691/1700, 1701/1800 respectively; [11]Town in Hesse; [12]Figures for 1631/50, 1651/1700, 1701/30 respectively.

half of the 16th century (27.0 years), it went up to 29.4 years between 1650 and 1699 (see Table 17). As Colyton also saw a decline in marital fertility, it has been conjectured that people there practised certain forms of birth control.

It was in these ways that control mechanisms established themselves in response to changing economic and social conditions. They were designed to prevent a further widening of the gap between population size and available resources. Yet, as these mechanisms became effective too late all too often, it was left to famines to reduce the population to a size which was commensurate with the means of subsistence. However, the crisis of the 17th century was evidenced by the fact that in some places the population continued to decline even after a new equilibrium between its size and the available resources had been established.

The general demographic trend which characterized the 17th century is marked by a number of deviations in regions where there existed concentrations of rural manufacturing. Here the mechanisms developed by European society to restrict its demographic growth were put out of action. The possibility of finding a steady subsistence in the rural cottage industries for generation after generation made it unnecessary to make the conclusion of a marriage conditional on the availability of a full-time occupation. Here the 'iron chain of biological reproduction and inheritance' was broken (Ch. and R. Tilly). Indeed it was a prerequisite of rural industrial activity to found a family since wife and children were indispensable contributors to the family economy. In other words, the marriage age tended to decline and the size of the population to increase in proto-industrial regions because the above-mentioned demographic control mechanisms were less strong and because the merchant

*Table 18:*

Growth of 62 agricultural and 40 cottage-industrial villages in Nottinghamshire, 1674–1801:

| | No. | Av. number of people | | | | | | | |
|---|---|---|---|---|---|---|---|---|---|
| | | 1674 | | 1743 | | 1764 | | 1801 | |
| | | abs. | Index | abs. | Index | abs. | Index | abs. | Index |
| Agricultural villages | 62 | 166 | 100 | 187 | 113 | 199 | 119 | 276 | 176 |
| Cottage-ind. villages | 40 | 230 | 100 | 340 | 148 | 462 | 201 | 908 | 395 |

capitalists had installed a production system in the countryside which suited their requirements. The weavers of Schweidnitz reported in 1619 that the number of *Pfuscher* (workmen) was growing in the villages: 'What happens is that the son of a small-holder or cottager, once a mere 17 or 18 years of age, will be poorly trained by a *Pfuscher* and will learn to weave in the shortest of time; he will then find himself a woman and will produce more *Pfuscher* who will all sit in their cottage like swallows in the rafters.' Figures from England confirm this picture. In Nottingham the population of purely agricultural villages increased by 12.7% between 1674 and 1743; villages with cottage industries, on the other hand, grew by 47.8% (see Table 18).

## 2.2 Agriculture: Crisis and Resurgence

The agricultural crisis of the 17th century did not assume the same proportions as that of the late middle ages. Nevertheless, there are many similarities, between the two periods. Prices for cereals began to drop. Thus the index for grain prices in France which had been at 100 points in 1625-50 declined to 59 in 1681-90 and, after a brief recovery, slumped to 50 in 1741-50. The picture was similar for the rest of Europe (see Figure 1, p. 4). However, the downward trend began to reverse in Germany and Austria as early as the end of the 17th century. Real wages rose slightly without being able to balance out their catastrophic fall during the 16th century. Agriculture thus came under pressure. Ground rents declined and pulled property prices down with them. There was less incentive to develop new land. In the northern parts of the Netherlands the index for land reclaimed from the sea reached its nadir between 1665 and 1730. France experienced a reduction of the gross agricultural product, as is demonstrated by the development of tithe yields. Following the serious crisis of the late 16th century, the ten-year averages had once more reached their 16th century level by 1680; but, as can be seen from Figure 12, the downward trend recommenced thereafter and lasted until the end of the reign of Louis XIV. In Poland, where the index of grain production had been at 100 in 1580, it had reached 87 some 75 years later. The destruction wrought by the Swedish-Polish War pushed the index even further down so that it finally reached a disastrous 43 in 1660.

Change also occurred in other respects. Thus a trend towards extensive agriculture in some areas was paralleled by a move towards more intensive cultivation elsewhere. On the one hand, fields were turned into pastures and grassland. Along the Alps where grain-

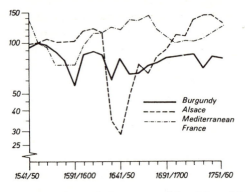

*Figure 12:*
Quinquennial averages of tithe income
using the index of grain production in
France 1541–1760 (1551/60 = 100)

growing had been expanded to considerable altitudes in the mountains in the 16th century, land was left to grow over to be used for stock-farming. The Limburg region east of Lìege presents a particularly extreme example: there the proportion of arable land fell from 67% to 19% between the 16th and the 17th century. Spain witnessed a further reduction of the influence of the *Mesta*, but this did not prevent a renewed expansion of sheep farming on a local basis. On the other hand, there was more intensive cultivation in parts of Spain and in the South of France where the vineyards were extended at the expense of agriculture. The wine-growing area around Sète and Montpellier increased by some 20% between 1676 and 1734. In Flanders, Brabant, Zeeland and Frisia grain-growing was reduced in favour of flax, hops, rape and other crops. The boom of tobacco cultivation in the central and eastern parts of the northern Netherlands was very impressive, particularly if compared with import figures of colonial tobacco from England (see Table 19). The expansion of tobacco was clearly linked to the crisis of the 17th century, as is also demonstrated by its decline a century later.

In Germany, but also in the Languedoc, the Roman Campagna and in Spanish Castille, villages, farmsteads and fields became deserted. In 1600 the proportion of land used for agriculture on East Prussian estates was 57.8%, by 1683 it had been reduced to a mere 32.4%. The wasteland on the estates of the Archbishop of Gnesen (now Gniezno in Poland) which comprised 34% of the arable land in 1685 increased to 65% by 1739.

Meanwhile international trade and commerce shrank. The annual

*Table 19:*

Production of tobacco in the Northern Netherlands and
imports of colonial tobaccos via England, 1675-1750
(mill. of Amsterdam pounds)

| Period | Prod. of domestic tobacco | English exports to Holland of colonial tobacco |
|---|---|---|
| ca. 1675 | 5− 6 | 4 |
| ca. 1700 | 9−10 | 8 |
| ca. 1701 | 15−18 | 7 |
| ca. 1730 | 8−10 | 10 |
| ca. 1750 | 11−12 | 17 |

*Figure 13:*

Volume of grain shipments to
Western Europe through the Sound,
1562-1780 (ten-year averages in *Last*)

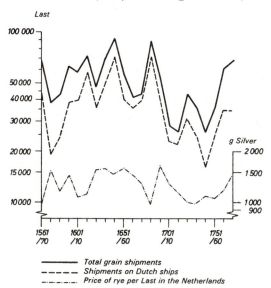

——— Total grain shipments
– – – – Shipments on Dutch ships
–·–·–·–·– Price of rye per Last in the Netherlands

averages of grain shipped westward through the Sound from the
Baltic region decreased from 68,500 *Last* in 1600-49 to 55,800 *Last* in
1650-99 and finally to 21,800 *Last* in 1700-49 (see Figure 13). Grain
exports from Danzig which had seen an enormous expansion in the
16th century stagnated as early as the first half of the 17th. Decline
followed from the middle of the century (see Figure 4, p. 29). The

downward trend for livestock exports from Denmark, Schleswig and
Southern Sweden began soon after the outbreak of the Thirty Years'
War. After 1630 these regions exported no more than 20–30,000 head
.per annum (see Figure 5, p.31). Nor did the Hungarian livestock
trade experience anything but a marked decline.

The crisis of the 17th century widened the gap between the two
geographic poles while pushing the evolution of European
agriculture in different directions. At one end, in Eastern and East-
Central Europe, the system of serfdom was tightened. England, at the
opposite end of the spectrum, on the other hand, made decisive
progress on the path towards a commercialized agricultural system.
The English farmers' response to the crisis which had started from the
middle of the century enabled him to gain an advantage over virtually
all other European countries. With prices for animal products rising
faster than the price for grain, there were clear benefits in growing
forage crops like *sainfoin*, clover and turnips. These crops were
interchanged with different cereal crops as part of a new system of
crop rotation which had not existed outside the Netherlands up to
now. The most famous among these was to be the Norfolk System
with its four-yearly sequence of wheat, turnips, barley, and clover.
The production of animal fodder made it possible to keep larger
and better nourished herds. This, in turn, meant larger quantities of
manure which contributed to higher agricultural yields. The
growing of forage crops also increased the fertility of the soil, thus
avoiding the earlier cycle of diminishing returns. The introduction of
crop rotation was accompanied by a growing regional differentiation
and specialization in respect of agricultural production. Stock
rearing and dairy farming concentrated in the Lowlands which had
plenty of water and rich soil. Grain growing became the speciality of
areas with light soil which were better suited to the new methods.

The transition to crop rotation was predicated on the at least
partial dissolution of the older types of communal agriculture. The
land had to be enclosed or, where 'open fields' existed, to be put in
severalty. This meant that 'common rights' could no longer interfere
with cultivation. However, there were also the property titles of
peasants which stood in the way of the new system. Buying up their
land hence became a prerequisite of successful enclosure.

More importantly the crisis contributed to the decline of the
peasantry less through the above-mentioned improvements than
through another and more direct mechanism. It was stagnant, if not
sinking, incomes, violent price fluctuations and heavy taxation
which pushed the peasants into a situation in which the sale of land

to a landlord appeared to be the only way out. Gregory King has estimated that in 1688 there were some 150,000 families with an income of £6.6 million on tenant farms as against 180,000 families with freehold properties and an income of £10.36 million (see Table 30, p. 100). But around 1790 some 85% of the land was farmed by tenant farmers. Those of the gentry with smaller holdings found themselves in similar difficulties, and not infrequently they were forced to sell out. All this tended to favour the large-scale landowners, and once the expropriation of the peasants had been more or less completed, English agricultural society was divided into three groups: the landlords, the land labourers and tenant-farmers who rented land to run their farms on a commercial basis.

At the other end of the spectrum, in Eastern and East-Central Europe, the trend was not towards expropriation but towards what was called *adscriptio glebae*. In other words, the crisis of the 17th century accelerated the process of refeudalization to the east of the River Elbe. What promoted this process was above all the shortage of labour, the losses of lives resulting from the wars of the 17th century and migration to the Black Soil region of Russia. It is also important to remember that the devastation inflicted by war broke the capacity of the peasants to resist. Thus the legal framework of serfdom was extended and further strengthened. The Compromise which the Great Elector concluded with the Brandenburg Estates in 1653 and which was to become the basis of the Brandenburg-Prussian military state pushed the peasants in to the hands of the *Junker*. It was now up to a peasant who claimed to be free to prove that he was not a serf. In a number of Eastern German territories, the peasants were treated as persons who were excluded from the right to inherit land or property; alternatively they were pressed to become short-term tenants whom the nobility could remove from the land at will. David Mevius, a lawyer from Mecklenburg, admitted around the middle of the 17th century that it had become 'almost common practice to trade and deal in serfs in the same way as was done with horses and cows'. With the help of rigid manorial regulations the landlords moreover tried to lay their hands on the labour of peasant children.

A fully-fledged system of serfdom finally developed in Russia. The distinction between bondsmen and peasants who were personally free disappeared. Labour services increased. To have to render these services for six days of the week was no exception in Russia. Polish peasants in the 17th century were obliged to work between four and five days per *Hufe* and week on the landlord's *Vorwerke* (see Table 6, p.28). But there were also discrepancies between the legal norm and

*Table 20:*

Wage labour and serf labour on the 'Vorwerke' of the Korczyn
district in Poland, 1533–1660 (days per 'Vorwerkshufe')

|  | 1533/38 | | 1564/72 | | 1600/16 | | 1660 | |
|---|---|---|---|---|---|---|---|---|
|  | days | % | days | % | days | % | days | % |
| Wage lab. on *Vorwerk* | 268 | 35 | 200 | 19 | 181 | 15 | 85 | 5 |
| Draught services | 490 | 65 | 551 | 53 | 475 | 40 | 598 | 33 |
| Manual services | – | – | 280 | 28 | 540 | 45 | 1102 | 62 |
| Total | 758 | 100 | 1031 | 100 | 1196 | 100 | 1785 | 100 |

actual practice which, in many cases, were considerable. For example,
in 1650 a number of villages in the Łukóv administrative district
complained that they were expected to render 12 days' service per
*Hufe* and week although the legal obligation was for no more than
four days, the 12 days' service being the equivalent of the labour force
of two serfs. In the long run the number of servants on the estates was
reduced, to be replaced by members of the landless rural proletariat
who rendered manual services (see Table 20).

Bohemia and Moravia likewise saw an extension of *robot* services,
as serfdom was called here. The land registers of estates of the
Imperial Count of Colonna of 1674 state that 'the peasants are obliged
daily to undertake with their draught animals all work which is
allocated to them. By the special grace of the Count and for the better
conservation of his subjects, the *robots* are given one day of the week,
usually the Saturday, off so that they may look after their own land'.
This would seem to indicate five days of serf labour per week. In
Russia there was also an increase in the *Vorwerk* acreage which a
farmstead or a male 'soul' was expected to work.

## 2.3 Proto-Industrialization and Merchant Capitalism

One of the most significant developments of the 17th-century crisis is
the shift away from the Continental countries and towards the sea
powers as the centres of economic growth. The Mediterranean
countries fell behind and lost out against their rivals to the North.
The first signs of this North-South split can be discovered in the
commercial field as far back as the 16th century. The North Sea and
Baltic Sea regions, as we have seen, developed their trade in products
for mass consumption at this time. The Mediterranean region, on the
other hand, continued to be dominated by its traditional trade in
spices and luxury goods from the Orient, however important the

grain trade may otherwise have been. Nor did the colonial trade of Spain and Portugal diverge fundamentally from this pattern. It both reflected the level of socio-economic development of the Iberian peninsula and helped to perpetuate the existing feudal mode of production. But in the 17th century the structure of intercontinental trade, and of trade with the Americas in particular, began to change. Increasingly, America gained importance as a market for manufactured goods from Europe while, on the other hand, the New World emerged as an exporter of sugar cane to Europe. The countries which benefited from these developments were not the ones which promoted the expansion overseas in the 16th century, but Holland and England. This was not an illogical shift, as the restructuring of the inter-Continental trade had essentially been the work of the Northwestern European sea powers. Holland had succeeded in bringing the trade in the Baltic, the North Sea and along the Atlantic coast under her control as early as the 16th century. With England on their heels, the Dutch plugged themselves into the inter-continental trading network. They began to adapt it to modern requirements and to the exchange of bulk commodities, even if as competitors and successors of the Portuguese in the Far East they remained wedded to the colonial practices of the 16th century. The evolution of commerce was completed by England which thus created one of the preconditions for her susbequent rise to the position of the 'First Industrial Nation' (Ph. Deane).

The share of East-Central Europe in the international trading system declined in parallel with the vigorous expansion of the trans-Atlantic trade. The demand for agricultural goods decreased on the Western European markets. The long-term fall in grain prices also worsened Eastern Europe's terms of trade, as prices for manufactured goods did not decline as sharply. Just as East-Central Europe, Southern Europe was also negatively affected by the shift in the international trade pattern. But worse was to come. Like the East-Central European regions before it, the South was demoted to the position of a supplier of raw materials. The Mediterranean was incorporated, by the metropolitan centres of merchant capitalism in the North-West (which were soon joined by France), into their system of an unequal division of labour. This system left the South, just as the overseas territories, with little room for manoeuvre. The rerouting of the sea lanes which occurred from the 16th century onwards was no accidental development. Rather it refers us back to the phenomenon of economic growth which proceeded at a different pace in different parts of Europe. Rapid commercial expansion overseas obviously provided an additional stimulus to the economic growth of the metropolitan centres at the hub of the system.

There are various similarities between the decline of Italy and Spain in the 17th century. Nevertheless, it would be wrong to compare the two countries in one breath. In Italy textile manufacture as a whole was affected by the crises. Venetian cloth production which had reached its peak in 1602 at 28,729 pieces dropped to little more than 2,000 pieces by the beginning of the 18th century (see Figure 14). Between 1560-80 and 1589-1600 output in Florence had already slumped from about 30,000 to 13,500, only to reach a new low by 1641-45 with an average of 6,114 pieces. In Milan losses in production were even more drastic. Around 1600 some 60-70 firms had produced about 15,000 pieces there. Yet in 1709 only one was left which sent a mere 100 to the market. Textile manufacture in other Italian towns met a similar fate. The silk trade also began to suffer. In Genoa the number of silk looms declined from about 10,000 in 1565 to 2,500 in 1675. Export markets in the Mediterranean, especially in the Levant, were lost to Holland and England. As early as 1611, the Venetian ambassador to Constantinople reported that English fabrics were

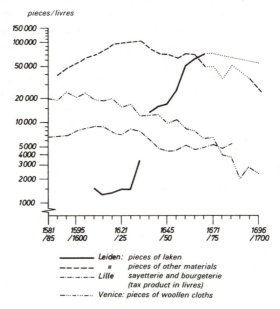

*Figure 14:*
Quinquennial averages of cloth production,
1581-1700

pieces/livres

Leiden: pieces of laken
          ʺ     pieces of other materials
Lille     sayetterie and bourgeterie
           (tax product in livres)
Venice: pieces of woollen cloths

given preference to Venetian ones in Turkish markets because they were cheaper. Venetian observers also pointed to the fact that English cloths were more attractive both in shape and colour. It turned out to be a disadvantage that Italian fabrics were of better quality. The way to overcome this disadvantage would have been for Italy to move into the 'new draperies' market which had made it possible for the Northwestern European manufacturers to strengthen their position. Yet the guilds prevented all innovation. High taxation, high wage levels and, above all, a rigid guild structure made it impossible for the Italian cloth manufacturers to respond flexibly to the new conditions. What ultimately sealed the fate of the industry was that the weavers successfully avoided their subordination to the merchant capitalists and established a system of production which was dominated by small workshops and the guilds. By the end of the 17th century, Italy was well on her way to becoming a country which imported primarily finished goods and services and exported raw materials.

This is also true of Spain and in particular of Castille, the main base of the Spanish monarchy. The Spanish artisans shared the fate of their Italian counterparts. Cloth manufacture is Segovia, next to Cordoba the country's most important manufacturing centre, fell from about 13,000 pieces in 1570-90 to some 3,000. Spain's American colonies quickly lost their significance as a market for the country's products. Seville's trade with the New World had begun to lose much of its earlier dynamic from the 1550's, although it reached its peak in absolute terms only in 1608. But after the crisis of 1619-1622 the city likewise began to fall behind (see figure 8, p. 41). The demographic disasters which had ravaged Spanish-America in the 16th century now reduced the size of its markets. Moreover production structures became so similar to those of the mother country that the basis of close commercial relations began to disappear. Ships that left Seville on the voyage across the Atlantic were filled with goods of non-Spanish origin. Foreign merchants gained control of the trade. By the end of the 17th century a mere 5% of the trans-Atlantic trade were still in Spanish hands. The trade with other countries was in no better shape. At the end of the 17th century only the Spanish balance of trade with the Hanseatic cities was in surplus. Meanwhile the trade deficit of the city of Barcelona increased from 285,000 to 721,000 Catalan pounds between 1664-65 and 1695-96. Imports consisted of luxury goods and goods destined for the Americas; raw materials were being exported. The Spanish manufacturers who were unable to survive foreign competition; they became the victims of the new international division of labour which separated individual countries into the industrial nations, on the one hand, and the suppliers of raw materials, on the other.

Nor did the manufacturing economy of Central and Western Europe escape the impact of the crisis; but the response to it was different from that of Spain and Italy. These were the regions which saw an expansion of rural industries. The Upper German economy had lost much of its dynamism since the decline of silver and copper mining (see Figure 7, p. 37). There was also the deterioration of the relationship between the Upper German merchant capitalists and Portugal as well as the crisis of fustian manufacture. The urban economy of the 17th century was badly hit by the Thirty Years' War in Central Europe and by the *Fronde* in France. These events resulted in a drain of capital and reduced demand. In Nuremberg the number of workshops dropped by one third; not even in the 18th century did they regain their former level. The fustian weavers of Augsburg suffered badly. The number of masters declined from 3,024 in 1612 to 468 in 1720; their output slumped from 430,636 pieces to 60,500. Similar figures pertaining to other towns in Germany could be added.

Textile production stagnated in France throughout the reign of Louis XIV. Virtually nowhere were the high production figures of the years 1625–1635 ever achieved again. In Beauvais, to the north of Paris, output of expensive fabrics fell by roughly one half between 1624–34 and 1710–20. Serge, on the other hand, which was lighter and cheaper, stood up well to the competition. The slump in production was no less dramatic in Amiens and, from 1667, in Lille. In both cities, and more so in Amiens than in Lille, textile manufacturing enjoyed a marked recovery after 1680, the first signs of which can be discerned between 1660 and 1680 (see Figure 14). The decline of Hondschoote which had been annexed by France in 1688 proved irreversible. The town had seen record exports of 60,720 pieces in 1630, before its position began to deteriorate rapidly on account of the Franco-Spanish War of 1635–59.

There were also elements promoting changes to the feudal mode of production itself. The long-term upswings furthered accumulation. The rise in grain prices and the above-mentioned drop in real wages favoured larger farms and opened up possibilities for enlarging the land held by them. Underproduction crises which occurred with greater frequency, especially at the end of a long-term growth period, tended to accelerate the concentration process. Large farms profited from the crisis; deliveries to the market, it is true, declined; but, thanks to the high level of grain prices, returns were higher. Small-holdings, on the other hand, were pulled down by the crisis. Small peasants not only had to abandon their deliveries to the market, but in many cases they were even forced to provide their most basic needs through purchases on that market and to go into debt in order to be able to do so. At the end of the day, the sale of parts of the land was frequently the only choice, and if neither the landlords nor the communities could stop this decline, accumulation was bound to continue. However, the fibre of peasant society was threatened with destruction only if attempts were made at the same time to secure the property titles to the land against claims by other village members. That such attempts should be made in the first place was a response to the population explosion and the increased use of communal privileges which this explosion had unleashed. But soon they went beyond their original objective and the aim was now to obtain free disposal of land, untrammelled by communal rights of any kind; to achieve what became known as 'enclosure' in England. It was these tendencies which challenged the viability of peasant society in a very fundamental way. Yet, at the same time, they represented one of the decisive preconditions for the introduction of new farming techniques and for an increase in agricultural productivity.

It also happened quite frequently that accumulation by the peasants was undermined and ultimately nullified by accumulation in the hands of the feudal lords. For, in search of maintaining his income in the face of an agricultural crisis, the landlord might expand his own holdings by withdrawing land from the peasants and incorporating it as part of his demesne. This opened up two possibilities: (1) The nobles managed these enlarged holdings themselves, relying on serf labour, as in Eastern and East-Central Europe (known as *Gutswirtschaft* or *Vorwerkswirtschaft*). (2) The landlord released the confiscated land again, but this time on terms which made it easy to adjust rents to the current price level.

The first solution, and in particular the reintroduction of the *Vorwerk* system, was of course nothing but a refeudalization of agriculture. The second alternative, on the other hand, pointed towards solutions which transcended the feudal mode of production, and very definitely so if it were supplemented by enclosure, as happened in England. In this case the peasants were virtually expropriated. The market became the mechanism which regulated the relationship between the landowner and those who rented his land. The feudal rent had been transformed into a capitalist ground-rent. Thus, seen in historical perspective, the 'English solution' of eliminating the peasantry was the major alternative to what E. Hobsbawm has called the 'peasant path towards capitalism'.

The twists and turns in the fate of urban textile manufacturing under the impact of foreign competition and proto-industrialization emerge from the case of Leiden. There the *nieuwe draperie*, after a period of prosperity, lost ground in the 1630s. It was squeezed out by English competition which disposed over better raw materials and a proto-industrial rural labour force. On the other hand, the *oude Leidsche draperie* enjoyed a revival in this period which lasted into the first decade of the 18th century. These draperies were made with Spanish wool and 'Turkish' camel hair. They were relatively expensive and less labour intensive, and this secured them a niche in the market. Ultimately they shared the fate of the 'new draperies' of Leiden when they were overcome by their competitors in the area of Verviers, Eupen and Monschau south of Aachen whose organization was proto-industrial. In the final analysis the victory of proto-industry was thus total. And as far as the struggle between the English and the Dutch textile industries is concerned, it appears to be a harbinger of later developments: England conquered the markets for relatively cheap goods of mass production; her competitors managed to survive only in the markets for luxury goods (see Table 21 and Figure 14, p. 72).

Leiden was probably the largest textile centre of the time, but the northern parts of the Netherlands were also important in other respects. And again they were threatened by foreign competition,

*Table 21:*

Estimated volumes and values of textile production at Leiden,
1630–1701 (%)

|  | 1630 | | 1654/55[1] | | 1701 | |
|---|---|---|---|---|---|---|
|  | Vol. | Value | Vol. | Value | Vol. | Value |
| *Old draperies* | | | | | | |
| Woollen cloths | 1.6 | 2.7 | 16.3 | 43.7 | 34.7 | 71.1 |
| *New draperies* | | | | | | |
| Greinen | ? | 2.8 | 26.8 | 32.8 | 33.0 | 20.3 |
| Fustians, etc. | 84.9 | 62.5 | 36.8 | 13.6 | 16.2 | 3.7 |
| Warpen, bayen | 13.5 | 29.5 | 20.1 | 9.4 | 16.1 | 4.6 |
| Others | ? | 2.5 | ? | 0.5 | ? | 0.3 |
| Totals (in %) | 100.0 | 100.0 | 100.0 | 100.0 | 100.0 | 100.0 |
| Totals (in prices | | | | | | |
| resp. 000s guilders) | 108 156 | 4 000 | 113 583 | 9 160 | 74 682 | 5 910 |
| Index | 100 | 100 | 105 | 229 | 69 | 148 |

[1]Vol. for 1655, value for 1654

dependent as they were on raw materials from abroad and on external markets for their finished products. The Dutch frequently succeeded in taking charge of those stages in the production process which were particularly profitable and which enabled them to control the markets for finished products. German, Flemish and French linen was bleached in Haarlem; Italian silk was prepared in Haarlem, Amsterdam and Utrecht. This was bound to generate animosities in other countries. Thus in 1614–17, a group of London merchants led by Alderman Cokayne tried to prevent the outfitting of English wool fabrics in Amsterdam by inducing the King to ban the export of undyed cloths. They failed. Sugar refineries and the tobacco trade emerged because Holland became the world's warehouse until it was squeezed out by England in the 18th century. A proto-industrial development took place only in Twente and was started by the local linen trade there.

Unlike in Holland, the development of manufacturing in England was more firmly rooted in a growth of the domestic economy; it was not just a product of a previously achieved strong position in world trade. This was to be of some importance for the future, because it helped industrial capitalism in England to emancipate itself from the grip of the merchant capitalists.

Gregory King has estimated that in 1688 some 70–80% of the English population was predominantly employed in agriculture. Yet agriculture generated no more than about 56% of the national income. Next to agriculture, textiles made the largest contribution to the gross national product among the manufacturing branches of the economy. But decline appears to have set in. Although textile exports increased absolutely, their share in total exports by England (excluding re-exports) fell from 80–90% at the beginning of the 17th century to 70.9% in 1699–1701. The process of restructuring which affected the English economy in this period may be gauged even more clearly by looking at the growing importance of coal as a source of energy. The rise in coal output between 1551-60 and 1681-90 was around 1,400%, but most of this increase happened in the 17th century. In 1651 Newcastle was celebrated as the English Peru. Both the private and commercial use of coal expanded. London became the largest consumer once coal was established as a domestic fuel. It was carried to the capital from Durham and Northumberland by sea. It has been calculated that the coal industry employed some 8,000 people in 1650. A hundred years later, the figure was 15,000 of whom 3,500 were miners. The advance of coal was particularly fast in those industries in which the substitution of wood by the new fuel posed few or no problems. This was true of soap-making, brick manufacture, brewing, refining of salt, alum and sugar and glass-making. The smelting of ores was more complicated. Thus the question of producing iron with the help of coal remained technologically unresolved, although processes using the new fuel had been developed by the end of the century for the production of lead, tin and copper.

Those industries which replaced wood by coal were able to increase their output considerably. But the iron manufacturers, having recovered from the crisis of 1620-60, also did well. The number of furnaces declined, but overall capacities rose. All in all, production went up by 30-40% in the course of the 17th century. On the other hand, there were almost no technological innovations or structural changes in the manufacturing sector throughout the century. Output increased as much in individual branches as the available equipment permitted. Changes occurred in this respect only towards the end of the 17th century. As far as their organization was concerned, textiles and large parts of metal manufacturing remained dominated by either the *Kaufsystem* or the putting-out system. More modern modes of production developed only in those branches, such as brewing, glass-making, paper manufacture, refining of salt and sugar, which required a high concentration of fixed capital.

Merchant capitalism, not industrial capitalism, thus continued to be the force that shaped the 17th century. Amsterdam rather than London remained the centre of the world trading system. Exchange with the Baltic region was Amsterdam's *moeder commercie* (as a contemporary source put it), i.e. the city's economic basis until its decline in the 18th century. By 1670 the Dutch fleet had a capacity of about 568,000 tons. Some 36.4% of this were taken up by the Baltic trade and only half of this percentage in shipping on the routes to Guinea, the West Indies and East India. However, it was precisely the Baltic connection which did not remain untouched by the crisis of the 17th century. It was first hit by a crisis which lasted from 1618-21 to 1630. There followed a long drawn out depression in the 1650s which, punctuated by a brief upturn in the 1680s, continued into the second decade of the subsequent century. Between 1641 and 1650 some 2,139 Dutch ships sailed through the Sound out of a total of 3,597. By 1711-20 this figure had declined to 880 ships out of a total of 1,755.

The reason for this drop would appear to be, above all, the reduction in grain shipments from the Baltic region which has already been mentioned. It must be added, though, that, whereas the total amount of grain fell by 18.5%, the amount transported by Dutch ships between 1600–49 and 1650–99 decreased by a mere 8.0% (see Figure 3, p.11). In other words, Dutch grain traders were affected less seriously by the crisis than their competitors. We have as yet no knowledge of whether and how far the losses in the Baltic trade were made good by gains from the prosperous colonial trade, even if the former continued to be the cornerstone of the commercial empire which the Dutch established in the 17th century.

Meanwhile the Spanish and Portuguese colonial systems experienced major upheavals. The colonial and quasi-colonial settlements of the 16th century in Asia and the Americas began to emancipate themselves from their mother countries. Spanish-America became independent of Spanish food supplies and thereby gained a greater measure of autonomy. However, contrary to a view which was widely accepted until recently, exports of precious metals did not decline, but continued to rise in the second half of the 17th century (see Figure 10, p. 49). The *Estado da India* was less and less concerned with promoting exports to the mother country. Rather it tried to secure its own survival by subjecting the inner-Asian trade to its authority to extract tributes from it. To put it crudely: it was not the route around the Cape, but that through the Red Sea which became its main artery.

These tendencies were reinforced by the pressure which the Northwest European sea powers—Holland, England and France—exerted on Spain and Portugal. These countries not only disrupted the trade of the Iberian powers with Asia and America, but also built up commercial networks of their own. They occupied the Caribbean islands one after the other and set up on them plantation colonies like those in Maryland, Virginia and the Carolinas. And along the east coast of North America these colonies were complemented by settler colonies. By 1700 British North America had as many as 275,000 white inhabitants.

The plantations of Brazil and the West Indies which were based on slave labour became the most important new element of the 17th century colonial system. With the products of this economy appearing on the world market, intercontinental trade assumed a more modern structure based on a division of labour. Sugar cane had reached Brazil from the Mediterranean via Madeira, the Azores and the Canary Islands. The first sugar plantations were founded there before the middle of the 16th century. In 1576 there were some 40 of them. But by the end of the first quarter of the 17th century, this figure had risen to 180. By 1576 no more than 60 sugar mills were in operation. By 1629, there were 346 of them, rising to 528 in 1710.

Production rose from 2,050 tons in 1570 to 22,700 tons a hundred years later. Sugar plantations spread from Brazil to the West Indies which had meanwhile been taken over by the French and the English. Around the middle of the 17th century they succeeded in squeezing out tobacco-growing whose main centres thenceforth were Maryland and Virginia.

Tobacco had at first been a 'free man's crop' (R. Pares) and up to about 1700 this was true as far as Virginia was concerned. But soon tobacco production, like that of sugar, became inseparably connected with the slave trade—one of the most brutal chapters in the history of merchant capitalism. The link can be most conclusively established by looking at the English colony which was founded on Barbados in 1627. Initially the main crop there was tobacco which was grown with the help of white labour. But the overproduction crisis of the 1630s induced the planters to switch to sugar production. The white population declined. On the other hand, the black slave population, which had been very small as late as 1629, rose to 20,000 by 1655. In 1684 Barbados numbered 19,568 white and 46,602 black inhabitants.

It was the emergence of sugar plantations which led to the use of slaves, imported from Africa, in Brazil was well as in the West Indies. When the native Indian population, in so far as it had not yet been decimated as in the West Indies, failed to withstand the strains of

*Figure 15:*
Imports of slaves in 25-year, 20-year and 10-year
averages, 1451–1870

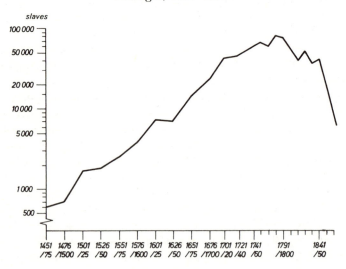

*Table 22:*

Estimated imports of slaves into the Americas, 1451–1870 (000s)

| Region | 1451/1600 | 1601/1700 | 1701/1810 | 1811/70 | Totals |
|---|---|---|---|---|---|
| Brit. North Am. | – | – | 496.0 | 51.0 | 547.0 |
| Spanish Am. | 75.0 | 292.5 | (623.1) | 606.0 | (1596.6) |
| Brit. Caribbean | – | 263.7 | (1513.5) | – | (1777.2) |
| French Caribbean | – | 155.8 | (1448.9) | 96.0 | (1700.7) |
| Dutch Caribbean | – | 40.0 | 380.0 | – | 420.0 |
| Danish Caribbean | – | 4.0 | 24.0 | – | 28.0 |
| Brazil | 50.0 | 560.0 | 1909.7 | 1145.4 | 3665.1 |
| Eur./São Thomé/Atl.Is. | 149.9 | 25.1 | – | – | 175.0 |
| Totals | 274.9 | 1341.1 | 6395.2 | 1898.4 | 9909.6 |
| Annual averages | 1.8 | 13.4 | 58.1 | 31.6 | 23.6 |

working in sugar cane production, Brazil's plantation owners increasingly used African slaves since the beginning of the 17th century. The crucial precondition for the operation of the plantation system was the provision of slaves in sufficient numbers and at a low price.

The origins of the slave trade between West Africa and the Americas go back to the beginnings of colonization. Some 17 slaves are reported to have been shipped to the West Indies as early as 1505. The *asiento*, the granting of an import monopoly for slaves into Spanish-America, dates back to 1518. In the last quarter of the 16th century about 3,800 slaves were transported per annum to Europe, the Atlantic Isles, to Sao Thomé and America. One hundred years later the annual average was 24,100. Up to 1700 some two million Africans were forced to leave their homelands to be sent on the way into a terrifying future (see Figure 15 and Table 22). The mortality rate during the passage to America was around 20%. At first the slave trade was a monopoly of Portuguese merchants. They dominated the markets both in West Africa and in Brazil and the West Indies. The *asientos* were granted mainly to Portuguese citizens. In 1637 Portugal lost Elmina, a fort on the Gold Coast, and in 1641 Luanda on the Angolan coast to Holland. Moreover, in 1640, Spain abolished the *asiento* system after the secession of Portugal. Thenceforth the Portuguese merchants encountered a serious competitor in the shape of the Dutch East India Company. In 1654, it is true, the Company was forced out of Brazil which it had partially taken away from Portugal. But it now organized the illegal slave trade to the Spanish possessions and participated in the *asiento* which had been re-established in 1662. The

Company also supplied the French and English islands in the Caribbean with slaves. Yet even during its peak period, the Dutch slave trade continued to rank second behind the Portuguese. The Dutch share was about 20%. Around 1675 the English pushed them into third place, and at the end of the century the French had demoted them to the fourth rank.

Between 1673 and 1711, the Royal African Company which had been specifically established to trade in slaves in 1672 imported an average of 2,327 slaves per year to the West Indies. It sent metal goods,

*Table 23:*
The triangular trade of the Royal African Company,
1673-1713 (annual averages)

| | No. | Weight in tons | Value £ | % |
|---|---|---|---|---|
| *Exports to Africa (1673–1704)* | | | | |
| Metal and metal goods | | | 7 071,3 | 15,5 |
| Brit. woollens | | | 10 210,3 | 22,4 |
| East India textiles | | | 5 351,4 | 11,7 |
| Other textiles | | | 6 252,3 | 13,7 |
| Gunpowder, firearms, knives | | | 3 485,5 | 7,6 |
| Beads, corals, cowries | | | 4 323.9 | 9,5 |
| Misc. | | | 8 965,6 | 19,6 |
| Totals | | | 45 660,3 | 100,0 |
| *Imports from Africa to Engl. (1673/74–1711/13)* | | | | |
| Gold | | 0,10 | 14 042.5 | 81,1 |
| Ivory | | 21,7 | ca. 2 353.0 | 13,6 |
| Wax | | 8.5 | ca. 749.5 | 4,3 |
| Redwood | | 3.7 | ca. 180 | 1,0 |
| Totals | | 34.0 | 17 325,0 | 100,0 |
| *Imports of Slaves from Africa to West Indies (1673–1711)* | 2327 | – | ca. 35 700 | |
| *Imports from West Indies to England (1673–1707/11)* | | | | |
| Sugar | | 918.2 | ca. 28 437 | 68,0 |
| Ginger | | 10,6 | ca. 322 | 0.8 |
| Indigo | | 2.3 | ca. 1 181 | 2,8 |
| Cotton | | 3.9 | ca. 226 | 0.6 |
| Silver | | 0.21 | 1 894,5 | 4,5 |
| Bills of Exchange | | | 9 748.6 | 23,3 |
| Totals | | 935.2 | 41 809,1 | 100,0 |

textiles, including linen from Silesia, fire-arms, gun powder and knives to Africa. In return it acquired not only slaves, but also gold, ivory, timber, furs and wax which were shipped to England. In the West Indies the Company exchanged mainly sugar for its slaves; it was loaded onto the returning slave ships (see Table 23). The slave trade thus became the stimulus which gave rise to a triangular trade relationship between the European metropoles, Africa and the West Indies. This triangle demonstrates very clearly how the various production centres and markets of the Atlantic region were functionally orientated towards, and dominated by, the merchant capitalists of Europe.

The Far Eastern trade experienced major structural changes when both the English and Dutch East India companies penetrated the Indian Ocean. The Portuguese had more or less integrated themselves into the structures which they found upon their arrival in Asia. Consequently the overland trade routes between Asia and Europe were hardly ever seriously threatened. As late as 1600, between 60% and 80% of Asian exports to Europe (in terms of volume) reached the Occident on land. When the above-mentioned Companies appeared on the scene at the turn of the 17th century, these patterns changed dramatically. The land routes became almost totally insignificant. Hormuz, the Portuguese fort at the entry to the Persian Gulf which had been the departure point of the caravans to the ports along the

*Table 24:*

Trading activities of the Dutch East India Company in Asia in triennial periods, 1619/21–1693/1700 (%)[1]

|  | 1619/21 | 1648/50 | 1698/1700 | 1778/80 |
|---|---|---|---|---|
| Spices | 17.6 | 17.9 | 11.7 | – |
|  | – | 26.4 | 24.8 | 24.4 |
| Pepper | 56.4 | 50.3 | 11.2 | – |
|  | – | 32.9 | 13.3 | 11.0 |
| Tea, coffee | – | – | 4.3 | – |
|  | – | – | 4.1 | 22.9 |
| Textiles, silk, | 16.1 | 14.2 | 54.7 | – |
| cotton | – | 17.5 | 43.4 | 32.7 |
| Other | 9.9 | 17.6 | 18.1 | – |
|  | – | 23.2 | 14.4 | 9.0 |
| Totals | 100.0 | 100.0 | 100.0 | – |
|  | – | 100.0 | 100.0 | 100.0 |
| Totals in guilders (000s) | 2943 | 6257 | 15 026 | – |
|  | – | 8771 | 21 032 | 28 137 |

[1]First line of figures = purchases; second line = sales.

*Table 25:*

Trading patterns of the English East India Company with Asia, 1661–1760, (ten-yearly averages in pounds sterling)

|  | 1661/70 | 1691/1700 | 1721/30 | 1751/60 |
|---|---|---|---|---|
| *Exports* | 133 464 | 332 613[2] | 650 008 | 988 588 |
| — Precious metals[1] | 67.0 | 71.4 | 83.6 | 65.7 |
| *Imports* | 101 680[3] | 173 080 | 633 293 | 778 658 |
| — Pepper[4] | 20.0 | 8.3 | 2.8 | 4.7 |
| — Textiles[4] | 62.5 | 68.6 | 65.5 | 53.7 |
| — Tea[4] | 0.1 | 1.8 | 9.6 | 21.7 |

[1]As percentage of total;    [2]1692/1700;    [3]1664/70;    [4]As percentage of total

Levant coast, was captured in 1622. The Companies succeeded in bringing the trade with the Far East under their control.

At the same time, trade became more diversified. As far as imports from Asia were concerned, pepper and other spices lost their lead over textiles. The purchases of spices by the Dutch East India Company dropped from 74.0% in 1619–21 to 22.9% in 1698–1700 in terms of the Company's overall imports. The share of textiles and raw materials for textile manufacture, on the other hand, increased from 16.1% to 54.7% during the same period (see Table 24). Imports of calicoes to England increased on average from 198,815 to 295,755 pieces between 1664–70 and 1691–1700. By the 1690s they made up no less than 86.6% of Asian imports (see Table 25). The European balance of trade continued to be in deficit. Between 1660 and 1700 a mere 24% of the English East India Company's exports were in finished goods; some 76% were in precious metals. However, the Companies tried to reduce their exports of precious metals to Asia by engaging themselves increasingly in the inner-Asian trade. The profits they made in these ventures were used to finance their imports to Europe.

The overseas expansion of the European commercial metropoles obviously also required an organizational and financial corset. It was impossible for a private company to finance the protection of its trade, the establishment of agencies and overseas branches as well as to satisfy the demand for working capital for its trading activities. There were, moreover, great risks in this trade which were increased by the vast distances involved. The state had an interest in controlling overseas trade directly or indirectly and this was achieved with the establishment of monopoly organizations. In Spain and Portugal the authorities exercised this control through the *Casa de la Contratación* at Seville and the *Casa da India* at Lisbon. The difference between the two organizations was that the *Casa da India* was not merely a supervisory and control institution, but also exercised a trade monopoly for such important commodities as spices, copper and silver.

In the countries of Northwestern Europe more or less private firms, most of which were joint stock companies, were granted by the state a trade monopoly in a certain overseas territory together with sovereignty rights. The most famous of these companies were the English East India Company which received its charter in 1600 and the Dutch *Verenigde Oost-Indische Compagnie* of 1602. Others were the Dutch West Indies Company of 1621, the English Hudson Bay Company of 1670, the Royal African Company of 1672 and the French *Compagnie des Indes Orientales* of 1664 which was hapless at first and merged with the *Compagnie des Indes* in 1719.

The common feature of these Companies was that, being chartered, they were quasi-public bodies. However, their actual *raison d'être* was to maximize profits. Thus the state, by granting a charter, created the organizational preconditions for the accumulation of commercial capital. Another common characteristic of the Companies was that they were no longer organized as 'regulated companies' but as 'joint-stock companies'. They were equipped with a capital stock which could be subscribed. Initially the funds thus accumulated were used exclusively for particular trade expeditions to be repaid, plus any profits, after the expedition had been completed. The Dutch East India Company had a permanent capital stock from the start. It was only in 1657 that the English East India Company also adopted this form of financial organization. The dividends paid by these Companies were considerable. The average dividend of the Dutch East India Company, which existed from 1602 to 1798, was 18.2%. In thirteen of these years, investors received 40% and more. The dividends of the English East India Company averaged out at 20.3% between 1661 and 1691. But in the 18th century they dropped to 10% and below. The reasons for the impressive successes of the Companies may be found in the 'internalization of the protection costs' (N. Steensgaard). In order to protect their trade, they built up forces of their own. This made them independent of those powers which had hitherto provided the protection for caravans and ships. The price at which this latter protection was offered was not only well above their own costs, but could largely also not be calculated in advance.

While Dutch and English overseas trade continued to prosper, Spain and Portugal suffered considerable losses. In 1641-50 total Spanish tonnage on the trans-Atlantic route had been 22,528; by 1701-10 this figure had declined to a mere 4,950 tons carried by 15

*Figure 16:*
Volume of sea traffic from Europe to Asia,
1491/92–1700/01 (ships sailing to Asia in ten-year
periods and by country)

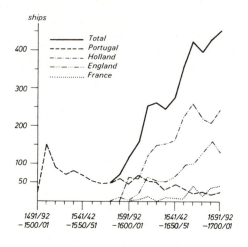

ships (see Figure 8, p. 41). The fall in the tonnage was partially made good because the products sent to the Americas tended to be more valuable. Between 1601–2 and 1610–11 some 69 ships sailed to Asia from Portugal. By the final decade of the 17th century there were just 23. Meanwhile Dutch, French and English figures showed a steep increase. Again, taking the first and the last decades of the 17th century, Dutch, English and French traffic to Asia rose from 59 to 241, 20 to 134 and 2 to 40 ships respectively (see Figure 16). The purchases of the Dutch East India Company in Asia increased five-fold between 1619–21 and 1692–1700. Turnover in Amsterdam shot up by 140% between 1648–50 and 1698–1700. Imports by the English East India Company saw a 70% rise from 1664–70 to 1691–1700. Unfortunately there are no figures relating to the total overseas trade of the northern parts of the Netherlands. English exports increased by more than 50% between 1663–69 and 1699–1701. Whereas the share of exports to West Africa, America and Asia in terms of total English exports (excluding re-exports) was no more than 14.9% around the turn of the century, imports from these regions already amounted to 31.9% of total imports (see Table 26, also itemizing London's share which was 74.3% of England's foreign trade in 1699–1701). However, the really dynamic element in this trade were not so much imports and exports, but re-exports of products from the under-developed and colonial

*Table 26:*

Share of Europe, Asia, Africa and America in foreign trade of London and of England, 1663/69–1699/1701 (%)

| | Europe[1] | | | Asia, Afr., America | | | Totals | | |
|---|---|---|---|---|---|---|---|---|---|
| | 1663/69 | 1699/1701 | | 1663/69 | 1699/1701 | | 1663/69 | 1699/1701 | |
| | I | I | II | I | I | II | I | I | II |
| Exports | 65.9 | 50.3 | 58.7 | 6.9 | 12.0 | 10.3 | 72.8 | 62.3 | 69.1 |
| Re-exports | ? | 31.7 | 25.9 | ? | 6.0 | 5.0 | 27.2[2] | 37.7 | 30.9 |
| Totals | ? | 82.0 | 84.6 | ? | 18.0 | 15.3 | 100.0 | 100.0 | 100.0 |
| Imports | 76.3 | 65.3 | 68.1 | 23.7 | 34.7 | 31.9 | 100.0 | 100.0 | 100.0 |

I = London, II = England
[1]Incl. Ireland and Turkey;   [2]Estimate

world like tobacco, sugar and calicoes which went primarily to the European Continent. The share of these re-exports in terms of total English exports rose from 22% in 1663–69 to 30.9% in 1699–1701.

Holland, not England was the warehouse of Europe in the 17th century, though. This activity formed the basis of its dominating position in trade and finance. In 1728 Daniel Defoe gave an apt description of Holland's role in international trade when he wrote: 'The Dutch must be understood as they really are, the Carryers of the World, the middle Persons in Trade, the Factors and Brokers of Europe: that, as is said above, they buy to sell again, take in to send out: and the Greatest Part of their vast Commerce consists in being supply'd from all parts of the World, that they may supply all the World again.'

Amsterdam was the centre of trade and finance in this period. Its population grew from about 30,000 in 1567 to over 200,000 by the early 1780s. Its exchange, which was accommodated in a splendid building erected between 1609 and 1611, took the same development as Antwerp's before it: it created a commodities market, but also a system of payment which was independent of the fairs, even if it did not operate through its own framework, but through a bank of exchange which will be mentioned in a moment. In 1585 some 205 different commodities were traded at Amsterdam; in 1675 there were as many as 491. In the same year the London exchange listed the prices of 305 commodities. From 1609 a weekly bulletin was published which gave the prices of various products. The stock exchange soon emerged side-by-side with the commodities trade. Initially it was above all the shares of the Dutch East India Company, soon also those of the West Indies Company, which changed hands. Later still, bonds issued by the two Companies were added, but above all loans of the City of Amsterdam, the Province of Holland and the United Provinces. Towards the end of the century, foreign governments also tried to place their loans. Finally speculative futures markets developed in both commodities and shares against which all bans proved powerless.

One of the main reasons for Amsterdam's rise to the position of the largest financial market in Europe was the founding of the *Wisselbank* in 1609. It was this bank which broke the hegemony of the Genoese markets, until then the most important international clearing centre. Being a clearing bank, the *Wisselbank* was nothing new, but formed the terminal point on a 'tradition-bound axis' (H. van der Wee) in the history of European banking. It was only the Antwerp-London axis which opened up new perspectives. The number of deposit accounts held at the *Wisselbank* rose from 708 in 1611 to 2,698 in 1701. Total deposits increased from 925,562 guilders in 1610 to 16,248,849 guilders in 1700.

The *Wisselbank* was not a credit bank. It gave credits only to either the City of Amsterdam or generally the Dutch East India Company. The *Wisselbank* made Amsterdam the most important market for precious metals in Europe. Between 15% and 25% of the silver which reached Spain from the Americas was sent directly to the Netherlands. It was used for balancing the accounts for trade and services between Spain and Spanish-America, on the one hand, and the northern Netherlands, on the other. A roughly similar percentage of American silver probably got to Holland through other channels. This means that the financial world of Amsterdam was able to dispose over a significant part of the Spanish silver imports. In the second half of the 17th century a fleet of 30–50 ships accompanied by war ships sailed into Amsterdam harbour every autumn. The city's dominant position in international finance was reflected in an enormous export of capital which was related to investments abroad. Governments in need of funds turned to Amsterdam and sought to place loans on its capital market. It was in connection with such financial transactions that the Dutch capitalists gained control of Swedish copper and the mercury deposits in Idria. Louis de Greer established a financial empire in Sweden the likes of which did not exist elsewhere.

The leading role of the Northern Netherlands in international trade and finance mobilized their neighbours. The English tried to oust the Dutch from their position as intermediaries and to gain control of world trade. They also aimed to establish a system of *entrepôts* of their own. The Navigation Acts of 1651 and 1660, the acts of 1662, 1669, 1673 and 1696 as well as the trade wars of 1652-54, 1665-67 and 1672-74 are reflections of these policies. Above all, England was keen to disrupt the trade links which the Dutch had established with the English settlers in the West Indies and along the eastern seaboard of North America and to take the foreign trade of the colonies into their own hands. The English colonial system whose constitutional foundations had been laid in the Restoration period left little room for the trade relations of other nations. However, the significance of the Navigation Acts and the legislation that followed lay in something else. These laws established a tradition of trade policy-making which was no longer based on the monopoly of individual companies, but on 'a national trading interest' (Chr. Hill). There was no place in this system for monopolistic trade companies, unless they were prepared to subordinate themselves to the 'national monopoly'.

The outcome of the Anglo-Dutch Wars cleared the way for England to become the dominant trading nation in Europe. Between 1629 and 1686 her commercial fleet trebled, even though its size in 1686 of 340,000 tons was still well below that of the Dutch fleet. However, English re-exports rose from 100 index points in 1663-69 to 221 in 1699-1701, reflecting England's growing importance as the emporium for goods from the under-developed and colonial world. Capital which would have been invested in landed property only a century ago was now put largely into foreign trade. Issues of shares for joint-stock companies were frequently subscribed with surprising speed. Nor was it difficult to place debentures. In many cases shares were held by very few people. In 1675 some 700 investors owned the capital of the three most important trading companies, the East India Company, the Africa Company and the Hudson Bay Company. The medium-size investors tended to dominate the Africa Company. The East India Company, on the other hand, was increasingly controlled by a few very wealthy merchants. In 1691, more than a quarter of the total capital was held by eight people. Josiah Child, the Governor of the Company, owned 6.9% of it, amounting to £51,150.

As far as the development of financial institutions was concerned, England was even farther behind Holland than in her trade. A noteworthy stock-market did not emerge until the 1690s. But thereafter it expanded very quickly and assumed modern features. Antwerp rather than Amsterdam became the model for the structure of the English system of credit and finance. Antwerp's financial techniques, in particular those of endorsement and the discounting of debt certificates and bills of exchange, spread throughout England, soon giving the English a lead over the Dutch. Next to the acceptance of deposits and the issue of bank notes, the discounting business became the most important activity of the London bankers, most of whom were goldsmiths by professional origin. The Bank of England also adopted these practices after it had been founded as a joint-stock company in 1696 to reorganize the English state debt. This made the Bank of England the most modern financial institution in Europe which left the exchange banks of the Continent well behind.

The 17th century was the high noon of merchant capitalism both in the Northern Netherlands and in England. In a few places it got involved in manufacturing, but this did not mean that these interests received much attention. The circulation sphere and the production sphere moved on different levels and an identity of interests between trade and manufacturing was lacking. Free Trade prevailed in the one sphere; protection of the domestic market against foreign competition, in the other. The growing volume of re-exports in Dutch and English foreign trade benefited the manufacturing sector only in a very limited way. The expansion of merchant capitalism threatened to hold back the development of manufacturing. However, in the 18th century industrial capital succeeded in establishing itself as an independent factor in England next to merchant capital. And once the Government had abolished the controls over the country's economic life during the Revolutionary period and had scrapped the monopolies in trade and industry, the system of industrial production could be put on a new footing. Moreover, in February 1700, the domestic manufacturers achieved an important victory against the commercial interests of the East India Company when they succeeded in getting legislation passed which was directed against the imports of Persian, Indian and Chinese silk and cotton products.

Nothing like this ever happened in the Netherlands. There the merchant capitalists and the financiers upheld their hegemony. As Marx put it succinctly: 'The history of the collapse of Holland as the dominant trading nation is the history of the subordination of commercial capital to industrial capital'. Proto-industrial developments within the national boundaries of their competitors deprived Dutch manufacturing with its low adaptability of its foreign markets. By the beginning of the 19th century textile production at Leiden was down to 30,000 pieces. Other crafts did not fare much better. Although the volume of trade declined but marginally, Holland's strong position in world trade was undermined. Between 1701–5 and 1771–75 her share of imports into England slumped from 11.2% to

*Table 27:*

Anglo-Dutch Trade, 1701/05–1771/75

(quinquennial averages)

|  | 1701/05 | | 1771/75 | |
|---|---|---|---|---|
|  | £(000s) | % | £(000s) | % |
| Total Brit. exports | 2 048.0 | 34.9 | 1 846.0 | 11.7 |
| Exports to Holland | 5 866.4 | 100.0 | 15 832.6 | 100.0 |
| Total Brit. imports | 562.0 | 11.2 | 457.0 | 3.5 |
| Imports from Holland | 4 794.2 | 100.0 | 12 884.4 | 100.0 |

3.5%. Only 11.7% instead of the previous 34.9% of English exports still passed through the Dutch *entrepôts* (see Table 27). By 1771–80 a mere 27.6% of the ships sailing through the Sound flew the Dutch flag. International finance now became the focus of the country's economic activity. But unlike in 19th-century England, Dutch foreign credits were not accompanied by stepped-up exports of manufactured goods. It is one of the ironies that the northern parts of the Netherlands should be overtaken again by their southern counterparts. As Maurice Dobb has rightly emphasized: 'The launching of a country on the first stages of the road towards capitalism is no guarantee that it will complete the journey.'

## 2.4 The Crisis of the 17th Century in its Socio-Economic Context

The crisis of the 17th century started off as an agricultural crisis which was rooted in the price revolution of the previous century. It is possible that it was exacerbated by climatic changes. Some people have spoken of the 'little ice age' which is assumed to have afflicted Europe. The demographic aspects of the 16th-century history have already been analysed (see above p. 18). However, by the turn of the 17th century and definitely by the middle of that century there was a reversal of earlier population trends. The size of the population began to stagnate or even declined. It did not take long for the economic repercussions of this development to be felt, above all in agriculture. Demand for basic foodstuffs dropped, because, as we have seen before, it was more directly linked to varying population sizes than were more expensive manufactured goods.

It might be objected that, as the size of cultivated land was also shrinking, food supplies would presumably have fallen in proportion to the demographic losses. However, it must be taken into consideration here that the food crisis of the 16th century had led to large areas of marginal soil which yielded very little being taken under the plough. When the economy turned around, these fields were probably the first to be abandoned. This meant that the production of cereals did not decline to the same extent as the population had done and that the marginal cost of agricultural production also decreased. In other words, when the supply was greater than the demand and productivity saw at least a slight increase, prices were bound to fall. And this is precisely what happened up to the early decades of the 18th century (see Figure 1, p. 4). A further factor must be added when one looks at the development in England and the northern parts of the Netherlands. There the decline in prices was presumably due not merely to demographic change, but also to a growing agricultural output. This stepping-up of production was the specific manner in which the Dutch and English farmers responded to the crisis.

However, the crisis of the 17th century was not just and not exclusively a 'Malthusian' crisis. It also gave rise to tremendous social problems. There are many indications that the growing subsistence crisis became exacerbated because the feudal lords tightened their grip on agricultural incomes. They increased their pressure in the struggle for the distribution of these incomes once it became clear that their own losses could not be made up from other sources. Thus the Languedoc witnessed a 'rent offensive' (E. Le Roy Ladurie) in the first six decades of the 17th century. Rents increased from 1–1.5 hecto-litres of grain per hectare around 1550 to three or more hecto-litres. Increases by 100% occurred in the Paris region and in the Soissonais. In some other regions such as the Hurepoix and the Poitou, south of the River Loire, 17th-century levels had been reached as early as 1560. In some parts of England payments to the landlords rose more steeply than the price of grain (see Table 11, p. 50). The feudal lords, it is true, were forced, as the crisis deepened, to reduce the contributions if they wished to avoid their own ruin. But in many cases the state appeared on the scene to grab what the lords had left. Soon indirect state taxes surpassed the reductions in direct rents, squeezing the peasant economy even further. Everything pointed towards an irresistible downhill slide. In the Languedoc rent rises came to a halt by 1675–80 at the latest; there now followed a fall in rents which amounted to 20% in some cases and 50% in others. Meanwhile, the *taille* which had doubled between 1580–90 and 1650 from 6.2% to 13% of the gross agricultural product was pushed up even more massively after 1690. These new burdens spelt the doom for many a peasant. If one calculates the tax burden of the French population in terms of work days, it becomes clear that it trebled between 1588 and 1683. The tax rate rose from 5.0% to 15.5% (see Table 28). In the Beauvaisis north of Paris the share was even 20% to which must be added another 20% for rent.

*Table 28:*

Growth of tax burdens in France, 1515–1683

|      | Total taxes levied (A)[1] | Gross agric. product (B)[1] | (A) as a % of (B) | Taxes per head of family (C)[2] | Taxes calcul. in workdays (D)[3] |
|------|------|------|------|------|------|
| 1515 | 3.5  | 53.7 | 6.5  | 0.8  | 6.4  |
| 1547 | 7.4  | 178  | 4.2  | 1.4  | 7.0  |
| 1588 | 24   | 480  | 5    | 6    | 10.0 |
| 1607 | 31   | 389  | 8.0  | 4.8  | 13.6 |
| 1641 | 78   | 533  | 14.6 | 28   | 34.4 |
| 1661 | 79   | 744  | 10.6 | 18.1 | 20.8 |
| 1675 | 98   | 514  | 19.0 | 25.2 | 34.0 |
| 1683 | 106  | 690  | 15.4 | 23.6 | 31.2 |

[1] = millions of 'livres tournois';    [2] = 'livres tournois'; for a family of four; [3] Based on wage levels of Parisian building-workers.

In Western Europe the agricultural crisis resulted partly from the combined pressure of landlords and the state. In Eastern Europe, on the other hand, it was an outgrowth of the more traditional feudal mode of production and its contradictions which had undergone a fresh twist when the landlords decided to rely primarily on serf labour services. Thenceforth the *Vorwerk* became the focal point of the rural economy and its constitution. The peasant economy found it impossible to expand production the more it lost control of its labour process and the more it was incorporated into the seigneurial economy. With the end of the 16th century boom approaching, feudal pressures on the peasants increased. The landlords tried to meet the reduction in the returns from the sale of their produce with increased production and a cutting of their costs. Hence they enlarged their *Vorwerke*, reduced the workforce and the number of animals and relied on the services of the peasants. The consequences were pernicious for both the demesnes and the peasant economy. Yields declined and so did the number of peasants. The size of cultivated land and of livestock contracted. Ultimately the landlords even had to provide the peasants with draught animals to be maintained by the latter, if they did not want to jeopardize production on the *Vorwerke* (see Table 29). Thus excessive exploitation helped to trigger off the crisis.

*Table 29:*

Index of changes in the structure of agriculture in the Kalisz province (Poland), ca. 1600–ca. 1650

|  | ca. 1600 | ca. 1650 |
|---|---|---|
| 1. Land farmed by peasants | | |
| 1.1 Total acreage | 100 | 64–72 |
| 1.2 Land per peasant-holding | 100 | 80–85 |
| 2. *Wüstungen* (total acreage) | 100 | 400–500 |
| 3. *Vorwerk* land | | |
| 3.1 Noble demesnes | 100 | 113 |
| 3.2 Ecclesiastical demesnes | 100 | 116–130 |
| 3.3 Royal demesnes | 100 | 126–145 |
| 4. Total cultivated land | 100 | 87–89 |
| 5. Population size of villages | 100 | 75–80 |
| 6. Draught animals | | |
| 6.1 Total | 100 | 60–70 |
| 6.2 Per peasant-holding | 100 | 80–85 |
| 6.3 In relation to acreage | 100 | 95–100 |
| 6.4 Supplied by demesnes | 100 | 200 |

War and uprisings also contributed to the pressures on the peasants and to seal the collapse of the rural economy. These were of course factors which cannot always, and sometimes no more than partially, be included in a discussion of the socio-economic aspects of the crisis. The Thirty Years' War or the various wars in Northern Europe in the second half of the 17th century were more extraneous. The *Fronde* in France, on the other hand, was both a reflection of, and an element in, the crisis. Other factors, above all plagues and epidemics, must be added. And again it will have to be left to further research to decide how far they represented the culmination of a long-drawn-out crisis.

The manufacturing sector followed the general course of the agricultural depression. But its specific characteristics prevented it from following exactly the same path. Exceptions always admitted, prices for manufactured goods did not decline as sharply as those for grain. As before, these goods proved less susceptible to demographic fluctuations. Moreover, once the economy began to slacken, purchasing power became available which had thus far been absorbed by the higher cost of food and drink. On the other hand, it must be remembered that the gains made in the purchasing power of wage earners and small craftsmen were counterbalanced by losses on the part of the agricultural producers. In the long term, however, changes in the demand structure were more important than those which, like the ones mentioned above, can be directly related to the ups and downs in the economy. There was the disproportionately large growth of the cities from the 17th century, the incipient commercialization of agriculture and proto-industrialization. These developments led to an increase in the number of households which were dependent on the market.

Even more important than the fall in prices and wage rises was the manner in which the merchant entrepreneurs and *Verleger* reacted to the fact that their profit margins were being reduced at both ends. This reaction took three forms:

(1) Rising labour costs induced them to move manufacturing to the countryside on an even larger scale and to rely on the rural labour potential.

(2) Falling prices led them to turn to mass production which reduced unit costs through higher output and thus enabled the merchant capitalists to maximise profits by means of a larger turnover rather than by trying to increase their gains through higher unit prices. The changeover from expensive 'old draperies' to cheap 'new draperies' and from fustian to linen, which have been discussed earlier (see above p. 34), are cases in point.

(3) The merchant capitalists stepped up the expansion of trade with the underdeveloped and colonial world in an attempt to shore up the precarious demand situation in the domestic markets. In this process, the 'old colonial system' based on extraction was replaced by a 'new form of colonialism' represented by the plantation economy (E.J. Hobsbawm).

These responses of the merchant capitalists to the crisis stimulated the production of goods. On the other hand, the crises tended to deepen where the new methods were not adopted. The extension of craft production into the countryside was a very serious blow to the urban export economy which was constrained by the guild system. Those regions which did not switch from old to new draperies in time, were badly hit by the crises. With the emergence of Holland, England and France as the centres of the embryonic capitalist world system, the countries of the Mediterranean slipped into a position half way towards the periphery. The expensive goods of their manufacturers were squeezed out of the international markets. A proto-industrial development which might have put them in a position to keep up with their competitors in North-western Europe failed to take place. How far the manufacturing sector in the Northwest began to diverge from that of the South may be gauged from the output of the Tolfa alum mining works near Rome and the customs accounts of the Sound. The Tolfa works held a quasi-monopoly of alum which was indispensable for the dyeing of textiles. But after 1614 production at Tolfa declined steadily. On the other hand, exports of raw materials such as iron ore, flax and hemp from the Baltic region rose from the middle of the 17th century, while the grain trade fell behind (see Figure 17). Iron ore exports from Stockholm rose by 85% between 1648 and 1700. Some 44% of all these exports went to England.

*Figure 17:*
Index of exports by volume of different commodities to Western Europe through the Sound, 1562/66–1770/80
(1731/39 = 100)

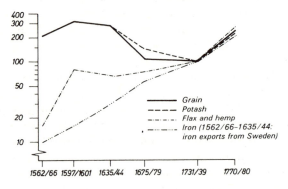

Eric Hobsbawm has argued that 'the "crisis" itself created the conditions which were to make the industrial revolution possible'. In making this statement he thought above all of the concentration movements and shifts which were unleashed by the crisis and then sharpened that crisis. It appears that these shifts occurred on the international and interregional level, i.e. from the land powers towards the sea powers and from grain production towards stock-farming and proto-industry. The interregional shift was accompanied by a move away from urban manufacturing towards rural cottage industries. These developments accelerated a division of labour on an international, interregional and societal plain and boosted the exchange of goods. Thus the flow of information was improved within the trading network which emerged in North-western Europe, and which was soon to stretch across the globe. At the same time the costs of commercial transactions decreased. The emergent interregional division of labour made intensified agricultural production a more attractive proposition. But it also led to a reallocation of rural labour either in favour of farming or of proto-industrial production. In either case the rural populations ceased to produce goods or food for their own consumption. The system of partial barter which had been a feature of a peasant economy began to disintegrate. The latter became a demand factor of the national economy concerned. The market principle established itself, and the division of labour became firmly entrenched.

Once the population trend had been reversed, the demographic problem which had caused the most serious tensions in the social structure of Europe in the 16th and early 17th centuries began to disappear. The slight rise in the level of real wages worked in the same direction. This rise was due to the fact that the supply and demand of labour started to converge while per capita output rose and the cost of living declined. And yet neither the demographic shift nor the short-lived increase in real wages were able to arrest a long-term pauperization process. There was no relief for peasants whose burdens continued to increase as taxation or feudal services rose in Western and Central Europe and in East-Central and Eastern Europe respectively. Famines and wars had permanently weakened the productive potential of the peasant economy. Indebtedness assumed enormous proportions. For the Beauvaisis the records of some 60 suits have been investigated which were initiated between 1683 and 1685 in protest against high tax demands. These cases showed that the indebtedness of only nine peasants was less than one quarter of their total assets; in 14 cases it was half and in 29 slightly above that; in the case of eight peasants it was even above that percentage. Thus indebtedness became a decisive stage on the road which ended in expropriation. And indeed expropriation made rapid strides unless the landlords or the village were prepared, and able, to stem it. In some regions of France the percentage of peasants farming their land dropped to less than one third. the new owners were the *noblesse de robe*, the Church and—especially in the vicinity of larger towns—the bourgeoisie. Up to a point, the French peasants therefore shared the fate of their English counterparts.

Central and Eastern Europe were spared from the process of expropriation. Where it can be demonstrated to have taken place, it remained within the rural community. Indebtedness did not result in dissolution, but led to the transfer of property titles within peasant society. The Thirty Years' War had put no more than a temporary halt to the process of differentiation within the peasantry, and although this process amounted to an expropriation of some peasants, it nevertheless remained internal to the rural economy. In general, those peasants who actually owned their land remained unaffected and in fact stood up to economic pressures relatively well. East of the River Elbe, on the other hand, they did not always escape the effects of the proliferating *Vorwerk* system. Thus in 1569 tenants of the King in Masovia holding more than half a *Hufe* made up 36% of the peasant population. By 1616 they had been decimated to 10%, and by 1660 they had all but disappeared. At this time 40% of the farms had a size of between a quarter and one half of a *Hufe;* 43% had a quarter and 17% even less than that. But these figures assume their significance only if one remembers that a peasant on half a *Hufe* of land lived on the verge of the subsistence minimum.

Expropriation, pauperization and differentiation created the preconditions for the emergence of proto-industrial regions. Once rural manufacturing had established itself in a particular area, the number of people living on the margins of peasant society grew quickly, ultimately to reach a size which society as a whole proved unable to cope with. In 1660 some 62.1% of the households of Rossendale and four other villages in the textile region of Lancashire held plots of land worth less than £5. In large parts of East-Central and Eastern Europe, on the other hand, where the demesne monopolized the labour market the path for a proto-industrial development was necessarily blocked.

The pressures which the peasants were forced to live under led them to stage innumerable uprisings in the 17th century. These uprisings broke out all across Europe, from England to the frontiers of the Russian Empire in the Southeast. They were most numerous in France, where one uprising followed the other between 1624 and 1675. The rebellions of the *Nouveaux Croquants* of 1636 in the Southwest, of the *Nu-pieds* of 1639 in Normandy, of the *Sabotiers* in the Sologne (1658), of the *Lustucrus* in the Boulonnais (1662) and of the *Bonnet Rouges* in Brittany (1675) are just a few examples in a long chain. Resentments against the *seigneurs* combined in these uprisings with resistance to taxation, with the latter being the decisive cause except for the 1675 rebellion in Brittany.

The dominant classes did not remain completely unscathed by the crisis of the 17th century either. However, unlike the peasants, they succeeded in developing policies which cushioned them against its effects comparatively well and which are best described as 'nationalization' and 'oligarchization'. What is meant by these terms is that the nobility formed an alliance with the state. This enabled the aristocracy to participate in the distribution of tax revenues extracted by the state from the peasantry and thus to make up the fall in feudal rents. However the nobles had to pay for this by allowing the state to divest them of their original feudal privileges, to recruit them into its service and to emasculate them politically. On the other hand, in order to cement the social status hierarchies, they sealed themselves off from inferior social groups.

The tendency to form oligarchies which can be observed throughout Europe at this time even reached England and the northern parts of the Netherlands. The successful revolt of the Netherlands against Spain saw the rise to power of the wealthy merchants who represent the upper crust in the cities, with major changes taking place only in Amsterdam in this respect. These oligarchies determined the political fate of the Republic until 1795. The nobility was ousted and since then lived no more than a shadow existence. The conduct of state business had been taken over by the merchant capitalists. However, there was a reversal of this development from the second half of the 17th century. The patricians turned their backs on commerce, lived as *rentiers* and tried to establish themselves as a new aristocracy.

England's unprecedented social mobility of the years 1540–1660 lost its momentum with the end of the price revolution, the growth of the population and the contraction of the property market. The aristocracy and the upper gentry succeeded in expanding their holdings of land at the expense of the lower gentry and the peasants. Moreover, they tried to erect barriers between themselves and the social groups below. The exercise of political power was in the hands of this extremely wealthy and influential land-owning class. But side-by-side with the 'feudal' hierarchies which they promoted there emerged other status hierarchies which had a decisive impact on the shape of English society. In 1688, Gregory King counted as many as 10,000 'merchants and traders by sea', 10,000 'persons in offices and places', 10,000 'persons in the law', 10,000 'clergy-men', 15,000 people 'in liberal arts and sciences' and 9,000 army and naval officers. King estimated that their combined income surpassed that of the 16,586 noble households by as much as 36% (see Table 30). These groups and the first four in particular increasingly enjoyed recognition by the aristocracy, not least because many sons of aristocratic families who were excluded from inheritance by the system of primogeniture were accepted into these other groups. Intermarriage was no exception. The merchant capitalists, it is true, remained excluded from the centres of political power. On the other hand, monied and landed interests had already become too closely intertwined for the ruling oligarchies to be able to ignore the former completely. To this extent the emergent status system of England is a pointer of later developments. Meanwhile the blatant inequalities in the distribution of wealth remained untouched by these developments (see Table 30).

*Table 30:*

Gregory King's scheme of social structure and income of England for 1688

| | No. of households | | Income in pounds | | |
| | abs. | % | per household | total | % |
|---|---|---|---|---|---|
| Aristocracy | 186 ⎱ | | 2 590.3 | 481 800 | |
| Gentry | 16 400 ⎰ 1.2 | | 315.5 | 5 174 000 | 13.0 |
| | | | | | |
| Merchant and Traders by Sea | 10 000 | | 240.0 | 2 400 000 | |
| Persons in Offices and Places | 10 000 | | 180.0 | 1 800 000 | |
| Persons in the law | 10 000 | | 140.0 | 1 400 000 | |
| Clergy-men | 10 000 | | 48.0 | 480 000 | |
| | | 4.8 | | | 17.7 |
| Persons in Lib. Arts & Sciences | 16 000 | | 60.0 | 960 000 | |
| | | | | | |
| Naval & Military Officers | 9 000 | | 71.1 | 640 000 | |
| Freeholders | 180 000 | | 57.6 | 10 360 000 | |
| Farmers | 150 000 | 31.6 | 44.0 | 6 600 000 | 48.6 |
| Shopkeepers, Tradesmen, Artisans | 100 000 | | 42.0 | 4 200 000 | |
| Labouring People, Outservants | 364 000 | | 15.0 | 5 460 000 | |
| Cottagers and Paupers | 400 000 | 62.4 | 5.0 | 2 000 000 | 20.6 |
| Common Seamen and Soldiers | 85 000 | | 17.5 | 1 490 000 | |
| Vagrants | [30 000][1] | | [2.0][1] | 60 000 | 0.1 |
| Totals | 1 360 586 | 100.0 | 31.9 | 43 505 800 | 100.0 |

[1] No. of persons, resp. income per person

# 3. The Upswing of the 18th Century

Just as the crisis of the late middle ages was followed by the price revolution of the 16th and early 17th centuries, the crisis of the 17th century led to a new phase of economic expansion in the 18th. Once the tensions within the productive sectors of the economy had been removed, once the balance between population and food supplies had been restored and the ravages of the wars overcome, a longer period of growth could begin. This upswing was reinforced by the process of industrialization which started in England in the 18th century and somewhat later on the European Continent and which resulted in the largely self-sustained, though still crisis-prone, growth of industrial capitalism. Periodic food crises, to be sure, continued until the middle of the 19th century—the last one of the traditional type being the crisis of 1845–47 which preceded the 1848 Revolution; but the agricultural revolution gradually began to flatten out the fluctuations of the harvest cycle. The growth period spread to Central Europe around the turn of the 18th century. The economies of other countries followed suit in the 1730s and 1740s.

## 3.1 Population: From Crisis to Growth

The demographic trend underwent another shift in the 18th century. The growth which set in at this time ultimately reached its climax in the population explosion which accompanied the Industrial Revolution. It lasted until the late 19th century when a different balance began to emerge which was characterized by declining birth and mortality rates as well as a smaller demographic surplus.

All in all, the population growth of the 18th century took place within quite narrow limits. As can be seen from Table 31, it did not surpass that of the 16th century. Nor did the divergent growth patterns change which were characteristic of North and North-western Europe, on the one hand, and Central, Western and Southern Europe, on the other, and which we had occasion to observe for the 16th and 17th centuries. This did not prevent some regions, in particular in East-Central Europe, from developing growth rates

*Table 31:*

Index of population change, 1700–1800

|  | 1700 | 1800 |
|---|---|---|
| Northern and Northern Europe | 100 | 166 |
| Central, Western and Southern Europe | 100 | 138 |
| Totals | 100 | 144 |

which outpaced those of England and the southern parts of the Netherlands. Germany, on the other hand, recovered but slowly from the population losses of the Thirty Years' War. It appears that they had not been made good even as late as 1700. Württemberg reached its pre-1618 level only in 1730. Similar figures apply to the Electorate of Hesse. Thus, while the population of the western German territories increased relatively slowly, that of East Elbia grew all the more rapidly. Between 1748 and 1800 the population of the Prussian core provinces (i.e. excluding the Prussian possessions in Western Germany) rose from 100 index points to 161. In France, though she remained the most populous state of Europe, the size of the population went up from 100 in 1700 to 134 in 1800. The figures for Italy are similar: 100 in 1700, rising to 135 in 1800.

Meanwhile the population of the northern parts of the Netherlands was almost stagnant, growing from 100 in 1700 in 111 in 1800. But the country's southern parts saw an extraordinary expansion from 100 in 1700 to 194 a hundred years later. These rates were considerably higher than those for England and Wales which rose to 157 by 1800. Broadly speaking, the rate of expansion accelerated not insignificantly in the second half of the 18th century. To quote but one example: the English rate shot up from 0.10% to 0.79% per annum. This must be taken as an indication that demography in the 18th century is part of a more comprehensive process of change. In this respect it differed fundamentally from the population growth of the 16th century.

As far as the causes of the 18th-century expansion are concerned, everything appears, at first glance, to point to the importance of falling mortality rates. The plague, having raged in Marseille for the last time in 1720, retreated from Europe. The advance of medical knowledge continued to be small. Nevertheless, inoculation against small-pox which was pioneered in England in the late 18th century was not without effect. Famines became less severe without, however, disappearing completely. The food crisis of 1771—72 was particularly serious in Central Europe. For example, in the Electorate of Saxony mortality rates doubled in 1772. Until then there had been a surplus of births over deaths. But now 64,532 more people died than were born. Yet such crises were no longer able to determine the broader demographic trend in any decisive way. Mortality rates, calculated over the century as a whole, were on the decline, particularly in the second half. Average life expectancy increased.

However, it would be rash to explain the population growth of the 18th century exclusively in terms of falling mortality rates. The marriage age, as we have seen, had gone up again from the end of the 16th century. It would therefore not be illogical to assume that people married younger again once the new growth cycle had set in. Indeed there are a number of examples of this, such as Colyton, Shepshed and Heuchelheim (see Table 17, p. 63). But large parts of France did not follow this pattern. Instead, from the middle of the century a further rise occurred in the average marriage age. Birth control continued to spread so that in 1778 a French writer felt obliged to speak of 'dark secrets' which had reached the countryside. 'Nature is being outwitted even in the villages', he wrote. It would seem plausible that birth control was a response to a growing population. Above all, it is not sufficient to explain regional differences in population growth in terms of economic fluctuations and variations. We must search for factors which were operative only in the region concerned. Proto-industrialization and the commercialization of large-scale agriculture in East-Central Europe were such factors.

Proto-industrialization became one of the most important engines of population growth. Whereas Silesia had no more than 49 inhabitants per sq. kilometer, the figure for some districts in the mountainous parts of that region was 71–80, rising to 135 inhabitants per sq. kilometer in zones of concentrated manufacturing. Thus in the Upper Eichsfeld region southeast of Göttingen, the production of textiles had spread to the countryside, and in 1792–3 Johann Wolf, in his *Political History of the Eichsfeld,* described the situation as follows: 'Precisely the opportunity of making a living from weaving and spinning, has made marriage, on which agriculture and the absence of anything beyond essential crafts had imposed their limits in earlier times, very much easier and has filled the countryside with people.' Wolf's explanation of these developments was essentially correct. The marriage age came down and the number of children per marriage went up. These trends emerge very clearly, especially for the second half of the 18th century, from a glance at Table 32 and Figure 18 which juxtapose the demography of Shepshed, a stocking weavers'

*Table 32:*

## Indices of population change in the villages of Shepshed and Bottesford in Leicestershire/England, 1700–1824

|  | Shepshed | | Bottesford | |
|  | 1700/49 | 1750/1824 | 1700/49 | 1750/99 |
|---|---|---|---|---|
| No. of births per female[1] | 3.94 | 5.53 | 4.65 | 4.10 |
| Percentage of surviving children | 66.8 | 68.6 | 63.3 | 70.2 |
| Percentage of children marrying | 85.2 | 91.8 | 85.0 | 87.0 |
| Marrying daughters per mother[2] | 1.12 | 1.74 | 1.25 | 1.25 |
| Annual growth rate (%) | 0.35 | 1.74 | 0.70 | 0.69 |
| No. of years for population to double | 200.6 | 40.1 | 100.0 | 101.4 |

[1]Revised Gross Reproduction Rate (GRR);   [2]Net Reproduction Rate (NRR)

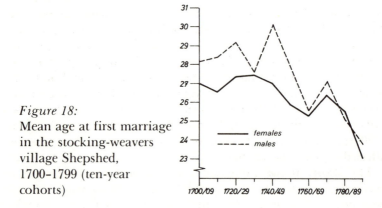

*Figure 18:*
Mean age at first marriage in the stocking-weavers village Shepshed, 1700–1799 (ten-year cohorts)

village, with that of Bottesford, a peasant village. It was proto-industrialization which freed population growth from its traditional constraints. It thus prepared the way for living conditions which were to become the dominant pattern in the phase of capitalist industrialization.

In East-Central Europe another factor stimulated population growth no less than proto-industrialization. This was the replacement of the *Vorwerke* (using serf labour) by self-managed estates based on wage labour, the beginnings of which can be traced back to the middle of the 18th century. We have seen how the system of agricultural production in the East had come to rely primarily on serf labour. Only a small force of unattached land labourers and domestic servants was required under this system. But things began to change again from the second half of the 18th century, and landlords started to employ wage labourers in larger numbers for whom a multitude of small jobs, together with living quarters, had to be created. And once these had become full-time positions capable of supporting a family, it is not surprising that the birth rate should rise and the population grow quite rapidly. The commercialization of the large estates of East-Central Europe unleashed a population boom.

### 3.2 Agriculture: Expansion or Revolution?

The upturn on the agricultural markets set in around the 1730s and 1740s. It was only in Central Europe that it started as early as the late 17th century, and only to experience a serious setback at the beginning of the 18th. Starting from an index position of 100 for 1730-41, grain prices rose to the following figures up by the 1790s: Germany = 169; Austria = 130; Poland = 123; Northern Italy = 182; New Castille = 230; France = 150; England = 190; northern parts of the Netherlands = 200 (see Figure 1, p. 4). Prices for animal products and manufactured goods did not keep up with those for grain. Higher grain prices were bound to affect ground rents. Land and rents became more expensive. The cost of leases for land which had not been enclosed rose by around 40-50% in England between 1750 and 1790; they doubled and trebled in France between 1730-39 and 1780-89. Only towards the end of the century was Central Europe affected by a similar boom.

The slowly improving price and cost positions of agriculture encouraged the expansion of agricultural production, and not only in respect of the acreage taken under the plough, but also in respect of the amount of capital and labour deployed. This expansion reached its limit when marginal yields began to balance out marginal costs although the pressures of poverty frequently pushed small units, run by a family without wage labour, beyond this limit.

As in the two earlier periods of growth in European agriculture, the use and cultivation of land was extended. Thus the 18th century is the third great period of agricultural expansion in European economic history. Reclaiming work assumed considerable dimensions in Brandenburg-Prussia where it was supported by the state. The swampy regions along the rivers Oder and Warthe (*Oderbruch* and the *Warthebrüche*) as well as the *Havelländische Luch* near Berlin were drained. Of more immediate benefit to the farmer than these ambitious undertakings was the reclaiming work done around the estates and farms by the owners themselves. In Schleswig-Holstein acreage increased by 20% when parts of the region's moors and heaths were taken under the plough. As was reported in 1811: 'Just as wastelands were ploughed up and woodlands which were economically useless were cleared, trenches were dug in moor-like fields, on which up to now nothing but miserable reeds had grown (which, whether green or dried, did not provide good fodder for the animals); drained of its acids, the soil was made available for the cultivation of rye.'

Agricultural land in the Breisgau in Southwestern Germany increased by nearly 74% between 1699 and 1798. The percentage growth of newly cultivated vineyards and vegetable gardens as well as of pastures was even larger. In Catalonia, too, agricultural land was extended, ponds were drained and forests were cleared. The institution which was to become the Academy of Sciences at Barcelona asserted in 1770 that the extension of agricultural land had continued without interruption since 1720. In the northern parts of the Netherlands efforts were stepped up after 1765 to reclaim land through the construction of dykes. The index of reclaimed land rose from 94.8 in 1740-64 to 168.3 in 1765-89. France went so far as to introduce a number of laws in 1761, 1764 and 1766 which promoted an extension of agricultural land by granting tax relief. However, the scheme did not have much success. The size of agricultural land probably increased by much less than 10% between 1730 and 1789. It is more likely that 'social tensions' rose (E. Labrousse) as a result of these policies because the clearing of woods and wastelands tended to impinge upon common rights.

In England the enclosure movement experienced a veritable boom from the middle of the 18th century. Between 1721 and 1750 Parliament passed no more than 100 bills of enclosure. However, their number went up to 156, to 424 and finally to 642 in the following three decades respectively. The movement reached its climax during the Napoleonic Wars (see Figure 19, which also relates enclosures to the price of grain). These figures do not include 'enclosures by agreement' even if these, too, were frequently effected under pressure. It has been estimated that about half of the land changed hands by agreement, with the other half being enclosed by Acts of Parliament. The enclosure of 'open fields' did not affect the total amount of cultivated land. Only where enclosures included wasteland and common land was this amount pushed up. The motives behind the

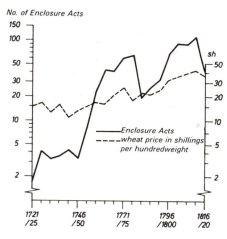

*Figure 19:*
Number of enclosure acts of Parliament and development of wheat prices in England, 1721–1820 (quinquennial averages)

enclosure movement were mainly financial. Income from leases of enclosed land were on average twice as high. Yields on investments which were related to enclosure were between 15% and 20%.

For the first time, common land came under pressure also on the Continent. A policy known as *Verkoppelung* made considerable progress in the Duchies of Schleswig and Holstein as well as in the regions bordering on them. *Verkoppelung* related to fields and commons *(Koppeln)* which were removed from collective use. The Allgäu and the area north of Lake Constance saw an accelerated *Vereinödung*, i.e. the depopulation of villages and hamlets in connection with the creation of larger units and the abolition of common rights. In other places changes such as these proceeded much more slowly, however vigorously the authorities and agricultural experts may have advocated them. What generally frustrated their efforts was the resistance of those who thought they had most to lose. They were usually people from the lower strata of the peasantry, but not infrequently also landlords, especially where they owned large flocks of sheep which they sent across the peasants' grain fields after the end of the harvest.

The intensification of agricultural production at first developed along the lines with which we are already familiar from our analysis of the 16th century. Grassland was taken under the plough; stock-farming gave way to agriculture. The 'greed for agricultural land' assumed proportions that shocked many contemporaries; but this was not even the end of it. This time the rural economy broke out of the narrow framework of intensification alternating with extensive agriculture. Thenceforth intensification did not merely amount to extending the acreage of the land under cultivation, but it also began to affect the structures of agricultural production as a whole.

The fallow was the first to catch the attention of those who aimed to increase the productivity of agriculture. The method was to replace the three-field-system by what was called the 'improved three-field-system'. The triannual rhythm was retained, but the fallow was planted with summer crops such as peas, beans, sweet peas, clover, lupins and flax. Potatoes were also grown, though only in limited quantities at this time. Western Germany was the region in which the fallow was vigorously reduced through the introduction of fallow crops. However, the farther east one moved, the smaller was the proportion of these crops in relation to the total area under cultivation. Around 1800 the share of these crops was 14% for the whole of Germany; but it was 25% in the *Schwarzbrache* (fallow) regions. The traditional three-field-system remained the predominant mode of production in East-Central and Eastern Europe. Attempts to modify the system in these parts of Europe were few and far between. Little progress was also made in France. As late as 1840 the fallow comprised 27% of total acreage. To some extent this may be due to the setbacks which the process of agricultural innovation suffered during the French Revolution. There were not just technical difficulties preventing a reduction of the fallow. The changes met with resistance because they were predicated on the abolition of grazing rights on the fallow which were held by villagers and the landlords. The new methods ultimately called the entire rural system of production into question.

To this extent, the introduction of *Koppelwirtschaft* in Schleswig-Holstein, Denmark, Mecklenburg and Brandenburg was a much bigger step forward than the growing of summer crops on the fallow. This type of system had been developed in Schleswig-Holstein as early as the 16th century. In the 18th century, then, it spread north and from there further east. The term derives from the practice of turning cultivated land into pastures. After a number of years in which the land had been used for grain-growing there followed a period in which it was left for grazing. Under certain circumstances it was also left fallow for one or two years. But as Johann Heinrich von Thünen, the famous agronomist of the 19th century, noted, *Koppelwirtschaft* was economical only in periods of high grain prices, since it was considerably more intensive than the three-field-system. The 18th century was such a period. *Koppelwirtschaft* began to establish itself in Mecklenburg towards the end of the 17th century. But it was only a century later that it had become the dominant system of land cultivation. It then spread to Brandenburg where it became known as *märkische Koppelwirtschaft* because of the introduction of root crops into the cycle.

The most intensive form of agriculture, known as crop rotation, gained a foothold on the European Continent but very slowly. In line with Thünen's model—the Thünen Circles—it was to be found primarily in the vicinity of large towns. A few estates adopted crop rotation around the turn of the 19th century, after a variant, the so-called *'englische Wirtschaft'* (English System) had proliferated from the 1760s onwards. The first beginnings of crop rotation can be traced to the Netherlands in the 16th century, and here it also established itself most widely by comparison with other Continental countries. In England the transition to crop rotation was completed during the crisis period of the late 17th and early 18th centuries. Tull, Townshend and Coke of Norfolk who were once seen as the inventors of the new methods were the ones who popularized them in the 18th century. By the time grain prices began to rise again in the second half of the century, crop rotation had firmly established itself. There was hence no danger that forage crops might be restricted again in favour of grain production. On the contrary, the enclosure movement which accelerated under the impact of the agricultural boom created the preconditions for the use of crop rotation even in those areas where the fragmentation of the land had prevented its introduction until then. Thus enclosure contributed not merely to an extension of arable land, but also to an intensification of agricultural production.

The gap between England and the Netherlands, on the one hand, and the rest of the Continent, on the other, is very clearly reflected in the ratios between seeds and yields for grain. The figures in Table 3 (see above p. 22) show that the ratios were around 1:10 in the Netherlands and 1:7.5–8 in England. In France they were 1:6 and a mere 1:4.9 in Germany. The figure for Schleswig-Holstein was 1:6.5, which provides an indication of the progress made there when *Koppelwirtschaft* was introduced.

Stock-farming in the 18th century, not unlike that of the 16th, was very much in the shadow of the booming grain trade. Prices for animal products lagged behind those for cereals. Regional exceptions apart, stock-farming was put in the service of agriculture. In Prussia animal products amounted to no more than 24% of the total cash value of agricultural production as a whole. However, some of the developments which took place in agriculture were also to the benefit of animal husbandry. The transition to the improved three-field-system, to *Koppelwirtschaft* and to crop rotation provided increased quantities of forage. Thus the notion of round-the-year indoor feeding was no longer a remote possibility. Indeed it was already being practised in some areas. In England there was also a greater emphasis on systematic breeding. The number of animals increased, and this in turn had a beneficial effect on agriculture which could not contemplate a marked increase in production without the availability of additional manure. 'Progress has the smell of manure' was therefore a very apposite contemporary saying.

Production relationships in the 18th century moved along the tracks which had been laid by developments of the two previous centuries. England approached the completion of a rural society differentiated into landlords, lease-holders and land labourers. By the end of the 18th century, peasants owned no more than about 15% of the land used for agricultural production. This decline, as we have seen, is closely linked with the crisis of the 17th century. The enclosures of the second half of the 18th century do not appear to have been of major importance anymore as far as the disappearance of the peasantry is concerned. Rather they represented the terminal point in a process of erosion which had gone on for a long time before. The rest of the agricultural land, i.e. about 85%, was in the hands of lease-holders. But also the number of small lease-holders decreased in parallel with the decline of the peasantry. We have figures for a number of estates which show that farms of between 21 and 100 acres diminished by half, whereas those of over 100 acres saw an increase (see Table 33). This development was in the interest of the landlords who desired a consolidation of their estates, as only large farms could be run efficiently. The cottagers and squatters, on the other hand, were demoted to the position of pure wage labourers who were forced to seek employment with the lease-holders. Another alternative was to make a living in the cottage industries although this choice was not always available. Common lands and wastelands had disappeared

*Table 33:*
Changes in the size of farms in the Bagot Estates
(Staffordshire), 1724–1764

| Year | Farms of 21–100 acres | | Farms of more than 100 acres | |
|---|---|---|---|---|
| | No. | Av. acreage | No. | Av. acreage |
| 1724 | 49 | 46 | 16 | 135 |
| 1744 | 31 | 54 | 21 | 173 |
| 1764 | 24 | 55 | 23 | 189 |

with the enclosure movement, and an essential source of maintenance had thus been destroyed. As the Hammonds put it succinctly, 'before the enclosure the cottager was a labourer with land; after the enclosure he was a labourer without land'.

While the seigneurial structures survived in Germany west of the River Elbe, they were increasingly challenged in France. On the eve of the Revolution and with marked regional variations, only just over one third of the cultivated land was held by peasants, as against 90% in West Elbian Germany. Of the rest, the nobility owned about 20–25%, the Church 6–10% and the bourgeoisie 30%. This land was also worked by the peasants, the difference being that he was not the tenant. In most cases the French peasant was an 'occupant', as well as a lease-holder, with both legal arrangements frequently being caught up in an impenetrable tangle. The expropriations which had begun to hit the peasantry assumed a new quality in the 1740s, when the seigneuries became 'modernized' (E. Le Roy Ladurie). Whereas the peasants were more or less successful in defending their 'occupancy' of the land against outside attempts to take it away from them, the landlords also tried to enlarge their estates mainly at the expense of the common land. Thus common lands were carved up, forests were closed and grazing rights suspended. Production on the estates became more rationalized, also in the sense that the landlords tended to rely on the *gros fermiers*. The latter in turn usually leased the land to the peasants, thus interposing themselves between the landlords and the mass of the peasants. They were, as E. Le Roy Ladurie has put it, 'agents of seigneurial repression and capitalist modernization' at the same time. It seems that France was about to take the same route as England. However, it should not be overlooked that the transition to leasing was a stimulus to a modernization of the system of agricultural production only in a very limited sense. Rents were often combined with contributions which were typically feudal. Lease-holders did not pay in cash, but made payments in kind, in particular in the form of *métayage*. Leasing became an instrument for pushing up the rate of exploitation of the peasant masses. Thus about 20% of the income was siphoned off in cash payments, whereas by and large some of the net yield had to be handed over as payments in kind. For this reason alone the system was unable to function as a pace-maker for the transformation of agricultural production.

In East-Central and Eastern Europe the *Vorwerk* economy survived beyond the 18th century. But the labour relations on which it was based were slowly modified and called into question. The transition to new forms of land cultivation increased the demand for workers on the large estates beyond the capacity of the traditional system of serf labour. It became necessary to supplement serfs with wage labourers. Ultimately the latter came to replace the former, as the landlords, having begun to manage their estates themselves, did not want to demand further labour services which would threaten the viability of the peasant economy. These developments made the emergence of an agrarian capitalism unavoidable. How far this new system had advanced in some areas may be gauged from the case of the Boitzenburg Lordship which is situated on the northern fringe of the Brandenburg Mark (see Table 34).

*Table 34:*
Estates of the Lordship of Boitzenburg (Brandenburg),
ca. 1800

| | Size of arable land[1] | Land cultivated in 1799[1] | No. of villages provid. serf lab. | No. of Peas. and small-holders | Size of land worked by serfs[1] |
|---|---|---|---|---|---|
| 4 estates with serf and wage lab. | 8 129.2 | ca. 3 417 | 9 | 156 ps 6 sm | 1908 |
| 9 estates with wage lab. only | 5 847.6 | ca. 3 800[2] | – | – | – |
| | 13 976.8 | ca. 7 217 | 9 | 156 ps 6 sm | 1908 |

[1]In Magdeburg *Morgen;*   [2]Probably much less.

These four demesnes were worked partly by serfs who provided some 55.8% of the labour and partly by wage labourers. Another nine demesnes relied exclusively on wage labour. If all thirteen are taken together, three-quarters of the land in the district were worked by wage labourers and no more than one quarter by serfs. Nevertheless, the conservative forces prevailed. The growth potential of the older system had not yet been exhausted. Nor were the landlords prepared to abolish serfdom. Yet the negative effects of these attitudes on the system of agricultural production and on the domestic market became more and more obvious. This is why the authorities were under some pressure to reform the *Vorwerk* system. Thus the Prussian minister Friedrich Leopold von Schroetter wrote in 1802: 'Serfdom and true industry are clear contradictions. Serfdom does not exist in any country or province in which agriculture and manufacturing prosper. Wherever it does exist, creative and manufacturing industriousness is really being smothered.' Yet for the time being the Prussian authorities merely decided to introduce some reforms on the royal demesnes. From 1799, serfdom was replaced by payments in cash; the legal rights of peasants were improved, though not in all districts. Joseph II did away with serfdom in the Habsburg Empire through his decree of 1789. This decree went well beyond the Prussian solution because it affected the land ownership of the nobility at large and not just his own estates. The abolition of serfdom had first got underway on the royal demesnes in the mid-1770s. However, the decree of 1789 was rescinded immediately after the untimely death of the Emperor. Finally, there is the Polish case. On 7 May 1794 a famous decree was issued in Połaniec during the Kościuszko Uprising. It granted personal freedom to the Polish peasants, but left the *Vorwerk* economy and its labour system untouched.

The emergence of an agricultural capitalism and government efforts to reform the traditional relationship between peasants and landlords notwithstanding, trends even within the larger countries of East-Central and Southern Europe did not all point in the same direction. In Poland serfs were being replaced by wage labour on a large scale on the latifundia. But the lesser nobility did not participate in this development; indeed they relied even more heavily on serf labour. Mecklenburg and Russia deviated most from the general pattern, though they moved towards opposite extremes. When the Mecklenburg landowners introduced *Koppelwirtschaft* on their *Vorwerke*, they reallocated peasant holdings on a large scale. Above all, they pushed the peasants off the land. Clearly the fragmentation of the land into *Vorwerk* fields interspersed with peasant holdings impeded the creation of *Koppeln*. Nor were the landlords as dependent on serf labour as before once more wage labourers became available. Hence the equilibrium of the *Vorwerk* economy was no longer put in jeopardy as a result of the removal of the peasants. By the turn of the century, the decline of the peasantry in Mecklenburg reached its nadir. In 1719 the number of peasant holdings in the manorial villages of the Stargard district was 319; some eighty years later, in 1801, no more than 140 were left.

Meanwhile the expansion of Russian agriculture occurred exclusively within the framework of serfdom. Rising grain prices induced the nobility to extend their estates and to give preference to *barshchina* (serf labour) rather than to *obrok* (rent). At first grain exports to Western Europe, which began to gain major importance in the second half of the 18th century, were of little significance in this

*Table 35:*
Forms of feudal obligations by region in Russia,
1765/67–1858 (%)

| | Serf labour | | Rent | |
| | 1765/67 | 1858 | 1765/67 | 1858 |
|---|---|---|---|---|
| Northwestern Russia | 66.2 | 66.5 | 33.8 | 33.5 |
| Smolensk district | 66.5 | 73.0 | 33.5 | 27.0 |
| Central non-Black Soil region | 40.8 | 32.5 | 59.2 | 67.5 |
| Central Black Soil region | 75.0 | 72.7 | 25.0 | 27.3 |
| Middle Volga region | 66.2 | 77.2 | 43.8 | 22.8 |
| Totals | 54.7 | 56.6 | 45.3 | 43.4 |

respect. These exports came from Livonia, Lithuania, Bielorussia and the Ukraine west of the River Dniepr. At the same time Russia tightened the laws relating to serf labour. Serfdom assumed forms which were without parallel in East-Central Europe. The expansion of Russian agriculture was preceded by the emergence of an interregional division of labour. The seigneurial economy became concentrated in the Black Earth regions in the South East. The other, less fertile areas of Western Russia, on the other hand, turned to the production of manufactured goods. Accordingly, rents prevailed in these parts of Russia, whereas labour dues were typical of the Black Earth regions (see Table 35). A similar division can be observed in East-Central Europe: the *Vorwerk* economy dominated in the fertile plains; manufacturing, by contrast, was taken up in the more mountainous regions where the restrictions were fewer.

All in all, not only the feudal system, but also the collectivism of the village community were fast becoming the decisive impediments to a further expansion of the productive potential of agriculture on the European Continent. Major changes could only be expected to come, if this system was turned upside down. Such an upheaval was a prerequisite of an agricultural revolution on the Continent of the kind which had meanwhile begun in England. The upswing of agriculture, it is true, unleashed a number of developments which changed the system production; but at the same time there were other tendencies which worked in a retrograde direction. Many feudal lords continued to believe that they could participate in the blessings of the agricultural boom only if they maintained and even strengthened the traditional mechanisms of economic exploitation. The peasants, and in particular the lower strata of the peasantry, tenaciously clung to the village community and its economic rights. Both currents combined to block the evolution of the agricultural system.

### 3.3 Towards Industrial Capitalism

At the beginning of the 18th century manufacturing and trade found itself in a situation which was different from that of agriculture. A number of countries, especially in East-Central and Southern Europe, had been struck by severe structural crises in the previous century. These crises continued in the 18th century, even if there were sporadic improvements. The remaining countries had experienced a drop in prices for manufactured goods; but the results of this had been positive, especially in England, as the path towards industrialization in a capitalist framework was, to some extent, cleared by these developments.

The state, in responding to these crisis phenomena, had begun as early as the 17th century to protect the domestic market from foreign competition by erecting high tariff walls; it had also moved to support the merchant capitalists in their struggle for foreign markets and, especially in the countries of the European Continent, to introduce measures designed to further manufacturing and trade at home. These policies remained unchanged. The state saw it as its special task to make improvements to the country's infrastructure, and the road networks of today therefore go back to the 18th century. In 1747 the French founded the *Ecole des Ponts et des Chaussées* which stimulated the development of new techniques for the building of roads capable of coping with the heavier traffic requirements of the time. The French network expanded rapidly and became a model which was much admired in the rest of Europe. Other countries were also very active in this field. And it was not just roads that were being built. Europe was seized by a veritable canal-building fever. In France and in the northern parts of the Netherlands the beginnings of this building activity go back to the 17th century. Canal-building in Prussia reached its peak during the reign of Frederick II (Frederick the Great). Eighteenth-century England came to be the land of canals. The country's canal age became a precursor of the railway age. The first wave of canal-building in England occurred in the 1760s and early 1770s, followed by a second wave in the 1780s and above all the early 1790s. The boom was triggered off in the years 1759–61 when the Duke of Bridgewater constructed a canal between Manchester and the collieries at Worsley. In the same way, most other canals in England were used primarily for transporting coal. Where

England differed from the Continent was that her canal-building was privately financed. The same is true of road maintenance.

Mercantilist policies on the European Continent did not confine themselves to improving the general infrastructure of the economy; the state also intervened directly, even if the forms of intervention varied greatly. Mercantilism, as Alexander Gerschenkron has put it, was 'a function of the degree of economic backwardness of the countries concerned'. The aim of mercantilist interventionism was to buttress the foreign trade position of a particular country by promoting the development of the domestic economy. The hope was to catch up with the leading economic powers of Northwestern Europe. Mercantilism therefore differed from country to country and depended on the degree of relative backwardness. At the one end of the spectrum was Russia where the state was ubiquitous. There workers and entrepreneurs were virtually created by decree and the population was subjected to policies which aimed to increase the power of the state with the help of economic development. The establishment of *Manufakturen* (manufactures) became a special concern of state economic policy on the Continent. These centralized enterprises were, in the view of the governments concerned, particularly worthy of support. It seemed that with the help of such *Manufakturen* it became possible to reach the production levels of more developed rival nations in one step, as it were, by skipping the intermediate stages of *Kaufsystem* and putting-out system which have been discussed above (see p. 36). A host of separate measures was taken to promote these enterprises: workers and entrepreneurs were recruited from other countries; direct or indirect subsidies were paid by the Treasury; trade privileges and sales monopolies were granted. The success of these policies was limited. There was something artificial about many *Manufakturen*, especially if they had been established as prestige objects by some sovereign and were hence built up without much regard for market demand. In this case, they remained dependent on state subsidies. Other enterprises may have prospered at first. But as soon as they lost their privileges and monopoly rights, they were frequently pushed to the wall by their competitors and forced to close down. And in those places where the old feudal order was still more or less intact, government attempts to promote manufacturing tended to be frustrated from the start.

Growing demand both at home and abroad was a prerequisite of an expansion of industrial production. Population growth resulted in a growth of demand for items of mass consumption. However, there were limits to this nexus because real wages tended to decline in the face of rising food prices. On the other hand, price rises for food raised agricultural incomes and this, in turn, raised the demand for manufactured goods. It also seems that there was an increased demand from among the urban middle classes. Still more important was another development: the number of households which were dependent on the market increased very rapidly, once the commercialization of agriculture had set in and proto-industries as well as large cities proliferated. There was a gradual decline in the number of households which were removed from the existing market structures. The domestic market widened. Nor was it without significance that the impact of the traditional underconsumption crises in the manufacturing sector lost some of its force once agricultural productivity and technology had been improved and the recurrent supply crises had become less devastating than in the past.

The role played by foreign demand in economic growth differed from country to country. In England it assumed considerable importance, but must be seen in conjunction with a steadily growing domestic demand. England succeeded in gaining control of the sea, in ousting her competitors from the underdeveloped and colonial markets and in expanding her position on the world market to one of virtual monopoly. From the middle of the 17th century English merchant capitalists had no scruples to employ war as a means of politics. Their aim was to extend their economic activities for the purpose of capital accumulation in their struggle with their foreign rivals. Trade wars and accumulation entered into a close symbiotic relationship. In the 17th century Holland had been England's main enemy. France assumed that role from the end of that century. As a result of her struggle with France during the Spanish War of Succession (1701-1713/4), England succeeded in gaining hold of the *asiento*, the monopoly of the slave trade with Spanish-America, which had been held by the French Guinea Company since 1701. She had also gained access to the Portuguese and Brazilian markets as early as 1703 in the Treaty of Methuen. The Austrian War of Succession (1740-1748) and the Seven Years War (1756-1763) sealed the triumph of England over the French monarchy. The capacity of the French fleet in 1786-7 was estimated to be about 729,340 tons; England's was 1,055,000 tons in 1788. This meant that it had not only grown three-fold since 1686, but was also 42% larger than that of France.

The outlines of an asymmetrically organized world market had first emerged in the 17th century and now, in the 18th century, its contours were thrown into sharper relief. A capitalist world system came into existence which was based on the subjection of the peripheral regions of the globe to the production requirements of the metropolitan countries. In the 18th century its centre of gravity finally shifted towards England. France secured the second place for herself, while Holland fell back to the third rank. Spain and Portugal were able to hold on to their colonial empires; but their economic exploitation of these areas was increasingly organized by English and French merchant capitalists. There were indications of a reversal of this process in the second half of the 18th century, but these tendencies failed to assert themselves.

The economy of the Atlantic region, whose structures were determined by the triangular trade between Europe, West Africa and the plantations in the Americas, grew in the 18th century to become the most dynamic region of the world economy. Europe supplied the finished goods, Africa furnished the slaves and the Americas sent precious metals, raw materials and colonial produce. It was to be of great significance that the slave plantations of the West Indies and, from the 1790s, those of the American South, became the suppliers of raw cotton to the English textile industry. The slave trade was the vital element in this triangular system. It provided the urgently required workforce for the labour-intensive plantation economy. This is why Malachy Postlethwayt has called the slave trade 'the first principle and foundation of all the rest, the mainspring of the machine which sets every wheel in motion'. Accordingly there was a further rise in the number of slaves shipped across the Atlantic (see Table 22, p. 81 and Figure 15, p. 80). The trade reached its absolute maximum between 1781 and 1790 when some 88,600 slaves were exported per annum. Between 1700 and 1810 about 6.4 million Africans were imported as slaves to the Americas. In the 1730s, England succeeded Portugal as the leading slave-trading nation. Between 1761 and 1810 about 43.3% of the trade was English; Portugal's and France's share was 28.2% and 15.9% respectively. the remaining 12.6% were divided between North America, Holland and Denmark at 7.9%, 3.1% and 1.6% respectively. Liverpool and Nantes were the centres of the Western European slave trade, and the profits were sizeable. It has been estimated that, as far as England is concerned, they averaged around 9.5% between 1761 and 1807.

However, there were sharp fluctuations, as the slave trade involved great risks. The *Hawke*, a slave-ship from Liverpool, for example, made a net profit of 73.6% on her first voyage in 1779–80. In the following year she made a second journey in the course of which she seized the *Jeune Emilia*. Net profits this time were 147.1%. But the

*Table 36:*
## Outlays, insets and profits of the Liverpudlian slave trader William Davenport, 1757-1784

|  | Outlays (in pounds) | Net insets (in pounds) | Profits (in pounds) | Profit rate (%) |
|---|---|---|---|---|
| 1757/67 | 54 066 | 55 383 | 1 317 | 2.4 % |
| 1768/75 | 231 856 | 248 689 | 16 833 | 7.3 % |
| 1776/84 | 76 033 | 96 807 | 20 774 | 27.3 %[1] |
| Totals | 361 955 | 400 879 | 38 924 | 10.8 % |

[1]Without the "Hawke": 12.6%.

third journey which she started in December 1781 ended in a write-off: the *Hawke* became herself the victim of French pirates. This disaster notwithstanding, the ship still netted her owners a profit of £13,841, the equivalent of a profit rate of 66.4%. Such a performance was exceptional in every respect. The profit rate of the Liverpool slave-trader William Davenport and his associates, who also operated the *Hawke,* amounted to 10.8% for some 74 transactions in which they engaged between 1757 and 1784 (see Table 36). If the speed with which his firm's capital was turned over is taken into consideration, the profit rate was 8.1%. However, these figures mask considerable fluctuations from one year to the next.

As the 18th century wore on, there occurred a gradual shift in the balance and direction of the Atlantic trading links. In the case of England, direct trade with North America gained ground *vis-à-vis* the traditional exchange with the triangle. Imports to England from the West Indies were over three times higher than those from North America in the last decade of the 18th century. Exports to the West Indies, on the other hand, slowly fell back in comparison with those to North America. By 1791-1800 exports to the North exceeded those to the Caribbean by 71%. North America came to be the biggest overseas export market for English goods. In this respect it made little difference that the 13 American colonies had declared their independence from the Empire in 1776.

The enormous expansion of American silver mining and of Brazilian goods production gave a fillip to Spain's and Portugal's trade with their American colonies. At first this trade was of no more than limited benefit for the two mother-countries. The Western European merchant capitalists were the ones to profit from it in the first place. They were in a better position to satisfy demand in Central and South America for manufactured goods. Between 1698-1702 and 1756-60 English exports to Portugal (from where they were re-exported to Brazil) rose by 266%. The upswing of the Brazilian economy and above all the booming gold business played a key role in this impressive growth. Brazilian gold triggered an expansion of Anglo-Portuguese trade. It acted almost like a magnet for English merchants with their manufactured goods. Since wine was essentially Portugal's only export item, her imports from England had to be paid for in gold. This also explains why the expansion of Anglo-Portuguese trade came to an abrupt end in the 1760s when Brazilian gold production was struck by a crisis (see Figure 20). Spain, on the other hand, remained the domain of French merchants up to the 1760s.

*Figure 20:*
Quinquennial averages of Anglo-Portuguese trade, 1701/05–1796/1800
(£000s)

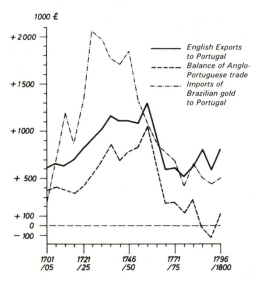

A new development began in the second half of the 18th century. From 1780, Portuguese overseas trade experienced a revival. In the meantime there had emerged a number of industries which exploited the drastic reduction in imports from England in the wake of the decline of Brazilian gold production. These industries were now able to profit from the renewed upswing. In 1796 some 45.1% of exports from Portugal to Brazil had been produced at home. The share of domestic industries in terms of total exports was 24.5%; that of foreign manufacturers amounted to 38.5%. Having taken Seville's place in the trade monopoly with Spanish-America, the monopoly was successively demolished from 1765; all Spanish ports became freely accessible to traders from 1765. The amount of commercial traffic trebled between 1778 and 1788. The extraordinarily vigorous expansion of Spanish-American silver production, which rose by about 179% between 1701–20 and 1781–1800, provided the decisive impetus for this traffic. A growing percentage of the goods which were shipped from Spanish ports to the American colonies, originated in Spain herself. In 1784 the share was 45%, rising to 50% five years later. Thanks to the trade with the colonies the accumulation of merchant capital also advanced in Barcelona. Economically speaking, Catalonia rose to become the leading province of the Spanish monarchy. It was only the wars at the turn of the 19th century which cut off these developments. Spanish-America as well as Portuguese-America fell prey to English merchant capitalism. Portugal became dependent on England once more.

Up to this point, Asia had remained a region 'external' (Immanuel Wallerstein) to the emerging capitalist world system. For the large-scale agrarian societies of Asia trade with Europe had no more than a marginal significance. Enclaves engaged in the export business developed around the factories established by European trading companies. The vast hinterlands of the Asian continent remained virtually untouched by their activities. It was only when colonization began that the decisive step was taken to incorporate Asia into the capitalist world economy. The Dutch were the first to proceed in this direction in Indonesia from the end of the 17th century. The English followed suit from the middle of the 18th century when they established themselves in India, with the Anglo-French conflict providing a welcome pretext for this move. The Dutch East India Company promoted the establishment of its territorial dominance over Indonesia in the hope of gaining control of the areas in which its commodities for export to Europe were grown. The territorial expansion of England in India must also be seen in this context. The main objectives of the two countries were to secure and to extend the supply markets for goods which formed the basis of the trade both inside Asia and with Europe. Thus the English merchants who had established themselves in India in the wake of the East India Company promoted the occupation of the Gujarat in Western India in order to obtain a hold over the cotton production of this province.

As before Europe's balance of trade with Asia remained in deficit throughout the 18th century. However, there was a marked improvement in the import-export ratio in Europe's favour.

*Table 37:*
Values of English exports to India and China,
1719/62–1763/1806 (annual averages)

|  | 1719/62 | | 1763/1806 | |
|---|---|---|---|---|
|  | £ | % | £ | % |
| Silver | 526 291 | 71.9 | 342 574 | 27.4 |
| Goods | 205 792 | 28.1 | 905 643 | 72.6 |
| Totals | 732 083 | 100.0 | 1 248 217 | 100.0 |

Gradually the markets of Asia were being opened up to textiles and metal goods from Europe. As is demonstrated by Table 37, silver exports to Asia declined, while exports of manufactured goods increased. Moreover England moved into the inner-Asian trade, and, by gaining a monopoly position in this so-called 'country-trade', English merchants also succeeded in financing their exports to Europe in part with the profits made inside Asia and hence to some extent at Asia's 'expense'. The exploitation of the Bengal had similar results. It has been calculated that, as a consequence of these practices, England between 1757 and 1780 received annual exports from India worth £1.6 million which were not offset by English exports to India, be it in silver or in the form of goods.

Finally there was also a change in the composition of Asian imports to Europe. Between 1698–1700 and 1778–80 the share of tea and coffee in relation to the total turnover of the Dutch East India Company at Amsterdam rose from 4.1% to 22.9%; the share of textiles and textile fibres, on the other hand, fell from 43.4% to 32.7% (see Table 24, p. 83). This shift emerges even more clearly if one looks at the types of goods imported from Asia to England. Although textile imports continued to rise absolutely, the percentages experienced a decline. In 1699–1701 textiles and textile fibres had made up 70.3% of all Asian imports into England; by 1772–74 the figure had slumped to 48.1%. Meanwhile the spice trade dropped in both absolute and relative terms. The share which had once been 15.4% was a mere 3.8% by the 1770s. Instead tea, which became something of a national beverage in England in this period, was imported in growing quantities. Its share of Asian imports shot up from 1.1% to 44.0%. The phenomenal success of the tea trade led to a shift in the balance of commerce within Asia. India declined in importance, at least for the time being. On the other hand, China moved up as a supplier of tea. Ships from Europe crowded the docks of the city of Canton, the only

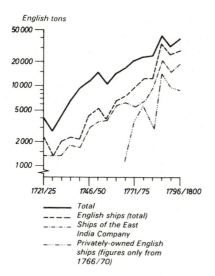

English tons

*Figure 21:*
Tonnage of European and North American ships docking at Kanton, 1721–1800 (quinquennial averages)

—————— Total
‒ ‒ ‒ ‒ English ships (total)
‒ ‧ ‒ ‧ ‒ Ships of the East India Company
‒ ‧‧ ‒ ‧‧ ‒ Privately-owned English ships (figures only from 1766/70)

port which the Chinese authorities had opened to foreigners (see Figure 21). And here, too, just like in India the English East India Company squeezed out all its rivals. In 1792–98 it dealt with 69.8% of all exports which left Canton for Europe.

The underdeveloped and colonial world as a whole was of growing significance to Europe in several ways. To begin with, it was an

*Table 38:*
Values of English re-exports, 1699/1701 and 1772/74
(000s of pounds sterling)

| | Re-exports (according to countries of origin)[1] | | | | | Imports (totals) % |
|---|---|---|---|---|---|---|
| | Manuf. products | Food-stuffs | Raw materials | Totals | % | |
| 1699/1701 | | | | | | |
| Europe | 302 | 100 | 232 | 634 | 31.9 | 68.2 |
| America | – | 732 | 47 | 779 | 39.2 | 18.9 |
| Asia | 444 | 109 | 20 | 573 | 28.9 | 12.9 |
| Totals | 746 | 941 | 299 | 1 986 | 100.0 | 100.0 |
| 1772/74 | | | | | | |
| Europe | 390 | 330 | 454 | 1 174 | 20.2 | 47.4 |
| America | – | 2 735 | 210 | 2 935 | 50.6 | 37.5 |
| Asia | 1 172 | 477 | 50 | 1 699 | 29.2 | 15.1 |
| Totals | 1 562 | 3 542 | 714 | 5 818 | 100.0 | 100.0 |

[1]Calculated from share of imports

*Table 39:*
Structure of England's foreign trade, 1699/1701–1772/74 (%)

| | Europe | | Asia, Afr., America | | Totals | |
|---|---|---|---|---|---|---|
| | 1699/1701 | 1772/74 | 1699/1701 | 1772/74 | 1699/1701 | 1772/74 |
| Exports | | | | | | |
| Woollen manuf. | 43.2 | 18.2 | 4.3 | 8.5 | 47.5 | 26.7 |
| Other manuf. | 3.5 | 6.2 | 4.8 | 21.2 | 8.4 | 27.4 |
| Foodstuffs | 6.7 | 2.7 | 7.6 | 3.7 | 0.9 | 1.0 |
| Raw materials | 5.3 | 4.7 | 0.3 | 0.4 | 5.6 | 5.1 |
| Totals | 58.7 | 31.8 | 10.3 | 31.1 | 69.1 | 62.9 |
| Re-exports | 25.9 | 30.5 | 5.0 | 6.6 | 30.9 | 37.1 |
| Exports & re-exports | 84.6 | 62.3 | 15.3 | 37.7 | 100.0 | 100.0 |
| Imports | | | | | | |
| Manuf. | 22.1 | 10.7 | 9.5 | 6.2 | 31.7 | 16.9 |
| Foodstuffs | 15.5 | 12.0 | 18.1 | 38.9 | 33.6 | 50.9 |
| Raw materials | 30.5 | 24.7 | 4.3 | 7.5 | 34.7 | 32.2 |
| Totals | 68.1 | 47.4 | 31.9 | 52.6 | 100.0 | 100.0 |

exporter of goods. In 1699–1701 some 31.9% of imports into England originated in America and Asia; by 1772–74 the figure had risen to 52.6% (see Table 39 and, for France, Table 40). Initially these imports were less important as such than as items to be re-exported by the commercial metropoles of Europe. In 1772–74 some 79.8% of English re-exports were of American or Asian origin, an 11.7% increase over the 1699–1701 figure (see Table 38). Profits from this trade (and the finishing business related to it) were extraordinarily high. In 1772–74 the re-export value of sugar, tobacco and coffee was 91%, 97.8% and 106.7% respectively above the import value. The re-export trade created dense networks, and via the respective *entrepôts* not only America and Asia were linked with Europe, but a connection was also established, albeit in one direction only, between Asia and America. These networks and the credit institutions supporting them fulfilled several functions and could also be mobilized at any time for the export trade of goods produced in England. As can be seen from Table

38, America's weight increased in comparison with Asia's in the course of the 18th century. The Asian share of imports earmarked for re-export began to stagnate; America's share, on the other hand, saw a marked rise.

Secondly, the underdeveloped and colonial world became a recepticle for European exports, even if it assumed this role for the European metropoles but gradually. In 1699–1701 a mere 15% of all English goods produced for export went to Asia and America; by 1772–74 the figure had gone up to 49.7%. The Americas, and North America in particular, were far more important than Asia as buyers of English export goods. Thus in 1699–1701 some 12.2% of all goods produced in England for export were shipped across the Atlantic, as against 2.8% which were sent to Asia; by 1772–74 America's share of 42.4% was way above the 7.3% for Asia. Indeed, this was the time when the Atlantic trade became the engine of growth in the European economy. As will be shown in a moment, the linen industries of Western, Central and East-Central Europe became the appendices of the trans-Atlantic connection.

Thirdly, the underdeveloped and colonial world promoted capital accumulation in Europe. It made a major contribution to this process, given the relations of unequal exchange which had traditionally existed between Europe and the non-European periphery as well as the enormous profits to be made through re-exports, slaves, the Asian 'country trade' and last, but not least, through plain plunder and looting, of which the exploitation of the Bengal is a good example. The surpluses which were not consumed in the metropolitan countries opened up fresh possibilities of reinvestment so that the exchange cycle continued on an even larger scale than before.

We have seen that the beginnings of this capitalist world system went back to the 16th century and that Europe remained its centre of gravity in the 18th. It was during this latter century that regions became incorporated which had hitherto been outside the system and that the system itself assumed greater inner cohesion. Europe's merchant capitalists built up a network which spread around the globe. The non-European world became part of a system of exchange whose rules were determined in the commercial capitals of Europe. The most important of these rules were: discrimination, an unequal division of labour orientated towards the imperial requirements of the metropoles and, in many cases, unashamed exploitation. The subjugation of the periphery to the needs of the European centre was not without significance as regards the revolutionary change that was to affect the manufacturing base of Europe. For the underdeveloped and colonial countries, on the other hand, European practices spelt stagnation and retrogression. This political economy of dependency experienced further solidification once the process of capitalist industrialization had set in. At this point it entered a new stage which was to determine the subsequent relations between the European centre and the non-European periphery.

The growth of Europe's foreign trade provides a gauge for the dynamism with which the capitalist world system unfolded itself. Thus England's foreign trade expanded but slowly in the first half of the 18th century. Its average annual growth rate between 1700 and 1745 was 0.5%. However, once the crisis which the American War of Independence had unleashed had subsided, the annual rate, which had been 2.8% between 1745 and 1771, jumped to an unprecedented 4.9% in 1779–1809 (see Figure 22). It is significant that re-exports continued to rise, but they ceased to be the crucial element in the dynamic economic process (see Table 39). Their role was taken over by the proliferating exports of goods manufactured in England (with the exception of woollen cloths). The phenomenal rise of the export trade was primarily due to a growing demand in the non-European world, above all in North America, even if by this time the latter region is no longer to be counted as part of the periphery. The

*Figure 22:*
Quinquennial averages of foreign
trade of England and Wales,
1697–1790 and of Britain, 1776–1800
(£000s)

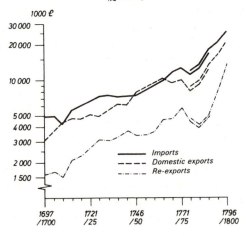

importance of the North Atlantic route emerges from the following set of figures: in 1699-1701 a mere 16.4% of English manufactured goods earmarked for export went across to America; by 1772-74 it was 55%. England's foreign trade entered into a new phase, once demand for her home-produced goods rose rapidly, especially in North America.

French foreign trade expanded even more vigorously than that of England. It grew three-fold between 1716-20 and 1784-88, as compared to a 2.4-fold growth of English foreign trade. On the other hand, it must be remembered that the respective patterns were reversed: unlike England's, France's average annual growth rates were as high as 4.1% in 1716-48, but decreased to 1.0% between 1749 and 1778, rising again only slightly to 1.4% from 1779. French links with the underdeveloped and colonial world were strengthened in the 18th century, especially after 1750. In fact M. Morineau has spoken of a 'colonialization' of France's foreign trade. By 1787 some 30.3% of her foreign trade was conducted with these regions, a marked rise on the 1716 figure of 17.1%. The corresponding figures for England were 23.3% in 1699-1701 and 44.4% in 1772-74. The nominal increase of trade with the French possessions in the Caribbean was 1350% between 1716-20 and 1787-89. And Table 40 demonstrates that French re-exports can stand comparison with those of England. Nevertheless, a decisive difference strikes the eye: on the eve of the Revolution, French foreign trade had reached a stage which England had long left behind her. In 1787 only some 34.2% of France's exports were in manufactured goods; in England these goods amounted to 54.2% as early as 1772-74. The reasons for this lag are to be found in the severe setbacks which France's ancient textile industries had experienced on the Southern European markets in the 1760s. Textile exports declined in relative terms, and it was only thanks to the colonial trade that they were able to maintain their absolute position within France's foreign trade structure in comparison to the base-line of 1750, when textile exports were 40.2% of total exports.

Holland's foreign trade went into decline from the 1740s onwards. Her 17th-century role as the warehouse of the world had largely come to an end. In the Central European region, Hamburg emerged as a serious rival of Amsterdam. For Hamburg's merchants the Seven Years' War of 1756-1763 meant the beginning of a period of great prosperity. The number of ships docking at Hamburg and the size of the city's merchant navy grew by leaps and bounds in the 1780s and 1790s. In 1780, some 2,084 vessels dropped anchor in the port of Hamburg. A considerable portion of English, French, Dutch and

*Table 40:*
Structure of France's foreign trade, 1716–1787 (%)

| | Europe | | Asia, Afr., America | | Totals | |
|---|---|---|---|---|---|---|
| | 1716 | 1787 | 1716 | 1787 | 1716 | 1787 |
| **Exports** | | | | | | |
| Textiles | 27.1 | 16.9 | 2.6 | 7.3 | 29.7 | 24.1 |
| Other manuf. goods | 5.6 | 6.5 | 1.4 | 3.5 | 7.1 | 10.1 |
| Foodstuffs | 30.0 | 17.4 | 3.0 | 6.2 | 33.0 | 23.6 |
| Raw materials | 4.5 | 4.6 | 2.0 | 1.7 | 5.2 | 6.3 |
| Misc. | 6.0 | 2.2 | – | 0.5 | 7.2 | 2.7 |
| Totals | 73.2 | 47.6 | 9.0 | 19.2 | 82.2 | 66.8 |
| Re-exports | 17.8 | 32.8 | – | 0.4 | 17.8 | 33.2 |
| Exports & Re-exports | 91.0 | 80.4 | 9.0 | 19.6 | 100.0 | 100.0 |
| **Imports** | | | | | | |
| Manuf. goods | 12.6 | 15.1 | 3.8 | 4.5 | 16.4 | 19.6 |
| Foodstuffs | 19.5 | 13.2 | – | 0.1 | 19.5 | 13.3 |
| Raw materials | 21.8 | 25.0 | 1.0 | 4.8 | 22.8 | 29.8 |
| Colonial goods | 12.2 | 7.5 | 23.1 | 27.7 | 35.3 | 35.2 |
| Misc. | 5.4 | 2.1 | 0.6 | – | 6.0 | 2.1 |
| Totals | 71.5 | 62.9 | 28.5 | 37.1 | 100.0 | 100.0 |

Spanish re-exports to Central Europe was channelled through this city. The main exports were linens from Central Germany and Silesia most of which went to Spain and Spanish America, to be supplemented by grain, once England had become an importer of cereals from the 1760s onwards. Hamburg also had close links with Leipzig in Saxony which acted as the main exchange and turntable for goods in the heart of Central Europe.

However, Amsterdam remained the financial centre of European commerce beyond the 17th century. It was only in the 19th century that the city was replaced by London. As Charles Wilson has put it: 'A bill [of exchange drawn] on Amsterdam was to the eighteenth century what the bill on London was to become to the nineteenth century. If a French merchant wished to import flax from Eastern Europe, he would mobilize his agent in Königsberg in East Prussia. Once the deal had been completed, the latter, in order to obtain his money, would draw a bill on an Amsterdam banking house with which he was accredited through his French partner. Thus a multilateral international credit system emerged by the second half of the 17th century. This system replaced the existing bilateral system of payment which had been rather cumbersome because it could not function without the export of precious metals. The bill of exchange now took the place of these metals in the new multilateral system. Bills facilitated cashless payments; they dispensed with the traditional bilateralism of trading relationships and 'internationalized' the latter. Thenceforth exports of precious metals were necessary only in exceptional cases.

The differentiation of the banking system into a public and a private sector suited the needs of commerce on the whole well. It served the interests of manufacturing only to a limited extent. The Amsterdam *Wisselbank* retained its lead among the traditional exchange banks. It provided the model for a number of other banks which were founded in the 18th century. These 'medieval' banks, as P. Léon has called them, were much less modern than the state banks which were beginning to assume the leading positions. After the establishment of the Bank of England in 1694 there followed the Bank of Scotland a year later, the Royal *Giro-und Lehnbanco* of Berlin in 1765 and the Bank of San Carlos at Madrid in 1782. A comparable institution was founded in France only in 1776 when the *Caisse d'Escompte* came into existence. The bank which had been founded by a Scotsman, John Law, in 1716/18 was dragged down by the collapse of the entire system established by him. Next to the municipal and state banks, private bankers remained indispensable. There were the London bankers in Lombard Street, the Huguenot bankers in France most of whom had immigrated from Geneva, or the private bankers of Frankfurt; all of them were harbingers of the age of high finance in the 19th century.

England also occupied first place among the European nations as far as the density of the branch network of private banks is concerned. In the course of the 18th century there emerged the so-called 'country banks' in the provinces which were connected with the London bankers. By the early 1780s, there were more than 100 of these banks in England. These institutions were designed to attract the savings of private individuals which would otherwise have remained untapped. And they facilitated capital formation in trade and manufacturing. However, their contribution to the Industrial Revolution was more indirect. They provided industry not so much with long-term investment credits as with short-term loans. This enabled the entrepreneurs to keep a comparatively large share of their own funds as fixed capital in their companies. Moreover, industrialization would have been unthinkable without the existence of a viable commercial network in the financing of which the banks were also involved. Indeed commerce and banking could not be clearly delineated from each other at this time. Finally, there were the various capital markets in London and the provinces, with something like a national capital market developing only towards the end of the 18th century. The influence of these markets extended far beyond the area which was controlled by the banks. It included the large joint-stock companies as well as insurance companies which began to mushroom in this period; it also comprised the multi-faceted world of commerce and stretched as far as the sphere of personal friendships and family ties.

The English public debt formed the bedrock on which the financial system of the London City rested. It had risen continuously from £14.2 million in 1700 to £78.0 million in 1750 and £167.2 million in 1780. It reached a staggering £426.6 million by the end of the century. This debt provided investment opportunities which were very secure. Furthermore the bonds which were issued by the state enabled the business world to erect 'a pyramid of loans' (A. H. John) upon the public debt. It is improbable that the London City would have risen to the position which it assumed in the 19th century had it not been for the enormous public debt of the English state. Nor, on the other hand, would it have been possible to conduct the wars of the 18th and early 19th centuries had the banking system not organized the cover for this debt. During these wars more than one third of state expenditure was at various times raised with the help of loans. The secret of this success was described by Isaac de Pinto towards the end of the Seven Years' War: 'The inviolable and scrupulous punctuality with which those interest payments were always made and the notion of a guarantee by Parliament have established the English credit system so strongly that loans could be floated which have surprised and astonished Europe.' The capital market which expanded so vigorously in this way was able to rely on the profits which were being made in commerce, and, above all, in overseas trade.

Looking at the problem with the benefit of hindsight, the accumulation of capital proved to be a necessary, though not exclusive, prerequisite of capitalist industrialization. As has been mentioned above, the merchant capitalists provided the nascent industries with the required working capital. Capital for long-term investments was not yet required on a larger scale. Certainly its lack did not present an obstacle when the transition to factory production was made. The ratio of working to fixed capital changed but slowly in favour of the latter. Industry was still a long way from the concentrations of fixed capital which were to characterize it from the 19th century onwards. It was not the supply side, but rising demand that unleashed the process of industrialization. This demand arose not only in England and Europe, but in those underdeveloped and colonial markets which the merchant capitalists, following the laws of accumulation, had created. It was not merchant capitalism as such which produced the factory system. Rather it emerged on the foundations of the world trading system which it had established. Once merchant capitalists had paved the way for the rise of industrial capitalism, their historical role had come to an end. Industry freed itself from the hold of the merchant capitalists. The process of industrial production, as Marx put it, 'absorbed the circulation of capital as one of its elements'.

The manufacturing industries responded to the growing demand both at home and abroad by increasing their output. While the production of cloths at Leiden had fallen to 29,434 pieces in 1800, France stepped up her production. Between 1700–4 and 1785–87 quantities rose by 126%; the increase in terms of value was even higher: 265%. However, there were considerable variations from region to region. The centre of gravity was the French North with a share of almost 50%. The English cloth manufacturers were able to more than double their output between 1695 and 1772. It was only in the last quarter of the 18th century that the annual growth rate began to slow down. Yorkshire emerged as the most important region of English woollen cloth manufacture. Around 1700 its share of exports had been less than 20%; by the early 1770s it was around 50%. Linen manufacture which had developed close ties with the markets of the underdeveloped and colonial world since the 16th century saw an even more impressive expansion. In France production doubled in some regions and trebled in others. In a few places it quintuplicated. English linen manufacture did not make more than moderate progress and even had to cut production from the 1780s. However, output of the newly-established Scottish linen industry which was completely unknown before 1700 rose seven-fold between 1728–32 and 1798–1802. The Irish linen manufacturers, who rose to the top rank of the British linen industry towards the end of the 18th century, succeeded between 1710 and 1800 in increasing their exports twentyfold. On the Continent, the centres of linen manufacture were, apart from those on the French west coast, in Flanders, Eastern Westphalia, Lower Hesse, Swabia, the Upper Lusatia northeast of Dresden and in Silesia. But up to now few statistics are available on these regions. We know that the number of pieces which the linen weavers in the villages around Ghent sent to the Ghent market doubled between 1700 and 1780. Linen exports from Landeshut in Silesia rose two-and-a-half-fold between 1763–65 and 1786–90.

If the growth rates of the traditional branches of the English textile industry began to decline in the last quarter of the century, this may be taken as a reflection of the rise of cotton manufacture. Rather insignificant until the 1760s, cotton experienced a staggering boom in the second half of the 1770s. Between the beginning of the 18th century and 1775–84 net imports of cotton rose seven-fold. The French cotton industry, it is true, reached comparable growth rates. But it must be remembered that France started from a lower level. In effect, by 1787–89 England used twice as much cotton as France. Cotton manufacture also flourished in Saxony, the eastern parts of Switzerland, in Catalonia and elsewhere in the second half of the 18th century. But nowhere else was the development as spectacular as in England.

Mining and the iron industry likewise participated in the general economic upswing. English coal production doubled between 1760 and the 1780s alone. This must be compared to an increase from just under three million tons to five million tons in the previous seven decades between 1681–90 and 1760. France, too, mined seven to eight times more coal in 1789 than she had done at the beginning of the century. But the quantities produced by her were no more than 6–7% English production. On the other hand, the French were ahead of their rivals across the Channel in iron production. Here output trebled up to 1789 and was 130,000–140,000 tons at this time; England's, on the other hand, was a mere 68,000 tons. However, the English iron industry, which more than doubled its output after 1760 following a period of slow growth, was well ahead of its French counterpart in technological terms. In England coke was used to smelt 79% of the iron; in France it was no more than 1.4–2%. It was due to this technological advantage that the English iron masters were able to overtake the stagnant French industry before the end of the century. By 1806, they produced around 250,000 tons. Pig iron production also increased in Germany. In fact, at the end of the 1780s it appears not be have been far below the English output. Yet here, too, technological change and the substitution of charcoal by coke were slow to come.

Calculations of the annual growth rates of industrial production are available so far only for France and England. According to these calculations, rates for the two countries between 1700 and 1790 were 1.5–1.9% and 1.17% respectively. But these figures are no more than rough estimates, and it may well be that the percentages were much closer together than is now known. What is more, however important exact quantification of economic performance may be, it does not answer the question of the forces that were behind these growth rates. Was growth due to a quantitative expansion of the existing production apparatus? Or was it made possible because of qualitative changes both in respect of technology and socio-economic organization?

At first the growth of manufacturing industry occurred along traditional lines. Proto-industrialization proliferated and reached its climax. Dense rural manufacturing industries which produced for supra-regional markets covered 18th-century Europe like a veil. Regions, which had hitherto depended on agriculture alone, were transformed into mixed zones in which agriculture and rural manufacturing existed side-by-side. Thus we read in 1797 in a report on the stocking weavers in the vicinity of Chemnitz in Saxony: 'At first they established themselves in the villages; Limbach, a manor two hours outside Chemnitz, was the first to have stock weavers among its inhabitants. From here they moved into the neighbouring villages and successively into the entire area. Their main residence have been the villages up to now. In the town of Chemnitz there are no more than 80 masters, 10 apprentices and around 50 journeymen. In 1709 there were a mere five looms in the town and not even 20 in the entire vicinity. Now some 2,500 looms are being operated in an area of not quite four sq. kilometers around Chemnitz'.

It was in this way that peasant villages were transformed into weavers' villages. The linen-weaving village of Großschönau in the Upper Lusatia presents a good case in point (see Figure 23). Until

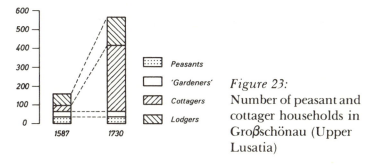

*Figure 23:*
Number of peasant and cottager households in Großschönau (Upper Lusatia)

1730, the share of the peasant population declined to 9% there. Cottagers and lodgers who outnumbered the peasants by 9.9:1 and 4.4:1 respectively dominated the village. Most of these people worked in the linen industry. Another example are the villages of the Gleichenstein district, a centre of the new draperie industry in the Upper Eichsfeld region southeast of Göttingen. Although the figures in Table 41 are probably not fully comparable, it appears that the proportion of weavers, spinners and wool-combers in terms of the total population rose from around 29% to over 58% between 1766 and 1796. By 1806 there were 96 looms there per 1,000 population. In the

*Table 41:*
Structure of the textile industry in the Gleichenstein district (Upper Eichsfeld, southeast of Göttingen), 1766–1796

|  | 1766 | | 1796 | |
|  | No. | % | No. | % |
|---|---|---|---|---|
| Raschmacher | 692 | 9.1 | 1 225 | 10.4 |
| Linen weavers | 74 | 1.0 | ? | ? |
| Wool spinners | 1 319 | 17.3 | 5 217 | 44.4 |
| Yarn spinners | 124 | 1.6 | ? | ? |
| Wool combers | ? | ? | 426 | 3.6 |
| Totals | 2 209 | 29.0 | 6 868 | 58.4 |
| Total population | 7 620 | 100.0 | 11 751[1] | 100.0 |

[1]Figure for 1792

*Table 42:*
Structure of the textile industry in the Picardie (France), ca. 1785

| Type of trade | No. of looms | | | |
|  | In towns (A) | In country (B) | Totals (C) | (B) as percent. of (C) |
|---|---|---|---|---|
| Wool | 5 700 | 5 300 | 11 000 | 48 |
| Fine linen | 500 | 5 500 | 6 000 | 92 |
| Rough linen | 500 | 3 500 | 4 000 | 88 |
| Stockings | 1 000 | 7 000 | 8 000 | 88 |
| Cotton | 100 | – | 100 | 0 |
| Totals | 7 800 | 21 300 | 29 100 | 73 |
| Total population |  |  | 533 000 |  |
| Looms per 1000 inhabitants |  |  | 55 |  |

French Picardy north of Paris about 73% of all looms were operated in rural areas around 1785. Some 30% of the local population were employed in the textile industry at this time (see Table 42). Between 1660 and 1710 about one third of the adult males whose professional status is known worked in the metal industries in the English West Midlands. They were nail-makers, lock-smiths, scythe-smiths etc. A further 27% found employment in other trades. In some cases such concentrations of rural manufacturing became conurbations which, in turn, attracted further villages into their orbit and permeated them with proto-industries. Roubaix near Lille, Verviers east of Liège and the Wupper River valley east of Düsseldorf are but a few examples. The Wuppertal became one of the most astonishing manufacturing regions in Europe. Friedrich Heinrich Jacobi, when submitting his report to the Electoral government at Düsseldorf in 1773, counted 100 bleacher's workshops, 2,000 hairlooms and 3,500 broad-looms; according to his estimates, the export value of the Wuppertal industry was 3,267,664 thalers. It was a common feature of these regions that manufacturing was not regulated by guilds. This was a point made in 1790 by the cloth manufacturers of Lennep south of the Wupper River valley who were permanently at loggerheads with the local shearman's guild. They argued: 'How much more flourishing, perfect and profitable are the factories of Verviers, Eupen [south of Aachen], Bourscheid [now Burtscheid southeast of Aachen], Monjoie [now Monschau southeast of Aachen]...and several other places...; and this is so only because in these factories there are no guilds and hence there is no compulsion; nor hence is there an opportunity to treat the fabrics incorrectly or even to ruin them; a reason for causing damage and for engaging the factories in legal quarrels which are so detrimental to them just does not exist.' The urban manufacturers were frequently unable to stand up to the competition of their rural counterparts and saw their position permanently weakened. The cloth makers of Aachen suffered considerable losses. They were due, as a contemporary observer, Georg Forster, put it, to the 'despotism of the craft guilds'. It was the latter who, he believed, were 'the immediate cause of the decline of the cloth industry' in the city, while the manufacturers of Vaals, Burtscheid, Stolberg and Monschau to the south-east continued to prosper. Elsewhere, as in Northern France, there developed a dynamic alliance between rural and urban manufacturers on the basis of a division of labour. This enabled the towns to partake in proto-industrial production, occasionally even in a prominent position.

The forces which promoted proto-industrialization were not

fundamentally different from those which had been at work since the
end of the 16th century. There was increased underemployment in the
countryside once population growth began to accelerate and the
trend towards greater accumulation and concentration of economic
power proved relentless. We have a submission, dated 1700, which
complains that the majority of the inhabitants of Viersen west of
Düsseldorf did not have more than 2–6 *Morgen* (= 0.6–1.9 hectares).
'This is why', so the document continues, 'they have to work in the
factories and workshops in order to be able to subsist.' The merchant
capitalists frequently had little choice but to mobilize the unused
labour potential in the rural areas, if the process of accumulation was
to continue without interruptions. The cloth manufacturers of
Monschau which must be regarded as a centre of proto-
industrial production put forward precisely this argument to defend
themselves against the reproach that they employed sub-contracted
putters-out (*Baasenmeister*) in the Limburg area. They replied: 'Just
as our factories have grown thanks to the use of *Baasenmeister* in the
region, they would lapse back into their former languid state if these
people were dismissed.'

Wherever proto-industry had taken root, the process continued in a
cumulative fashion. The small producers adopted a specific pattern
of reproductive behaviour which caused the existing balance
between demography and economy to collapse. It was replaced by a
new 'demo-economic high-pressure system'. This system secured the
further evolution of the proto-industrial process because it kept the
supply of labour flexible. In fact, the new patterns of demographic
behaviour provided the internal stimulus of proto-industrialization.
The external stimulus, on the other hand, was provided by the
demand for proto-industrial goods on supra-regional and international markets. Thus the European linen industry came to be an
integral part of the Atlantic economic system in the course of this
proto-industrial development. In 1787, C.L.P. Hüpeden, in writing
about the linen trade in Hesse, spoke of a 'Hessian Peru and East
India'. He added that this trade 'is the main channel through which
Spanish gold and silver flow into our coffers'. In the second half of the
18th century about 90% of the *bretañas*, which were exported from the
sea ports of Brittany, went to Spain and thence to Spanish-America.
Between 1748/49 and 1789/90 some 75.6% of Silesia's linen exports
went to Western Europe and overseas (see Fig. 24). By 1791/2 the
export quota of Silesian linen was around 75.5%. *Bretañas* were
produced almost exclusively for export from France. In 1695 the
English cloth manufacturers sent about 40% of their production

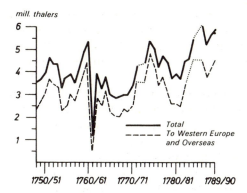

*Figure 24:*
Value of Silesian
linen exports,
1748/49–1789/90
(mill. Thalers)

abroad; by 1799 the quota was over 67%. That of Yorkshire alone
reached 72.3% in 1771–72.

Proto-industry was a cottage industry. In essence it was made up of
small manufacturers who produced for the market and who
organized their households as a family economy. Unlike the
household of the artisan who was organized in a guild, the proto-
industrial household mobilized its productive energies through the
co-operation of all family members, i.e. wife and children. In this
respect both the peasant household and the proto-industrial
household, which had after all emerged from the former, possessed
the same organization. But the proto-industrial family was only
partially market-orientated. Whenever its socio-culturally determined standards of subsistence were reached, it would abandon its
proto-industrial activity; the availability of labour began to
diminish. If the family's subsistence level was not secured, it was
forced to step up its labour input, often to a level of 'self-exploitation'
(A. V. Chayanov). This nexus did not escape contemporary observers.
Thus we find the following comment of 1785 on the Silesian linen
industry: 'Grain prices which are too low are detrimental to the linen
trade and reduce the diligence of the spinners and weavers . . . ; on the
other hand, business in the mountainous regions has never been
difficult in times of inflation (*teure jare*).'

However, once the putting-out system had established itself, the
preconditions began to disappear for the small producers to adopt an
anti-cyclical economic behaviour. These new realities are reflected in
a statement by the weavers of Monschau who complained in 1769:
'The entrepreneurs provide work for all weavers; but they distribute it
in such a way that, once one of them has been given a piece to do, he
will then have to wait and go hungry for 4, 5 or more weeks before
another order is placed with him.'

The production system which evolved in the course of proto-industrialization also took account of the fact that the rural producer-households were able to sell their goods directly to the consumer only in exceptional cases. The trader and retailer usually acted as the intermediary between the producer and the consumer, as the small producers were unable to reach the relatively remote markets with their goods. Nor did they have the working capital required to bridge the time-lag between production and marketing. They also lacked information on changing market conditions. All these things were provided by the merchant capitalists. Their role as go-betweens also enabled them to engage in 'exploitation through trade' (M. Dobb) and increasingly to dominate the small producers. The latter retained a degree of formal independence wherever the merchant purchased the goods from the producer (*Kaufsystem* as opposed to the putting-out system). The *Kaufsystem* obtained above all in the linen industry; but it was also operative in large parts of the Yorkshire textile industry. F. Zöllner described the system with reference to Silesia as follows: 'The merchants sit around in the exchange [*Kaufhaus*] on a slightly elevated chair. The weaver who would like to sell a piece of linen hands it to one of these gentlemen. The latter inspects and fingers it and states what he is prepared to pay; if the weaver is happy with the price, the merchant chalks the amount and his trade-mark on to the pieces; the weaver takes the linen to the merchant's office where he receives his money.'

The proto-industrial household lost the formal autonomy which it had under the *Kaufsystem*, if the merchant capitalist succeeded in subjecting the small producer to his control and in incorporating his workshop into a putting-out system. This happened when he advanced credit for the acquisition of raw materials and/or provided the raw materials, in some cases even the tools. The merchant thus intruded into the production sphere without, however, taking full control of it. The *Verleger* assumed control of the product; the small producer, on the other hand, kept control of the work process. Nevertheless, the production process was no longer self-contained. It was drawn into the circulation sphere which retained its dominant position. Especially in those areas in which the raw materials had to be delivered over longer distances and a segmentation of the labour process was unavoidable, the merchant was able to move into the production sphere as a buyer of raw materials and organizer of production. He became a *Verleger*. A book, published in 1796, on the cloth industry of Eupen which was organized on a putting-out basis described the system as follows: 'The merchant or the manufacturer is the mainspring, the heart of the whole system; he keeps many people active, all of whom work for him and receive their livelihood through him; . . . this merchant, in other words, acquires the raw materials of distant countries; he gets Spanish wool, oil, soap and hair for the loom and whatever else the workers need.'

The widely scattered workshops of proto-industry were often complemented by centralized enterprises which have come to be called *Manufakturen* (manufactures). They tended to organize the preparatory work processes and, more importantly, the finishing processes—the latter not least because they were decisive for the sales prospects of the product concerned. The cloth manufacturers of Monschau did the cleaning and dyeing of the wool in their own workshops; they then put it out to the local spinners and weavers. The final preparation of the fabrics was again undertaken under their own roof. As the author of the above-mentioned book on the Eupen cloth industry wrote: '. . . the merchant keeps . . . shearmen, pressers and happers in his house and under his supervision all of whom work for a wage.'

However, the number of workers employed in these centralized workshops was small in comparison to proto-industrial households organized in a putting-out system. In 1768, the Krefeld silk firm of von der Leyen had about 12% of all its employees directly on its pay roll; the same figure for the cloth industry of Vervier near Aachen in the 1780s was extraordinarily high, namely 25%. The capital which was invested in such workshops was in general not so large as to result in a situation in which it dominated, by virtue of its size, the production process. In 1789 a mere 5.8% of the balance-sheet total of the firm J.H. Scheibler & Sons, by far the most important enterprise of the Monschau cloth industry, were for buildings, tools and machinery (see Table 43).

Working capital was clearly dominant over fixed capital. It was also part of the *Verleger's* investment strategy to give preference to investments which, like buildings, were relatively versatile; nor, in view of the vagaries of the market, did they concentrate their capital in one area alone; rather they spread their investments so as to have several escape routes in a crisis. Thus for the *Verleger* the decisive criterion of his investment strategy remained the 'versatility' of his capital, to quote Werner Sombart.

Apart from *Manufakturen* which complemented proto-industrial production in the way described thus far, the 18th century also saw the establishment of other manufactures which were unconnected with rural industry and operated completely indpendently. Enterprises

*Table 43:*
Balance-sheet of J. H. Scheibler & Sons for the year ended
31.12.1789

| a) Assets Reich thalers | | % | b) Liabilities Reich thalers | | % |
|---|---|---|---|---|---|
| Factory buildings | 9 100 | | Creditors | 304 000 | 44,8 |
| Factory tools | 26 400 | | Cap. stock | 374 000[1] | 55,2 |
| Other | 4 000 | | | 678 000 | 100,0 |
| | 39 500 | 5,8 | | | |
| Raw materials | 80 500 | | | | |
| Finished/ semi-fin. cloths | 207 000 | | | | |
| | 287 500 | 42,5 | | | |
| Debtors | 346 000 | 51,0 | | | |
| Bills & cash | 5 000 | 0,7 | | | |
| | 678 000 | 100,0 | | | |

[1]Actual source gives: 374,301 Reich thalers

which were organised on this basis could be found above all in cotton printing as well as in the manufacture of porcelain, fayence and glass. The first of these was an industry which experienced its most dynamic development in the 18th century. Towards the end of that century, it employed more than 100,000 people. The largest of these enterprises had an annual output of between 20,000 and 40,000 pieces, with 500-800 workers on the payroll. Profit rates were exceptionally high in some cases. Capital multiplied within a few years. Thus the *Fabrique-Neuve* of Cortaillod, the most important cotton-printer in the Neuchatel region in Switzerland, achieved a profit rate (calculated in terms of the firm's productive capital) of 35% in 1783-91 and of 50% in 1792-98 (see Figure 25). Occasionally such a centralized *Manufaktur* became partially decentralized. This happened if, instead of using cotton fabrics made in India or elsewehere in Europe, it took production into its own hands and organized it on a proto-industrial basis. Finally, there were the porcelain manufactures which became the special concern of the German princes. The most famous among them in Germany was the one at Meissen in Saxony which was established in 1710. This *Manufaktur* employed 761 workers in 1765.

What was new about this type of enterprise was not the introduction of machines. Indeed the manufacturing process continued to be dominated by manual production. The advance consisted rather in a different organization of the process. As it was

*Figure 25:*

Quinquennial production averages of the cotton printing firm *La Fabrique-Neuve* in Cortalloid, 1754–1809

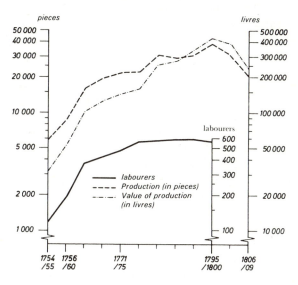

concentrated in a single building or complex of buildings, it became possible to compartmentalize and co-ordinate production, and occasionally this led to a marked increase in productivity. Seen in perspective, the significance of the *Manufaktur* lies above all in the fact that it represented an important link in the transition from proto-industrial production to factory production. This was less so in a micro-economic sense as few manufactures, in particular the cotton-printing enterprises among them, played a major role in the process of industrialization; but it is true in a macro-economic sense: *Manufakturen* pointed the way forward to the factory by bringing closer to a solution the problems raised by the centralization of production.

Centralized enterprises were not merely limited to the narrow area of *Manufakturen*. They were also to be found quite frequently in mining and the iron industry, and it was not rare for them to achieve a remarkable size. The Anzin mining company near Valenciennes in Northern France produced 310,000 tons of coal in 1790. This is the equivalent of about half the total production of the country. The Le Creusot iron works with its four blast furnaces, its forge hammers and steam engines was celebrated as 'one of the world wonders'. Le

Creusot also produced the first iron in France smelted with the help of coke.

As the end of the 18th century approached, there were growing signs that the prevailing system of production had reached the limits of its capacity. Under the increasing pressure of demand both at home and abroad the inner contradictions of the proto-industrial system, particularly in England, became so acute that its 'manageability' (M. Godelier) was called more and more into question. We have seen that the proto-industrial family had a propensity to reduce its output precisely in periods of boom; this was because, as the return per unit rose, its subsistence needs could be satisfied with a smaller labour effort. It was this behaviour which brought about the transformation of the proto-industrial system. In late 18th-century England a decline of proto-industrial productivity could only to a limited degree be made up with the help of additional labour. New forms of organization had to be found. Other problems were no less serious. The more a *Verleger* extended his putting-out network geographically, the sooner he was bound to reach the point at which his marginal costs per unit would rise. The speed with which his capital was turned over decreased; distribution costs rose. It became more and more difficult for him to supervise the proto-industrial producers and to protect himself against fraudulent use of the raw materials he was distributing to the families which were part of his network. There was also the problem that at least five spinning wheels were needed to supply sufficient yarn for one loom. This imbalance between yarn production and weaving capacity came to be a dysfunctional element, once labour to operate the spinning wheels was no longer plentiful in the centres of the textile industry. Wages rose (see Figure 28, pp. 147), and the inelastic supply of yarn threatened to block an increase in output beyond a certain level and hence to arrest the expansion of textile manufacturing. As R. Guest reported in 1823, it was not unusual for a Lancashire weaver in the 1760s 'to walk three or four miles in a morning and to call on five or six spinners before he could collect weft to serve him for the remainder of the day.'

The only alternative which promised a way out of the above difficulties of the proto-industrial system was greater mechanization of production, made possible through centralization. The cotton industry was the first branch to tackle these questions from the end of the 1760s. It thus became the 'pace-maker' (E.J. Hobsbawm) of the first phase of industrialization. Hargreave's 'Jenny' was still primarily operated in the proto-industrial workshop. But Arkwright's 'water

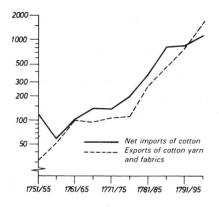

*Figure 26:*
Index of net cotton imports to England and exports of cotton fabrics from England in quinquennial averages, 1751–1800 (1761/65 = 100)

frame' and Crompton's 'mule' began to appear in factories and facilitated a solution not only of the traditional imbalance between yarn production and weaving capacity which has just been mentioned, but also of one of the central problems of proto-industrialization, namely the control and supervision of production. Arkwright opened his factory in Nottingham in 1769; three years later, some 300 people worked there. His 'Lower Mill' at Cromford near Matlock employed about 800 people at the end of the 1770s. Around 1780 there existed some 20 water-powered cotton mills. By 1797 their number had risen to about 900. They had an estimated fixed capital of £2.5 million. In facilitating this industrial break-through the importance of home markets and overseas markets varied at different times. Figure 26 shows that supplies of raw cotton rose more quickly than exports of cotton products during the crucial 1760s and 1770s. This lends support to the assumption that the home market was the decisive factor at this time. Only around the turn of the century were the scales tipped in favour of exports abroad.

The English iron industry was faced with difficulties which were no less formidable than those of the textile manufacturers. Charcoal became more scarce and expensive; marginal costs increased. The bottle-neck was overcome, however, when charcoal was replaced by coke. It was Abraham Darby who, around 1709, invented a process by which iron could be produced with the help of coke. Yet it took several decades before this technique was generally adopted. Its triumph came when Watt's steam engine made it possible to fit the first mechanized bellows to John Wilkinson's furnace at Willey south of the Coalbrookdale complex in 1776. Subsequently Henry Cort developed the puddling and rolling process which was patented in

1783–84, and this enabled the iron masters to use coal also for the next production stage, i.e. the making of wrought iron.

Thus coal became the primary source of energy of the 'First Industrial Revolution'; the steam engine converted coal into power for industrial use. The history of the steam engine is inseparably connected with the rise of the English coal industry. As the mines reached greater and greater depths, it became increasingly difficult to keep them free of water. The steam engine offered a solution to the problem. It could be used without great difficulty to drive water pumps. Its evolution started in 1698 with Thomas Savery's 'fire engine'; in 1712 Thomas Newcomen developed his steam engine; it then took until 1765 for James Watt to invent the separate condenser which enabled him to build a much more powerful engine at Boulton's factory in Soho in 1775. From now on the steam engine was also used outside the mines.

The growing demand for industrial goods enforced the substitution of scarce resources, such as labour, wood and water-power, by resources which were relatively abundant, such as capital, coal and steam power. It also brought about the transformation of proto-industrial production into factory production. The evolution of the productive forces had reached its ceiling in 18th-century England. These barriers could be removed only if improved steering mechanisms became available both in the field of technology and of the social organization of labour. It was precisely in these areas that the process of capitalist industrialization began.

Around 1790, the new system of production was still confined to a small part of the manufacturing sector. Nevertheless, the contours of a new age with new modes of production became discernible in the cotton industry. It was to be an age which was characterized by the deployment of capital and the division of society into capitalists and wage-labourers. However, the rise of the cotton industry marked not merely the beginning of a different social formation, but it also reminds us of the international context of the industrialization process.

To begin with, it was the calicoes which the trading companies had imported from India that stimulated demand for cotton fabrics in Europe. They had been re-exported by the European trading centres and this had led to the creation of a network which could equally well be used for the marketing of cotton fabrics which the metropolitan countries had themselves produced. Moreover the finishing of cotton products from overseas had given rise to the textile-printing industry which provided an important impulse for the industrialization of yarn production.

Secondly, it must be remembered that the raw cotton which was imported into Europe originated from the slave plantations of Brazil, the Caribbean and the American South. In 1786-87 some 69.3% of English cotton imports came from across the Atlantic; in 1796-1805 it was 87.5%. As Eric Hobsbawm has aptly written: 'The most modern centre of production thus preserved and extended the most primitive form of exploitation.'

Finally there is the fact that, in the 19th century, the cotton industry found markets in the underdeveloped and colonial world which facilitated its unprecedented expansion. In the course of this process occurred the destruction of the Indian domestic cotton industry which had been standing at the cradle of its later English rival.

### 3.4 Population Growth, Economic Growth and Society

Like the high middle ages and the 16th century, the 18th century was one of the great periods of economic growth in European history. The crisis of the 17th century had prepared the ground for renewed growth in the sense that it increased the margins of the peasant economy. Indeed from the middle of the 18th century the economy was once more on an expansionist course. The population grew. Agriculture and manufacturing increased their output. The volume of trade expanded. And yet fresh tensions arose in the pattern of supply and demand. Agricultural production could not keep pace with a growing population. Prices rose, especially those for basic foodstuffs where demand was inelastic. Prices for manufactured goods likewise experienced a rise, but it was less steep than that of grain. This was partly because demand for these goods was more elastic, but also because their supply can be organized much more flexibly than that of agricultural produce. On first impression it looks as if monetary factors were responsible for the inflationary development. Between 1701-20 and 1781-1800 production of precious metals in the Americas increased from around 369 tons to 1,065 tons per annum—an increase by some 189%. But on close inspection it seems more likely that, like in the 16th century, other, non-monetary factors were behind the long-term price rise. For it must be remembered that a growth in the circulation of money is just as little an autonomous element of the economic process as population growth. An expanding economy tends to create the money which it needs for its expansion. Thus, if one wishes to explain the inflation of the 18th century, one cannot avoid examining the supply of, and demand for, goods within the overall economic process. And the forces that were at work in this sphere were rooted in the phenomenon that a growing demand, in particular for basic foodstuffs, could be satisfied only at inflationary prices. Thus the growth of the population was initially a stimulus to economic growth; but it soon became detached from the economic process and began to overstretch the strength of the national economies of Europe.

Nor did demographic change and price development fail to have their effect on the distribution of incomes. Ground-rents rose because proceeds from agricultural production improved. By making this point, nothing has as yet been said about who pocketed the higher returns. Did they remain with the peasants or were they taken away by the landlords who succeeded in aligning incomes to the rising price level? We have the same difficulties to provide a clear-cut answer to this question as we have had for the 16th century. Favourable was above all the position of those peasants whose feudal contributions consisted, *inter alia*, of fixed cash payments. The value of cash payments made by East Prussian peasants between 1770 and 1800, calculated in terms of price equivalents for rye, declined by more than one third because grain prices kept rising. Their income, on the other hand, again computed on the basis of rye equivalents, improved by 15–25%. In other words, the percentage of feudal contributions declined.

We have seen how those landowners in England and, to some extent, in France who had extended their land in order to lease it again were best able to counter these economic developments. They could easily increase the rent and thus enforce an inflationary adjustment to the distribution of agricultural income. On the other hand, wherever there existed a *Vorwerk* economy like in East-Central and Eastern Europe, the nobility benefited directly and automatically from the rise in ground rents.

Wages took the opposite development from agricultural incomes. They fell, while marginal costs rose. As regards income distribution, this meant that labourers had their share reduced. Nominal wages held up in most cases and occasionally even experienced a rise; yet the abundance of labour, which was a consequence of the population growth, condemned to failure all attempts to adjust them to the rising cost of living. Thus the drop in real wages continued which, as we have seen, had started in the 16th century and which had temporarily been stopped in the 17th and early 18th centuries. In 1650–79 the daily wage of a worker in the quarries of Würzburg in Franconia was equivalent to the value of 12.7 kilograms of rye; by 1760–99 his daily wage would buy him no more than 4.8 kilos. The purchasing power

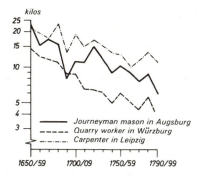

*Figure 27:*
Ten-year averages of daily real wages in three German towns, 1650-1799 (calculated in kilograms of rye equivalents)

of a journeyman mason from Augsburg for the same periods was the equivalent of 18.3 kilos and 7.9 kilos of rye respectively (see Figure 27). Ch.-E. Labrousse has calculated that the cost of living in France rose by 62% between 1726-41 and 1771-89, whereas nominal wages increased by about 26%. In other words, real wages declined by some 25% in comparison to their 1726-41 value. Meanwhile the predicament of the wage-earning population in England was somewhat less unequivocal. There real wages had actually risen up to the middle of the 18th century. The picture became more complex thereafter. Thus nominal wages in agriculture rose on average around 25% between the late 1760s and 1795. But the cost of living increased by about 30% and real wages hence actually experienced a decline. Calculated from a base-line of 100 in 1651-75 real wages of building workers in the English South also fell. In 1740-49 they had reached 67 index points and 59 in 1780-89. The English North, on the other hand, which was seized by the process of industrialization presented a different picture. In Lancashire real wages continud to rise overall in the second half of the 18th century, temporary setbacks notwithstanding (see Figure 28).

The social groups which lived on a higher income were much less directly hit be the rise in the cost of living because only a relatively

*Figure 28:*
Index of real wages in quinquennial averages in England, 1701/05-1791/95 (1701/05 = 100)

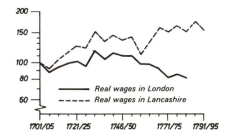

small percentage of their total budget was spent on these items. Merchants, *Verleger* and entrepreneurs moreover benefited from the general upswing of the economy, and fairly frequently they were able to net profits that were well above those made by the *classe propriétaire* in agriculture. Prices for manufactured goods rose and so did turnover. The volume of profit increased. In short, the growth period of the 18th century set in motion a redistribution of the gross national product: incomes from property were growing, whereas incomes from manual labour kept falling. Even England experienced a stagnation of her per capita income in the second half of the 18th century. There is hence good reason to presume that per capita income on the European Continent actually declined as it had done in the 16th century.

Finally, there occurred a shift in demand (and hence also in supply) as the general economic trend evolved. The lower classes in particular had to reduce the purchase of goods which were not essential to their livelihood the more food prices went up. In the early 1790s, miners in Durham·(Yorkshire), for example, spent 72.4% of their budget on food. A Berlin mason, who had to support a family of five, had to set aside 72.7% of his income for food around the turn of the century. The more nutritious, but expensive foods were replaced by cheaper ones. The consumption of meat declined even further. Demand centred on vegetables. We have seen above (p. 52) how meat had become replaced by cereals. Now potatoes began to substitute grain. Occidental nutritional standards reached their lowest level in the first half of the 19th century. People lived on the 'potato standard', as Wilhelm Abel has termed it. The shifts in the demand pattern were sooner or later bound to have a negative effect on the non-agricultural sector, especially in those countries which did not possess foreign markets worth mentioning. However, to some extent these problems were mitigated by the fact that the disproportional growth of the towns, the commercialization of agriculture and proto-industrialization had made a steadily growing section of the population dependent on the market. Thus socio-economic change provided a partial counterweight to economic recession. People could not survive without going to the market.

The effect of the triple pressure of population growth, inflation and redistribution of incomes was that the social structures of Europe were pushed and pulled in different directions. As these structures were still determined by functional and status hierarchies which were rooted in the feudal estates, demographic change, inflation and income redistribution had a highly destabilizing effect on the societies of Europe; for it was above all those lower strata which were not part of a society divided into estates that grew disproportionally both in the towns and in the countryside. By the end of the 18th century these strata made up more than half the population in some areas. Around 1750 the share of cottagers and *Inwohner* in terms of the total agrarian population was 61.1% in Saxony; the percentage of *Inwohner* in the towns was 45.4%. Nobles, clergymen, farmers and burghers added up to no more than 45.2% of the Saxon population. More than half the population there belonged to social groups which were outside the estates system (see Table 12, p. 55). Even more marked than in Saxony were the shifts in the social structures of Silesian villages. In 1577 56.8% of the rural population there were peasants. By 1787 the figure had slumped to 22.9%. The proportion of cottagers increased correspondingly (see Table 44). And these cottagers were particularly strongly represented in the mountainous region of Silesia with its large share of small-scale manufacturing.

*Table 44:*
Social structure of the Silesian village, 1577–1787 (%)

|  | Peasants | Small-holders obliged to render services | Cottagers |
|---|---|---|---|
| Totals for 1577 | 56.8 | 37.9 | 5.3 |
| Totals for 1787 | 22.9 | 25.2 | 51.9 |
| Districts (1787) |  |  |  |
| Eastern Silesia | 30.4 | 27.3 | 42.3 |
| Southwestern Sil. | 16.4 | 18.8 | 64.8 |
| Militsch-Ohlau | 18.8 | 27.2 | 54.0 |
| Central Silesia | 20.6 | 32.7 | 46.7 |
| Northwestern Sil. | 26.6 | 20.6 | 52.8 |

Further north, in the Swedish parts of Pomerania, a mere 10.1% of the rural population were peasants and small-holders in 1766; some 25.6% were lodgers and 51.3% worked as domestic servants and land labourers. The development took a similar course in other parts of Central Europe. Where, as in the Southwest, the land was divided up between the heirs, fragmentation continued and began to reach alarming proportions. In cities like Hamburg, Frankfurt and Basle, the burghers soon found themselves in a minority *vis-à-vis* those inhabitants and their families who enjoyed no citizen's rights.

A glance at the regions beyond Central Europe confirms this trend. On the royal estates of the Cracow Province no more than 35% of the farmsteads were held by peasants. The number of cottagers, on the other hand, who accounted for between 43% and 47% of the rural population in 1660, had meanwhile gone up to 56%. In the Dutch Overijssel region the share of peasants declined from 61.4% to 49.6% and that of cottagers from 38.6% to 34.8% between 1602 and 1795. At the same time there emerged a landles proletariat which amounted to some 18.3% of the population in 1795 and which was mostly employed in the textile industry. Nor did the French village in the 18th century escape a rapid process of proletarianization. According to statistics compiled by the Abbé Expilly, only around 13% of the rural population were *laboureurs* (peasants) in 1778. The remaining 87% were day-labourers, *manouvriers* and wine growers. Day labourers and *manouvriers* also made up more than 80% of the population in some villages in Burgundy. In England the ratio of lease-holders and peasants, on the one hand, and cottagers and land labourers, on the other, was 4:7 as early as the end of the 17th century. The number of the latter increased rapidly during the enclosure boom of the second half of the 18th century. Worse, their position deteriorated as they lost common rights and what little land they had been tilling. In 1803, over one third of the population were the 'labouring poor', the beggars, soldiers, sailors, land labourers and other desperately poor people at the bottom of the pile.

The accelerated growth of the lower class threatened to crush as with a steam-roller the traditional social structures. However, this did not mean as yet that these classes became the ferment of a new socio-economic order. At first their rise was no more than a symptom of decline of a social system which had reached the limits of its capacity to integrate divergent forces. However, the swelling of the lower ranks of society made the evolution of new forms of production unavoidable; for these additional people could find a livelihood only if more jobs were created for them in the non-agricultural sector of the economy. To be sure, the growth of the lower strata had been a factor in earlier times when manufacturing began to move into the rural areas around towns. However, these industries did not merely move to where there existed a reservoir of labour; as we have seen (above p. 136) they also stimulated demographic growth by undermining the traditional reproductive behaviour of the peasant family. It is in this way that the increasing population density in the major manufacturing regions of Europe may be explained.

The small producers, whom we encounter in these regions, occupy a peculiar intermediate position in European social history. In many ways they still lived in the world of the peasants. On the other hand, their daily life and the articulation of their socio-economic and cultural needs pointed frequently beyond the rural environment. Thus the products of the proto-industrial household were, unlike those of the peasantry, destined almost exclusively for the market, and this the more so the further rural manufacturing emancipated itself from its links with agriculture. This also implied that, conversely, the proto-industrial family had to rely on the market to buy in basic foodstuffs and other necessities. Small rural producers therefore needed what Rudolf Braun has called a '*bodenfremdes, exogenes Medium*', namely money, to pay for their livelihood. The agricultural seasons and the resultant pressure to engage in some kind of *ad hoc* economic planning lost their former importance. This occasionally promoted a happy-go-lucky approach to life or even an indulgence in luxuries which went beyond the means of the proto-industrial household. In 1765 the peasants of *Grossröhrsdorf* northeast of Dresden, for example, voiced the following complaint about the cottagers in the village, most of whom were ribbon makers and linen weavers: 'They showed off on all occasions and spent a lot of money. They dressed their daughters like burghers' daughters and certainly above their status·which had caused all sorts of things to be put into disarray.' And Solomon von Orelli reported on the weavers of the Zürich *Oberland* that 'sooner or later things began to go so far that a young weaver's woman could not be considered extravagant, if she bought from her earnings a bed, a chest, a nice colourful Sunday dress as well as a black one for the Holy Communion . . . Once these items had been acquired it depended on the greater or lesser degree of her vanity as to whether she would buy several attractive skirts or would blow her money in other ways.' Such behaviour was not just a consequence of the dissolution of a subsistence economy in which the peasant family consumed most of what it produced; it also testifies to an attempt on the part of the rural manufacturers to demonstrate their social difference to the outside world by 'symbolic and ostentatious consumption' (P. Bourdieu). By doing this, they tried to break through the confines of a society which was divided into feudal estates.

It was this mass of landless rural producers, small-holders and the proto-industrial manufacturers who came to be the labour force of the above-mentioned *Manufakturen* and early factories. The conditions under which they worked brought about the destruction of traditional life-styles and behaviour patterns; but new ones did not emerge immediately to replace them. Wage labour, to be sure, had existed for centuries before. However, it assumed a different quality in the 18th century. Those who were forced to sell their labour to entrepreneurs of factory owners found themselves working and living in conditions which had not existed in this form before. Thus they were subjected to a time- and work-discipline which could not be reconciled with the life-styles they were accustomed to. For the factory owners the irregular work rhythms of pre-industrial society were unacceptable. What had determined the time-consciousness of that society was the work that had to be done at a particular time of the day or the season. It was industrial capitalism that introduced the idea of measuring labour in specific units of time. It is no coincidence that clocks and watches became very widespread in the 18th century. But the work day was long and often extended beyond what was physically tolerable. In the *Manufakturen* of Berlin people worked for 14–16 hours per day. The figure for the English cotton mills was around 12 hours. Female and child labour was used on a large scale, above all in textiles, a practice which continued pre-industrial employment patterns. Children tended to be involved in the preparatory work, while women worked primarily as spinners. In 1789 only 14% of the work force in Arkwright's factories at Cromford were men.

The living conditions of this early proletariat were desolate. Whether it was the cotton weavers of the Zürich *Oberland*, the silk weavers of Lyons, the cotton printers of Chemnitz in Saxony or the female labourers in the English mills, they all vegetated at the poverty line. Only a small number of highly skilled workers were well paid. Most of these labourers found it impossible to put aside savings for emergencies so that they were without protection against the vicissitudes of life. If demand was slack, poverty and desperation became the general picture. When the Eichsfeld region southeast of Göttingen was struck by a severe crisis at the beginning of the 19th century, the authorities responsible for the area at Heiligenstadt reported as follows: 'The weavers are unable to find the large sums required for the purchase of wool; they are faced with the bitter necessity of having to sell and pawn their goods and chattels which they have worked hard to acquire in better times; and this enables them to buy a bit of wool from the agents (*Aufkäufer*) on whom they are dependent so as to be able to carry on their trade on a quite pitiful basis.'

Poverty increased the more the 'safety net' which state and society had traditionally provided was being dismantled in the course of the 18th century. The state no longer regarded it as a task of public welfare to help the poor. The poor were seen as a problem for the police and the judiciary. Poverty became a criminal offence. Poor-houses, orphanages, workhouses and penitentiaries were established whose objective it was to integrate the 'outcasts' into the production process. Most of these institutions supplied labour to the *Manufakturen*, and to those of the textile industry in particular. Occasionally the inmates were leased to the entrepreneur. The logical complement of the criminalization of poverty was the replacement of the 'old moral economy of provision' by the 'new political economy of the free market' (E. P. Thompson). The lower classes were forced to rely on their own resources and thus to offer themselves as wage labourers. The grain trade was freed from all restrictions. The regimentation of bread price was abandoned. State intervention in the economy with the aim of safeguarding the provision of food came to an end. The credo of *laissez-faire* which was characteristic of the dawn of capitalism triumphed.

The victims of these processes initially continued to cling to traditional thought patterns with which they tried to interpret and, under certain circumstances, even to respond to the new situation. As E. P. Thompson has shown, virtually uninterrupted chains of bread riots came to be the concentrated expression of 'the moral economy of the . . . crowd'. They all revolved around the question of 'setting' the bread price, i.e. they demanded its reduction. If the rulers failed to live up to the expectations of the crowd, the latter believed to be justified in its resort to violence in order to enforce the adoption of official measures to bring down the price of bread. The manufacturing population moreover evolved forms of struggle which went beyond the simple bread riot. Even if, like the latter type of protest, they amounted to a 'collective bargaining by riot' (E. J. Hobsbawm), the object of the struggle was no longer the price of bread, but the cost of raw materials, as in the case of the 1793 uprising of the weavers of Landeshut in Silesia. On other occasions the protest was against the low prices paid for manufactured goods by the merchants or piece-work wages. If tools and machines were smashed, this was done not merely to pressurize merchants, *Verleger* and entrepreneurs into making concessions, but also in order to enforce a sense of solidarity among the rioters. All of these uprisings were usually brutally suppressed by the authorities. Thus the state made its own specific contribution to the establishment of a capitalist system of production.

The genesis of an early proletariat was not a process which unfolded independently of the economy. Rather it was the result of the policies of employment and accumulation adopted by a nascent class of proto-industrial and industrial capitalists. However, it would be wrong to assume that these people were the decisive element within the bourgeoisie under the ancien régime. That system, on the contrary, was dominated by merchants, bankers, rentiers and officials. As the societies of Europe found themselves in a transition phase from one mode of production to another, a number of capitalisms co-existed side-by-side: merchant capitalism, agricultural capitalism and, pointing towards developments beyond the former, proto-industrial and industrial capitalism. Up to a point the 'bourgeoisie', with its divisions, was therefore a reflection of these divergent capitalisms. Investment in property, offices and state bonds in order to obtain a fixed annual return continued to be very important. According to recent estimates, more than 80% of private wealth in France was generated in this traditional way. Nor were income and property evenly distributed among this bourgeoisie. A small group of extremely rich merchants, financiers and officials must be sharply distinguished from a broadly-based lower and middle stratum within the bourgeoisie. In 1749 some 14.1% of the 'bourgeois' who appear in Parisian marriage contracts had assets worth less than 1,000 livres; on the other hand, 4.7% of this group held 100,000 livres and more. It is characteristic that 77.3% of these people were rentiers, bureaucrats and professionals who were not directly involved in commerce or production. Moreover, none of the large wealthy bourgeois families could stand comparison with the wealth accumulated by the nobility which resided in Paris. For one bourgeois with property worth 500,000 livres there were 11 aristocrats to match this figure (see Table 45).

It appears that wealth and income differentials between the nobility and the 'middle class' were just as marked in England as in France. Where England differed, was that social barriers between noblemen and 'bourgeoisie' were becoming less impenetrable. Daniel Defoe noted in 1726 that 'trade in England makes gentlemen and has peopled this nation with gentlemen'. In considering social mobility it is important, however, to remember that it worked in both directions. The strict application of primogeniture induced many members of the nobility to seek a 'bourgeois' livelihood. Property had so much become the dominant criterion of a person's status within the system of 18th-century English society that 'bourgeois' status hierarchies did not lag far behind the 'feudal' pecking order in complexity.

The bourgeoisie of the Central European towns had more simple structures. Mainz, for example, numbered 30,000 inhabitants at the

*Table 45:*

## Socio-professional stratification and distribution of wealth in Paris (based on marriage contracts for 1749)[1]

| Soc.-prof. category | Wealth (in 'livres tournois') | | | | |
|---|---|---|---|---|---|
| | <1 000 | 1 000– 9 999 | 10 000– 99 999 | 100 000 und mehr | Total |
| Wage lab. in crafts and commerce, small artisans | 280 | 353 | 9 | – | 642 |
| | *54.9*[3] | *31.2* | *3.0* | *–* | *32.1* |
| Master artisans and merchants | 72 | 357 | 120 | – | 549 |
| | *14.1* | *31.6* | *39.2* | *–* | *27.4* |
| Wealthy merchants | 1 | 6 | 5 | 5 | 17 |
| | *0.2* | *0.5* | *1.6* | *9.1* | *0.9* |
| Domestic servants | 94 | 245 | 29 | 2 | 370 |
| | *18.4* | *21.7* | *9.5* | *3,6* | *18.5* |
| Soldiers and petty officers | 8 | 11 | 4 | – | 23 |
| | *1.6* | *1.0* | *1.3* | *–* | *1.1* |
| 'Bourgeois'[2] | 55 | 155 | 116 | 17 | 343 |
| | *10.8* | *13,7* | *37.9* | *30.9* | *17.1* |
| Nobility | – | 4 | 23 | 31 | 58 |
| | *–* | *0.3* | *7.5* | *56.4* | *2.9* |
| No. | 510 | 1 131 | 306 | 55 | 2 002 |
| % | *100.0* | *100.0* | *100.0* | *100.0* | *100.0* |

[1]Not representative for population as a whole because most members of the lower classes did not conclude a marriage contract. Thus for 1749 contracts exist for 60.9% of the marriages;   [2]Professionals, officials, rentiers
[3]Percentages in italics

end of the 18th century and saw the rise of a new stratum of wealthy merchants and entrepreneurs. Yet their influence remained limited in view of the still strongly corporatist social structures of the time. Only in cities like Hamburg, Frankfurt and Berlin do we encounter a bourgeoisie whose weight is comparable to that of Western Europe. The concentration of wealth in these cities assumed considerable proportions. In the second half of the 18th century Frankfurt had no less than 183 families with assets of 300,000 guldens, with eight of these being millionaires. But the traditional status system had not yet lost its pull. Some 32 Frankfurt merchants acquired aristocratic titles in the course of the 18th century. As Dr. med. Johann Christian Senckenberg remarked mockingly: 'Wealthy merchants obtain ennoblement, blow up their cheeks and insist on being called "Gracious Gentleman". Once they held a yardstick in their hands; now they have a feather on their hat, having fixed the feather which they wore behind their ear to their hat.' And the farther we look towards Eastern Europe, the less significant was the 'bourgeoisie'. In 1775 Russian merchants obtained a higher status than the 'lesser burghers' who were taxed on a per capita basis. But they nevertheless continued to be strictly limited in their freedom of movement in the face of the power of Russia's 'state feudalism'.

However, only in those regions did the bourgeoisie genuinely leave behind the feudal world where it moved into the production sphere and succeeded in gaining control of it. The merchant capitalists and *Verleger*, as we have seen, directed production from the distribution sphere, and whenever there was a crisis they would be prone to retreat to their trading activities. The final and decisive step was taken only when they established a factory. Factories represented concentrations of fixed capital; when they emerged, the production sphere came into its own *vis-à-vis* the distribution sphere. Yet for this shift to occur, an important precondition had to be fulfilled. It was not enough merely to centralize production, if the existing mode of production was to be changed. Rather it had to be supplemented by a specific way of utilizing capital; capital had to be accumulated. It was not allowed to consume profits or to transfer them to the distribution sphere; profits had to be used for reinvestment and for an increase of the capital stock with the aim of expanding production. This type of economic behaviour required certain structural changes which have been discussed above; but there is also a subjective context in which the behaviour of the industrial capitalists must be seen. The system of societal norms and values had to be favourable and possibly even stimulating to an economic activity which was orientated towards profit and the productive reinvestment of economic growth. The same applied to the status system. Feudal society ascribed social positions on the basis of birth and social origin. But this type of status ascription was irreconcilable with social mobility without which a class of industrial capitalists could not come into existence. Status ascription had to be replaced by status achievement.

There can be little doubt that England had moved farthest from the feudal system of status ascription. However, that system also began to disappear, albeit slowly, on the European Continent, not-withstanding various attempts at reversing this trend. But economic activity was by no means the highest societal value yet. European society found itself in a period of upheaval in which several different modes of production cut across each other. This is also reflected in the criss-crossing of norms, values and status patterns of different countries. The farther a particular country had advanced on the road towards industrial capitalism, the more the traditional system of norms and values had lost its former rigidity; the more was the ascription of social positions within a feudal order being called into question. Slowly the class societies of the 19th century began to take shape within the framework of a capitalist-industrial economy, which ultimately affected Western as well as East-Central Europe and transformed even the landlords into a land-owning class. These observations are not meant to imply that early modern Europe lacked the elements of a class society. Pre-19th century European society was also organized according to the principle of labour and the appropriation of labour. But this reality was veiled by the fact that the mechanism of appropriation was not directly rooted in the production process. This is why the stratification system of this society could gain, tendencially at least, a degree of autonomy *vis-à-vis* its essential class character. However, this possibility began to disappear increasingly from the 18th century onwards.

# Conclusion

By the end of the 18th century agriculture was still clearly the most important creator of national wealth in Europe. According to J. Marczewski, the share of manufacturing in the physical national product (i.e. agriculture plus manufacturing) was 27% for France in 1803/12, 37% for Britain in 1811 (in both cases at British prices). Around 1800, some 65% of the Prussian working population was employed in the primary sector, with a mere 20% working in the secondary sector and 15% in the tertiary one. In Britain, by contrast, only 35.9% of the working population were employed in agriculture, forestry and the fishing industry. Manufacturing, on the other hand, absorbed 29.7%. These figures demonstrate just how large the gap between the British Isles and the Continental competitors had become.

The British lead became a factor which accelerated the revolution of the mode of production on the Continent. The more marked this lead was, the less the putters-out and merchant capitalists on the Continent could avoid taking over the technologies developed across the Channel and to enter the process of capitalist industrialization aided by them. Any procrastination would only lead to domestic and foreign markets being lost to their British competitors and to the indigenous industries being obliterated. The existence of a world market within which the production of manufactured goods occurred made it imperative to industrialize. Yet, industrialization could take place only in those regions in which favourable framework conditions prevailed, and this meant:

(1) Whenever the 'production factors' labour, land and capital had been freed from their hitherto feudal resp. collectivist constraints; i.e. wherever there existed free labour in a formal sense and, as Max Weber has put it, the free appropriation of all material goods as freely disposable property by autonomous private enterprises.

(2) Wherever there existed general conditions of production in the shape of a material, institutional and 'human' infrastructure, i.e. a network of transport and communications, a legal system and recruitable labour.

(3) Wherever there were markets which were expanding and capable of further expansion beyond the national frontiers and, above all, inside these frontiers. Capitalist industrialization hence not only amounted to a revolution of the mode of production, but was also predicated on the *sine qua non* that the first transitional stage had been achieved, i.e. that the feudal mode had already lost much of its impact and that the capitalist mode had developed in embryo. Thus at the end of this book the question is raised once again as to the forces that were at work during the period covered by it—a period which saw the transformation of European feudalism and which was at the same time the formative period of European capitalism. The following aspects are important here:

(1) The dynamic of the feudal mode of production which expressed itself in the long waves of European agricultural development unleashed processes of accumulation and de-accumulation in the countryside which, in certain circumstances, might turn into processes of modification and even of transformation, unless the balance of class forces or the intervention of the state blocked such changes. There emerged a process of capitalist commercialization. It took the form either of a peasant capitalism, like in Holland, or of a large-scale land-owners' capitalism, like in England. As a consequence, the feudal mode of production began to disintegrate. East-Central and Eastern Europe, on the other hand, moved in the opposite direction. There the re-feudalization of agrarian structures prevented the emergence of an agrarian capitalism. It was only the agrarian reforms of the late 18th and the 19th centuries which created the preconditions of what might be called the 'Prussian' variant on the path towards a capitalism in the countryside. Its basis was the large-scale agricultural enterprise which had evolved from the *Vorwerk* system.

(2) Merchant capital, which had initially been an integral part of the feudal system, began to prise open the guild structures of manufacturing and artisanal production once the pressure of demand increased. Wherever the merchant capitalists found it impossible to build up a production apparatus in the towns unhampered by guild restrictions, they moved production to the countryside and expanded it there on a large scale. In the countryside a labour potential had grown up which, representing the reverse side of the accumulation process described under (1) above, was the result of a process of de-accumulation. This potential was thus merely waiting to be used. But the merchant capitalists did not merely circumvent the policies of the guilds which prevented economic growth by locating production

outside the towns: they also externalized part of the production costs by burdening the agricultural sector with them. Large segments of the peasant population were in this way transformed into an 'accumulation fund' with which the merchant capitalists promoted the accumulation process in their hands. By the same token, the erosion of the feudal system was accelerated by them.

(3) The commercialization of agriculture, proto-industrialization and, not least, the disproportionate growth of the cities stimulated the development of a domestic market which was to be of fundamental importance for the triggering of industrialization. The more the process of specialization advanced, the more the people who were captured by this process were to become dependent on the market. The more these same people were under a pressure to concentrate their labour effort on the production for a market, the less they were able to avoid covering a growing percentage of their needs through purchases on the market. The market principle asserted itself; the markets expanded.

(4) In this process of transformation which seized hold of the societies of Europe, overseas expansion was to play an increasing role; but it was by no means the factor which decided everything. As is demonstrated by the inclusion of peasant society in the process of consumption and accumulation, the 'inner Americas' (I. Wallerstein) had by no means reached their limits. The movements of the European economy were not yet totally dominated by the nascent capitalist world system. Its genesis was a central element of the process of transformation; but it was not its determinant.

(5) Nor did the state act as the propellant behind the socio-economic transformation; but its contradictions certainly furthered this process. State taxes were initially an essential feature of a centralized feudalism; yet the more these taxes reduced the scope for, and superseded, the levy of feudal dues, the more they came into conflict with the feudal system. The pressure to develop the productive forces of society which moved the state's economic policy-making stimulated the growth of manufacturing and thus promoted the emergence of social structures which could no longer be integrated into the feudal system.

The French Revolution accelerated this transformation process, but not without retarding it at the same time. Its main direction and main consequence were 'bourgeois and capitalist' (B. Moore), once the popular revolution of the *sansculottes*, the last great protagonists of a 'moral economy' of welfare, had been defeated. On the other hand, it was in the countryside that this 'bourgeois' revolution suffered a serious defeat in its confrontation with that of the peasants: the beginnings of an agrarian capitalism were stunted and reversed; small-holding property emerged strengthened. Outside France, the Revolution and the popular movements which were partly connected with it forced governments into initiating reforms of the existing institutional framework. In this way decisive prerequisites were created for a thorough revolution of the mode of production. The upswing of the 18th century ended in a crisis at the beginning of the 19th. But it was a crisis of a new kind, which had little in common with those which had struck Europe from the late middle ages to the 17th century. Grain prices dropped, not because demand declined, but because too much was being produced. Proto-industry lapsed into agonies, not because markets for its goods disappeared, but because it was unable to cope with the competition of factory production. Pauperism was spreading, and for those affected by it the transition from an agrarian capitalist feudal system permeated by proto-industry to an industrial capitalism proved to be extremely painful.

# Annotated Bibliography

## Abbreviations

| | | |
|---|---|---|
| AnnESC | = | Annales. Economies, Sociétés, Civilisations |
| CEcHE | = | The Cambridge Economic History of Europe |
| EcHR | = | The Economic History Review |
| FEcHE | = | The Fontana Economic History of Europe |
| GG | = | Geschichte und Gesellschaft |
| JbWG | = | Jahrbuch für Wirtschaftsgeschichte |
| JEcH | = | The Journal of Economic History |
| JEuEcH | = | The Journal of European Economic History |
| Pb | = | Paperback |
| PP | = | Past and Present |
| VSWG | = | Vierteljahrsschrift für Sozial- und Wirtschaftsgeschichte |
| Z. | = | Zeitschrift |

## General Histories

The three most important **general histories** still are: *The Cambridge Economic History of Europe*, vols. 4-5, Cambridge 1966-1977; *The Fontana Economic History of Europe*, ed. C. M. Cipolla, vols. 2-3, London 1973-1974 (pb.); *Histoire économique et sociale du monde*, ed. P. Léon, vols. 1-3, Paris 1977-1978. See also P. Léon, *Economies et sociétés préindustrielles*, vol. 2: *1650-1780. Les origines d'une accélération de l'histoire*, Paris 1970 (an excellent introduction; vol. 1 by R. Gascon not yet published), and R. Davis, *The Rise of the Atlantic Economies*, London 1973.

Some of the older general histories are still useful: J. Kulischer, *Allgemeine Wirtschaftsgeschichte des Mittelalters und der Neuzeit*, vol. 2, München 1929; see also M. Weber, *Wirtschaftsgeschichte. Abriss der universalen Sozial- und Wirtschafts-geschichte des Mittelalters und der Neuzeit*, München 1923 (Engl. transl.: *General Economic History*, Brunswick 1981) and W. Sombart, *Der moderne Kapitalismus*, vol. 1, 1-2 and vol. 2, 1-2, München ²1916 (in contrast to Weber's study, this one is dated as regards its analytical framework, but continues to be thought-provoking in certain respects). C. M. Cipolla's *Before the Industrial Revolution. European Society and Economy, 1000-1700*, London 1976 (pb.) represents a systematic analysis, but neglects the relations of production; based on the "property rights"-concept: D. C. North and R. P. Thomas, *The Rise of the Western World. A New Economic History*, Cambridge 1973 (pb.); from various aspects of material culture to the genesis of the capitalist world system: F. Braudel, *Civilisation matérielle, économie et capitalisme, XVe-XVIIIe*

*siècle*, vols. 1-3, Paris 1979 (Engl. transl.: *Capitalism and Material Life, 1400-1800*, London 1973.) See also O. Hufton, *EcHR*, 2nd. Ser., 35, 1982, pp. 140-145.
**Individual countries: Germany:** *Handbuch der deutschen Wirtschafts- und Sozial-geschichte*, eds. H. Aubin and W. Zorn, vol. 1, Stuttgart 1971 (particularly important because of its annotated bibliography); F.-W. Henning, *Das vorindustrielle Deutschland 800 bis 1800 (Wirtschafts- und Sozialgeschichte*, vol. 1) Paderborn ³1977 (valuable as an introduction); H. Kellenbenz, *Deutsche Wirtschaftsgeschichte*, vol. 1, München 1977 (more detailed than the book by Henning); H. Mottek, *Wirtschaftsgeschichte Deutschlands. Ein Grundriss*, vol. 1, Berlin 1957 (the standard textbook of East German historiography); K. Borchardt, *Grundriss der deutschen Wirtschaftsgeschichte*, Göttingen 1978 (pb.; excellent, unfortunately too cursory for the early period).
**Britain:** E. Lipson, *The Economic History of England*, vol. 2, London 1931 (still interesting); S. Pollard and D. W. Crossley, *The Wealth of Britain, 1085-1966*, London 1968 (pb.); L. A. Clarkson, *The Pre-Industrial Economy in England, 1500-1750*, London 1971 (pb.; both useful surveys); D. C. Coleman, *The Economy of England, 1450-1750*, Oxford 1977 (pb.; short, but excellent outline); from *Social and Economic History of England:* W. G. Hoskins, *The Age of Plunder. The England of Henry VIII, 1500-1547*, London 1976 (pb.); and Ch. Wilson, *England's Apprenticeship, 1603-1763*, London 1965 (pb.; both stimulating analyses); finally vols. 2 and 3 of the *Pelican Economic History of Britain*, with a stronger political orientation: Ch. Hill, *Reformation to Industrial Revolution*, Harmondsworth 1969 and E. J. Hobsbawm, *Industry and Empire*, Harmondsworth 1969; see also R. Floud and D. McCloskey, *The Economic History of Britain since 1700*, vol. 1: 1700-1860, Cambridge 1981 (pb.).
**France:** *Histoire économique et sociale de la France*, eds. F. Braudel and E. Labrousse, vols. 1, 1-2 and 2, Paris 1970-1977 (the most important work); O. Goubert, *L'Ancien régime*, vol. 1: *La société*, vol. 2: *Les pouvoirs*, Paris 1969-1973 (excellent textbook; Engl. trans.: *The Ancien Régime: French Society, 1600-1750*, London 1973). W. Mager, *Frankreich vom Ancien Régime zur Moderne. Wirtschafts-, Gesellschafts- und politische Institutionengeschichte, 1630-1830*, Stuttgart 1980.
**Italy:** R. Romano, *La storia economica. Dal secolo XIV al Settecento (Storia d'Italia*, vol. 2, 2), Torino 1974, pp. 1813-1931; A. Caracciolo, *La storia economica* (ibid., vol. 3), Torino 1973, pp. 511-569.
**Netherlands:** J. A. van Houtte, *An Economic History of the Low Countries, 800-1800*, London 1977; J. G. van Dillen, *Van rijkdom en regenten. Handboek tot de economische en sociale geschiedenis van Nederland tijdens de Republiek*, Den Haag 1970.
**Austria:** F. Tremel, *Wirtschafts- und Sozialgeschichte Österreichs*, Vienna 1969.
**Poland:** J. Rutkowski, *Historia gospodarcza Polski (do 1864 r.) [An Economic History of Poland to the Year 1864]*, Warsaw 1953; B. Zientrara, A. Mączak et al., *Dzieje gospodarcze Polski do 1939 r. [An Economic History of Poland to the Year 1939]*, Warsaw 1965.
**Russia:** P. I. Liashchenko, *History of the National Economy of Russia to the 1917 Revolution*, New York 1949 (1939).
**Sweden:** E. F. Heckscher, *An Economic History of Sweden*, Cambridge, Mass. 1954.
**Switzerland:** A. Hauser, *Schweizerische Wirtschafts- und Sozialgeschichte*, Erlenbach-Zürich 1961; J.-F. Bergier, *Naissance et croissance de la Suisse industrielle*, Berne 1974.
**Spain:** J. Vicens Vives with the collaboration of J. Nadal Oller, *An Economic History of Spain*, Princeton 1969; J. van Klaveren, *Europäische Wirtschaftsgeschichte*

*Spaniens im 16. und 17. Jahrhundert*, Stuttgart 1960; see also the excellent regional study by P. Vilar, *La Catalogue dans l'Espagne moderne. Recherches sur les fondements économiques des structures nationales*, vols. 1-3, Paris 1962 (with the main focus on the 18th century).

**Demography:** A. E. Imhof, *Einführung in die historische Demographie*, München 1977 (a good survey of the history, problems and the literature of 'historical demography'); *Population in History*, ed. E. A. Wrigley, London 1969 (pb; the best introduction into a historical theory of population); P. Guillaume and J.-P. Poussou, *Démographie historique*, Paris 1970 (a useful systematic and chronological study); M. Reinhard et al., *Histoire générale de la population mondiale*, Paris ³1968 (a new edition of this standard work of the history of population is in preparation); E. A. Wrigley and R. S. Schofield, *The Population History of England, 1541-1871. A Reconstruction*, London 1981; Readers: *Population in History, Essays in Historical Demography*, ed. D. V. Glass and D. E. C. Eversley, London 1965 (pb.); *Population and Social Change*, ed. D. V. Glass and R. Revelle, London 1972; *Biologie des Menschen in der Geschichte, Beiträge zur Sozialgeschichte der Neuzeit aus Frankreich und Skandinavien*, ed. A. E. Imhof, Stuttgart 1978 (together with the reader by Glass/Eversley most highly recommended); *European Demography and Economic Growth*, ed. W. R. Lee, London 1979.

**Agrarian History:** W. Abel, *Agricultural Fluctuations in Europe from the Thirteenth to the Twentieth Centuries*, London 1980 (now considered a classic study in agricultural historiography, this book places the history of the agricultural economy within the long waves of the general economic development); B. H. Slicher van Bath, *The Agrarian History of Western Europe, A.D. 500-1850*, London 1963 (excellent introduction); see also F. Lütge, *Geschichte der deutschen Agrarverfassung*, vol. 3, Stuttgart ³1967; G. Franz, *Geschichte des deutschen Bauernstandes*, vol. 4, Stuttgart ²1976, and especially W. Abel, *Geschichte der deutschen Landwirtschaft vom frühen Mittelalter bis zum 19. Jahrhundert*, Stuttgart ³1978; F.-W. Henning, *Landwirtschaft und ländliche Gesellschaft in Deutschland*, vols. 1-2, Paderborn 1978-1979; *The Agrarian History of England and Wales*, vol. 4, 1500-1640, ed. J. Thirsk, Cambridge 1967 (vol. 5 in preparation); *Histoire de la France rurale*, vol. 2, 1340-1789, ed. G. Duby and A. Wallon, Paris 1975 (superbly illustrated); *Zarys historii gospodarstwa wiejskiego w Polsce [Outline of Polish Agrarian History]*, ed. J. Leskiewiczowa, vol. 2, *Warsaw 1964; Historia chłopów polskich [History of Polish Peasantry]*, ed. St. Inglot, vol. 1, Warsaw 1970; J. Blum, *Lord and Peasant in Russia. From the Ninth to the Nineteenth Century*, Princeton 1961 (pb.).

**Urban History:** *Town in Societies. Essays in Economic History and Historical Sociology*, ed. Ph. Abrams and E. A. Wrigley, Cambridge 1978 (pb.); P. Clark and P. Slack, *English Towns in Transitions, 1500-1700*, Oxford 1976 (pb.); P. Corfield, *The Impact of English Towns, 1700-1800*, Oxford 1982 (pb.); *Histoire de la France urbaine*, vol. 3: *La ville classique le la renaissance aux Révolutions*, ed. Le Roy Ladurie, Paris 1981.

**History of Technology:** *A History of Technology*, ed. Ch. Singer et al., vols. 3-4, Oxford 1957-1958; *Histoire des techniques. Technique et civilisations, technique et sciences*, ed. B. Gilles, Paris 1978 (good introduction); D. Furia, P.-Ch. Serre, *Techniques et sociétés, liaisons et évolutions*, Paris 1970 (useful textbook); *Moderne Technikgeschichte*, ed. K. Hausen and R. Rürup, Köln 1975 (excellent anthology, yet primarily focussing on the 19th and 20th centuries).

**Quantitative sources of economic history:** *An Introduction to the Sources of European Economic History, 1500-1800*, vol. 1: Western Europe, ed. Ch. Wilson and

G. Parker, London 1977 (with systematically structured chapters for individual countries, this is an excellent tool); for a survey of anthologies of the history of the development of prices and wages see W. Abel, *Fluctuations*; B. R. Mitchell, *European Historical Statistics, 1750-1970*, London 1975; for Britain see the indispensable book by B. R. Mitchell, with the collaboration of Ph. Deane, *Abstract of British Historical Statistics*, Cambridge 1962; see also Ph. Deane and W. A. Cole, *British Economic Growth, 1688-1959*, Cambridge ²1969. There are no comparable works for other countries. J. J. McCusker, *Money and Exchange in Europe and America, 1600-1775, A Handbook*, London 1978 (indispensable for the study of the development of currencies and exchange rates in the Atlantic economic area).

# Introduction

The so-called Dobb-Sweezy Controversy is the starting point of any analysis of the problems of transition. This controversy was carried on in the 1950s in the pages of *Science and Society* and arose from Dobb's investigations into capitalism: see M. Dobb, *Studies in the Development of Capitalism*, London ²1963 (¹1946; still the best study of the origins and history of capitalism) and M. Dobb et al., *The Transition from Feudalism to Capitalism (Introduction by R. Hilton)*, London 1976. The opposing position taken up by Dobb and Sweezy in the debate continue to determine the discussion to this day, as the controversy between R. Brenner and I. Wallerstein demonstrates. Dobb emphasized the inner dynamic of the feudal system and in particular the increasing exploitation of the peasants; Sweezy focused on commerce, i.e. on external factors, as the main driving force behind the dissolution of the feudal system. S. R. Brenner, 'Agrarian Class Structure and Economic Development in Pre-industrial Europe', in: *PP* 70, 1976, pp. 30-75; ibid., 78, 1978, pp. 24-55; 79, 1978, pp. 55-69; 80, 1978, pp. 3-65; 85, 1979, pp. 49-67; G. Bois, 'Against the Neo-malthusian Orthodoxy', in: ibid., 79, 1978, pp. 60-69; I. Wallerstein, *The Modern World-System 1. Capitalist Agriculture and the Origins of the European World-Economy in the Sixteenth Century*, New York 1974; idem, *The Modern World-System II. Mercantilism and the Consolidation of the European World-Economy, 1600-1750*, New York 1980; idem, *The Capitalist World-Economy. Essays*, Cambridge 1979; see also R. Brenner, 'The Origins of Capitalist Development: a Critique of Neo-Smithian Marxism', in: *New Left Review* 104, 1977, pp. 25-92, and *Kapitalistische Weltökonomie. Kontroversen über ihren Ursprung and ihre Entwicklungsdynamik*, ed. D. Senghaas, Frankfurt 1979 (excellent reader; see especially the editor's preface and the contribution by H. Elsenhans); in their extreme form, the arguments of both Brenner and Wallerstein would seem to go into the wrong direction. Brenner, because he puts so much emphasis on the respective class constellation to the exclusion of other factors, bars himself expressly from gaining an understanding of the dynamics of the feudal mode of production. Wallerstein, on the other hand, maintains that the capitalist world system emerged without any transitional phases from the crisis of feudalism in the late middle ages. This leads him not only to reduce the phenomena of the socio-economic process to this world system and to reject the Marxian concept of commercial capital, but also to deny that the Industrial Revolution had an epochal significance. As a result, the transitional period loses its multifaceted variety and janus-facedness. This study tries to restructure the problem of transition in a way which is inspired by the concept of proto-industrialization, on the one hand, and by G. Bois's attempt to incorporate the theory of agrarian crisis into a theory of the feudal mode of production, on the other; see G. Bois, *Crise du féodalisme. Economie rurale et démographie en Normandie orientale du début du 14e siecle au milieu du 16e siècle*, Paris 1976 (see also M. Aymard, 'L'Europe moderne: Féodalité ou feodalités?', in: *Ann ESC* 36, 1981, pp. 426-435; P. Kriedte, 'Spätmittelalterliche Agrarkrise oder Krise des Feudalismus?', in: *GG* 7, 1981, pp. 42-68) and P. Kriedte, H. Medick, J. Schlumbohm, *Industrialization before Industrialization. Rural Industry in the Genesis of Capitalism. With Contributions from H. Kisch and F. F. Mendels*, Cambridge 1981; idem, 'Die Proto-Industrialisierung auf dem Prüfstand der historischen Zunft. Eine Antwort an einige Kritiker', in: *GG* 9, forthcoming; see also the important work by C. Lis and H. Soly, *Poverty and Capitalism in Pre-industrial Europe*, Hassocks 1979.

**Feudal mode of production:** *Feudalismus. Materialien zur Theorie und Geschichte*, ed. L. Kuchenbuch in co-operation with B. Michael, Frankfurt 1977 (highly recommended as a reader); idem, 'Zur Struktur and Dynamik der "feudalen" Produktionsweise im vorindustriellen Europa', in: ibid., pp. 694-761; idem, 'Gesellschaftsformationen in der Geschichte' (special issue of *Argument*, vol. 32), Berlin 1978, pp. 137-144; P. Anderson, *Lineages of the Absolutist State*, London 1974; on peasant societies see also E. R. Wolf, *Peasants*, Englewood Cliffs 1966; T. Shanin, 'The Nature and Logic of the Peasant Economy', in: *Journal of Peasant Studies* 1, 173/74, pp. 63-80, 186-206.

On the **long waves of European agriculture,** whose discovery essentially goes back to Wilhelm Abel and which, at least as far as French economic historians are concerned, provide the basic structure for almost all their studies, see W. Abel, *Fluctuations, (Agricultural History)*; idem, *'Agrarkonjunktur'*, in: *Handwörterbuch der Sozialwissenschaften*, vol. 1, 1956, pp. 49-59; see also the attempt at theory formation by Bois, op. cit. as well as the alternative model developed by E. Le Roy Ladurie, 'L'histoire immobile', in *AnnESC* 29, pp. 543-567. **Short cycle:** Ch.-E. Labrousse, *Esquisse du mouvement des prix et des revenus en France au XVIIe siècle*, vol. 2, Paris 1933, pp. 543-567; idem, *La crise de l'économie française à la fin de l'Ancien Régime et au début de la Révolution*, vol. 1, Paris 1944, pp. XIII-XVI, 172-184; idem, in: *Histoire économique et sociale de la France*, (see above section on General Histories), vol. 2, pp. 529-563; W. Abel, *Fluctuations*, (see above section on Agricultural History); idem, *Massenarmut und Hungerkrisen im vorindustriellen Europa. Versuch einer Synopsis*, Hamburg 1974, pp. 267-301 and passim; P. Vilar, 'Réflexions sur la "crise de l'ancien type". "Inégalité des récoltes" et "sous-développement" ', in: *Conjoncture économique, structures sociales. Hommage à E. Labrousse*, Paris 1974, pp. 37-58.

**Production of manufactured goods:** K. Bücher, 'Gewerbe', in: *Handwörterbuch der Staatswissenschaften*, vol. 4, Jena ⁴1927, pp. 966-989 (still relevant today); M. Weber, *Economic History* (see above section on General Histories; still valuable in many respects); B. Geremek, *Le salariat dans l'artisanat parisien aux XIIIe-XVe siècles. Etude sur le marché de la main-d'oeuvre au Moyen Age*, Paris 1968, esp. pp. 13-25; R. Ennen, *Zünfte und Wettbewerb. Möglichkeiten und Grenzen zünftlerischer Wettbewerbsbeschränkungen im städtischen Handwerk und Gewerbe des Spät-mittelalters*, Köln 1971 (systematic survey); E. Schremmer, *Die Wirtschaft Bayerns. Vom hohen Mittelalter bis zum Beginn der Industrialisierung. Bergbau, Gewerbe, Handel*, München 1970, pp. 33-36, 472-479 (precise definitions of concepts); K. H. Kaufhold, *Das Handwerk der Stadt Hildesheim im 18. Jahrhundert. Eine wirtschaftsgeschichtliche Studie*, Göttingen 1968 (case study); on the gradual geographic expansion of manufacturing see Kriedte, Medick, Schlumbohm, *Industrialization*, pp. 6-9, 12-33.

**Commercial Capital:** K. Marx, 'Geschichtliches über das Kaufmannskapital', in: idem, *Das Kapital*, vol. 3 (Marx, Engels, Werke, vol. 25; still unsurpassed); see also J. Merrington, 'Town and Country in the Transition to Capitalism', in M. Dobb et al., *The Transition from Feudalism to Capitalism*, (see above), pp. 170-195.

**On the role of the state:** R. Robin, 'La nature de l'état à la fin de l'ancien régime: Formation sociale, état et transition', in: *dialectiques* 1/2, 1973, pp. 31-54; see also P. Anderson, *Lineages of the Absolutist State*, London 1974.

## Chapter 1

**Comprehensive studies:** F. Mauro, *Le XVIe siècle. Aspects économiques (Nouvelle Clio 32)*, Paris 1966 (with extensive bibliography); H. A. Miskimin, *The Economy of Later Renaissance Europe, 1460-1600*, Cambridge 1977 (useful survey); for the Mediterranean see esp. the main work of the Annales school: F. Braudel, *The Mediterranean and the Mediterranean World in the Age of Philip II*, vols. 1-2, London 1976.

**1.1 Surveys:** Reinhard et al., *Histoire générale*,(see abve section on General Histories), pp. 108-127; Guillaume, Poussou, *Démographie*, (see above section on General Histories), pp. 111-115.

**Specialized studies:** F. Koerner, 'Die Bevölkerungsverteilung in Thüringen am Ausgang des 16. Jahrhunderts', in: *Wiss. Veröffentlichungen des Deutschen Instituts für Landeskunde NF* 15/16, 1958, pp. 178-315; A. Croix, *Nantes et le Pays nantais au XVIe siècle. Etude démographique*, Paris 1974; idem, *La Bretagne aux XVIe et XVIIe siècles. La vie, la mort, la foi*, vols. 1-2, Paris 1981; see also below the literature for Table 2.

**Control of population growth:** G. Mackenroth, *Bevölkerungslehre. Theorie, Soziologie und Statistik der Bevölkerung*, Berlin 1953, pp. 408-432; J. Haynal, 'European Marriage Patterns in Perspective', in: *Population in History*, ed. E. A. Wrigley, (see above section on General Histories), pp. 101-143; see esp. J. Dupâquier, 'De l'animal à l'homme: le mécanisme autorégulateur des populations traditionelles', in: *Revue de l'Institut de Sociologie* 45, 1972, pp. 177-211; see also Bois, *Crise*, (see above Introduction), p. 331, note 5.

**1.2 General:** Abel, (see above section on Agricultural History); Slicher van Bath, *Agrarian History*, (see above section on Agricultural History), pp. 195-205, as well as the agrarian histories of individual countries listed above in section on General Histories.

**Enclosure movement in England:** See despite many qualifications which have since been added: R. H. Tawney, *The Agrarian Problem in the Sixteenth Century*, New York 1967 ([1]1912) and also L. Stone's introduction to the new edition; strongly influenced by Tawney: B. Moore, *Social Origins of Dictatorship and Democracy. Lord and Peasant in the Making of the Modern World*, London 1967, pp. 3-14; on improvements in agriculture see the somewhat controversial book by E. Kerridge, *The Agricultural Revolution*, London 1967; see also idem, *Agrarian Problems in the Sixteenth Century and After*, London 1969 (with documents); J. A. Yelling, *Common Fields and Enclosure*, London 1977; based on the 'property rights' approach: C. J. Dahlman, *The Open Field System and Beyond*, Cambridge 1980; J. A. Yelling, 'Rationality in the Common Fields', in: *EcHR*, 2nd Ser., 35, 1982, pp. 409-415.

**France:** Esp. the grand hypotheses in: E. Le Roy Ladurie, *Les paysans de Languedoc*, vols. 1-2, Paris 1966 (abr. pb. edition, Paris 1969) and J. Jacquart, *La crise rurale en Ile-de-France 1550-1670*, Paris 1974; see also L. Merle, *Le métairie et l'évolution agraire de la Gâtine poitevine de la fin du Moyen Age à la Révolution*, Paris 1958: G. Cabourdin, *Terre et hommes en Lorraine 1550-1635. Toulois et Comte de Vaudemont*, vols. 1-2, Nancy 1977 and G. Durand, *Vin, vigne et vignerons en Lyonnais et Beaujolais (XVIe-XVIIIe siècles)*, Lyon 1979; for a synthesis see E. Le Roy Ladurie, 'Les paysans français du XVIe siècle', in: *Conjoncture économique* (see above Introduction), pp. 333-352.

**Southern Europe:** J. Klein, *The Mesta. A Study in Spanish Economic History, 1273-1836*, Cambridge, Mass., 1920; B. Bennassar, *Valladolid au siècle d'or. Une ville de Castille et sa campagne au XVIe siècle*, Paris 1967, pp. 307-328; R. Romano, 'Agricoltura e contadini nell'Italia del XV e del XVI secolo', in: idem, *Tra due crisi: l'Italia del rinascimento*, Torino 1971, pp. 51-68; F. McArdle, *Altopascio. A Study in Tuscan Rural Society, 1587-1784*, Cambridge 1978, and the important anthology by C. Poni, *Fossi e cavedagne benedicon le campagne. Studi di storia rurale*, Bologna 1982.

**Western Central Europe:** D. Saalfeld, *Bauernwirtschaft und Gutsbetrieb in vorindustrieller Zeit*, Stuttgart 1960 (on the Principality of Brunswick) and A. Strobel, *Agrarverfassung im Übergang. Studien zur Agrargeschichte des badischen Breisgaus vom Beginn des 16. bis zum Ausang des 18. Jahrhunderts*, Freiburg 1972.

**Netherlands:** B. H. Slicher van Bath, 'The Rise of Intensive Husbandry in the Low Countries', in: *Britain and the Netherlands*, ed. J. S. Bromley and E. H. Kossmann, London 1960, pp. 130-153; see esp. J. de Vries, *The Dutch Rural Economy in the Golden Age, 1500-1700*, New Haven 1974 (based on the model of increasing specialization).

**Re-feudalization of agrarian structures east of the River Elbe:** J. Topolski, 'La réféodalisation dans l'économie des grands domaines en Europe centrale et orientale (XVIe-XVIIIe ss.)', in: *Studia Historiae Oeconomicae* 6, 1971, pp. 51-63 (survey); *Le deuxième servage en Europe centrale et orientale* (Recherches inter-nationales à la lumière du marxisme 63/64), Paris 1970 (a commendable anthology); M. Małowist, 'The Economic and Social Development of the Baltic Countries from the Fifteenth to the Seventeenth Centuries', in: *EcHR*, 2nd Ser., 12, 1958/59, pp. 177-189; for a critique of the 'colonial theory', as presented by Małowist in particular, see J. Topolski, 'Commerce des denrées agricoles et croissance économique de la zone baltique aux XVIe et XVIIe siècles', in: *AnnESC* 29, 1974, pp. 425-436. The East German debate of the fifties on the nature of the *Vorwerk* economy (feudal or capitalist) is still interesting; see J. Nichtweiss, 'Zur Frage der zweiten Leibeigenschaft und des sog. preussischen Weges der Entwicklung des Kapitalismus in der Landwirtschaft Ostdeutschlands', in: *Z. für Geschichtswissenschaft* 1, 1953, pp. 687-717; J. Kuczynski, 'Zum Aufsatz von Johannes Nichtweiss über die zweite Leibeigenschaft', in: ibid. 2, 1954, pp. 467-471; J. Nichtweiss, 'Reply to Jürgen Kuczynski', in: ibid., pp. 471-476, as well as further contributions in: ibid. 3-5, 1955-1957 (Engl. transl. of these articles now in: *Review* 3. 1, 1979); see also B. Zientara, 'Z zagadnień spornych tzw. "wtórnego poddaństwa" w Europie Środkowej' [Some problems of the "second bondage" in Central Europe], in: *Przegląd Historyczny* 47, 1956, pp. 3-47 (with abstract in French and an excellent survey of earlier research). Specialized studies: H. Harnisch, 'Die Gutsherrschaft in Brandenburg', in: *JbWG* 1969, 4, pp. 117-147; see also H. Rosenberg, 'The Rise of the Junkers in Brandenburg-Prussia, 1410-1653', in: *American Historical Review* 49, 1943, pp. 1-22, 228-242, now extended and published as: 'Die Ausprägung der Junkerherrschaft in Brandenburg-Preussen, 1410-1618', in: idem, *Machteliten und Wirtschaftskonjunkturen. Studien zur neueren deutschen Sozial- und Wirt-*

*schaftsgeschichte*, Göttingen 1978, pp. 24-82, 298-308; A. Wyczański, *Studia nad folwarkiem szlacheckim w Polsce w latach 1500-1580 [Studies on the 'Vorwerk' of the Nobility in Poland in the Years 1500-1580]*, Warsaw 1960 (synopsis in French in: *AnnESC* 18, 1963, pp. 81-87); L. Zytkowicz, *Studia nad gospodarstwem wiejskim w dobrach kościelnych XVI w. [Studies in the Agrarian Economy on the Estates of the Church in the 16th century]*, Warsaw 1962 (with abstract in French); J. A. Tichonov, 'Die Feudalrente in Zentralrussland zur Zeit der Entstehung der Leibeigenschaft', in: *JbWG* 1974, 4, pp. 184-201, as well as the superb survey by C. Goercke, in: *Russland*, ed. C. Goercke et al. (Fischer Weltgeschichte, vol. 31), Frankfurt 1972, pp. 130-138, 149-157. W. Kula's model of the *Vorwerk* economy in Poland is of fundamental importance; see idem, *Theorie économique du système féodal. Pour un modèle de l'économie polonaise, 16e-18e siècle*, Paris 1970 (Polish 1962; Engl. transl: *An Economic Theory of the Feudal System*, London 1976).

**Cattle trade:** H. Wiese and J. Bolts, *Rinderhandel und Rinderhaltung in nord-westeuropäischen Küstengebieten vom 15. bis zum 19. Jahrhundert*, Stuttgart 1966; *Internationaler Ochsenhandel (1350-1750)*, ed. E. Westermann, Stuttgart 1979.

**1.3 Upper Germany:** see the excellent surveys by E. Schremmer, in: *Handbuch der bayerischen Geschichte*, ed. M. Spindler, vol. 3, 1-2, München 1971, pp. 477-503, 1073-1100, 1371-1380; on the Fuggers (apart from the hardly manageable biographies by G. von Pölnitz): idem, *Die Fugger*, Frankfurt 1960; L. Schick, *Un grand homme d'affaires au début du XVIe siècles, Jacob Fugger*, Paris 1957; R. Hildebrandt, *Die "Georg Fuggerschen Erben". Ihre kaufmännische Tätigkeit und soziale Position 1555-1600*, Berlin 1966; R. Mandrou, *Les Fuggers, Propriétaires fonciers en Souabe 1560-1618. Etude de comportements socio-économiques à la fin du XVIe siècle*, Paris 1969, as well as the chapter on the Fuggers which is still interesting in: R. Ehrenberg, *Das Zeitalter der Fugger, Geldkapital und Creditverkehr im 16. Jahrhundert*, vols. 1-2, Jena ³1922 (¹1896); a much abridged version was published in English as: *Capital and Finance in the Age of the Renaissance*, New York 1928.

**Textile industry:** H. Heaton, *The Yorkshire Woollen and Worsted Industries*, Oxford 1920; E. Coornaert, *Un centre industriel d'autrefois. La draperie-sayetterie d'Hondschoote (XIVe-XVIIIe siècles)*, Paris 1930; W. Troeltsch, *Die Calwer Zeughandlungskompagnie und ihre Arbeiter. Studien zur Gewerbe- und Sozial-geschichte Altwürttembergs*, Jena 1897 (three fundamental regional studies); for the evolution of the "new draperies" see D. C. Coleman, 'An Innovation and its Diffusion: the "New Draperies"', in: *EcHR* 2nd Ser., 22, 1969, pp. 417-429; on the English textiles exports see R. Davis, *English Overseas Trade, 1500-1700*, London 1973, and the sources for Table 8 below; for the linen industry: E. Sabbe, *Histoire de l'industrie linière en Belgique*, Brussels 1945; G. Aubin and A. Kunze, *Leinenerzeugung und Leinenabsatz im östlichen Mitteldeutschland zur Zeit der Zunftkäufe. Ein Beitrag zur industriellen Kolonisation des deutschen Ostens*, Stuttgart 1940 (very important); on the origins of the relocation to the countryside see G. Heitz, *Ländliche Leinenproduktion in Sachsen (1470-1555)*, Berlin 1961; H. Aubin, 'Die Anfänge der grossen schlesischen Leinenweberei und -handlung', in: *VSWG* 35, 1942, pp. 105-178, and H. Kisch, 'The Textile Industries in Silesia and the Rhineland: A Comparative Study in Industrialization (with a Postscriptum)', in: Kriedte, Medick, Schlumbohm, *Industrialization*, pp. 178-200.

**Mining and Metals:** R. Sprandel, *Das Eisengewerbe im Mittelalter*, Stuttgart 1968; *Schwerpunkte der Eisengewinnung und Eisenverarbeitung in Europa, 1500-1650*, ed. H. Kellenbenz, Köln 1974; J. U. Nef, 'Silver Production in Central Europe, 1450-1618', in: *Journal of Political Economy* 49, 1941, pp. 575-591; E. Westermann, *Das Eislebener Garkupfer und seine Bedeutung für den europäischen Kupfermarkt, 1460-1560*, Köln 1971; *Schwerpunkte der Kupferproduktion und des Kupferhandels in Europa, 1500-1650*, ed. H. Kellenbenz, Köln 1977; of special interest: R. Hildebrandt, 'Augsburger und Nürnberger Kupferhandel, 1500-1619. Produktion, Marktanteile und Finanzierung im Verleich zweier Städte und ihrer wirtschaftlichen Führungsschicht', in: ibid., pp. 190-224; on the structure of enterprises and production relations see J. Strieder, *Studien zur Geschichte kapitalistischer Organisationsformen. Monopole, Kartelle und Aktiengesellschaften im Mittelalter und zu Beginn der Neuzeit*, München ²1925, and M. Mitterauer, 'Produktionsweise, Siedlungsstruktur und Sozialformen im österreichischen Montanwesen des Mittelalters und der fruhen Neuzeit', in: *Österreichisches Montanwesen. Produktion, Verteilung, Sozialformen*, ed. M. Mitterauer, München 1974, pp. 234-315; on Nürnberg in particular: H. Aubin, 'Die Stückwerker von Nürnberg bis ins 17. Jahrhundert', in: *Beiträge zur Wirtschafts-und Stadtgeschichte. Festschrift für H. Ammann*, Wiesbaden 1965, pp. 333-352; very important: M. Myška, 'Pre-industrial Iron-Making in the Czech Lands: The Labour Force and Production Relations circa 1350-circa 1840' in: *PP* 82, 1979, pp. 44-72; Mining: J. U. Nef, *The Rise of the British Coal Industry*, vols. 1-2, London 1932; J. Lejeune, *La formation du capitalisme moderne dans la principauté de Liège au XVIe siècle*, Paris 1939.

**Commerce:** P. Jeannin, *Les Marchands au XVIe siècle*, Paris 1957 (excellent synthesis); good surveys by K. Glamann, in: *FEcHE* 2, 1974, pp. 427-526, and *CEcHE* 5, 1977, pp. 185-289; complementary: P. Pach, 'The Shifting of International Trade Routes in the 15th-17th Centuries', in: *Acta historica* 14, 1968, pp. 287-321; for the Mediterranean see F. Braudel and R. Romano, *Navires et marchandises à l'entrée du port de Livourne (1547-1611)*, Paris 1951; for East-Central Europe see the anthology *Der Aussenhandel Ostmitteleuropas, 1450-1650*, ed. I. Bog, Köln 1971; A. Attman, *The Russian and Polish Markets in International Trade, 1500-1650*, Göteborg 1973; A. Maczak, *Między Gdańskiem a Sundem. Studia nad handlem bałtycki, od połowy XVI do połowy XVII w. [Between Danzig and the Sound. Studies in the Baltic Trade from the Middle of 16th to the Middle of 17th Century]*, Warsaw 1972 (with synopsis in Engl.); see also P. Jeannin, 'The Sea-borne and Overland Trade Routes of Northern Europe in the XVIth and XVIIth Centuries', in: *JEuEcH* 11, 1982, pp. 5-59.

**Overseas Expansion:** P. Chaunu, *L'expansion européenne du XIIIe au XVe siècle* (Nouvelle Clio 26), Paris 1969; idem, *Conquête et exploitation des nouveaux mondes (XVIe siècle)* (Nouvelle Clio 26 bis), Paris ²1976 (two superb textbooks with extensive bibliographies); for Spain see the work by H. and P. Chaunu (essential, but very difficult to use) *Séville et l'Atlantique (1504-1650)*, vols. 1-8, 2, 2, Paris 1955-1960; drastically abridged edition: *Séville et l'Amérique aux XVIe et XVIIe siècles*, Paris 1977; complementary: idem, *Les Philippines et le Pacifique des Ibériques*, vols. 1-2, Paris 1960-1966; for Portugal most important: V. M. Godinho, *L'économie de l'empire portugais aux XVe et XVIe siècles*, Paris 1969; see also the comprehensive study by C. R. Boxer, *The Portuguese Seaborne Empire, 1415-1825*, London 1969; important observations on individual aspects in P. Vilar, *Or et monnaie dans l'histoire, 1450-1920*, Paris 1974, pp. 57ff (Engl. transl.: *A History of Gold and Money*, London 1976) and idem, 'The Age of Don Quixote', in: *Essays in European Economic History, 1500-1800*, ed. P. Earle, Oxford 1974, pp. 100-112; on the involvement of foreign capital see the contributions by J. Heers et al. in: *Les aspects internationaux de la découverte océanique aux XVe et XVI siècles*, ed. M. Mollat and P. Adam, Paris 1966, pp. 273-374; on the system of unequal division of labour which emerged in the 16th century, see Wallerstein, *Modern World-System* (see above Introduction) and A. G. Frank, *World Accumulation, 1492-1789*, New York 1978 (quite close to Wallerstein's conceptualization).

**Antwerp and Amsterdam:** H. van der Wee, *The Growth of the Antwerp Market and the European Economy (Fourteenth-sixteenth Centuries)*, vols. 1-3, Louvain 1963 (indispensable); complementary: idem, 'Das Phänomen des Wachstums und der Stagnation im Lichte der Antwerpener und südniederländischen Wirtschaft des 16. Jahrhunderts', in: *VSWG* 54, 1967, pp. 203-249; on the rise of Holland see the works by M. Małowist, in: idem, *Croissance et régression en Europe. XIVe-XVIIe siècles. Recueil d'articles*, Paris 1972, pp. 91-173; H. Kellenbenz, 'Spanien, die nördlichen Niederlande und der skandinavisch-baltische Raum in der Weltwirtschaft und Politik um 1600', in: *VSWG* 41, 1954, pp. 289-332; see also A. A. Christensen, *Dutch Trade to the Baltic about 1600. Studies in the Sound Toll Register and Dutch Shipping Records*, Copenhagen 1941.

**Credit and Finance:** The work by Ehrenberg (see above 1.3) is still unsurpassed; see also the syntheses by G. Parker, in: *FEcHE* 2, 1974, pp. 527-594, and H. Van der Wee, in: *CEcHE* 5, 1977, pp. 290-392; for Antwerp: idem, 'Anvers et les innovations de la technique financière aux XVIe et XVIIe siècles', in: *AnnESC* 22, 1967, pp. 1067-1089; for Lyons the great study by R. Gascon, *Grand Commerce et vie urbaine au XVIe siècle. Lyon et ses marchands*, vols. 1-2, Paris 1971; for the Genoeses: J.-G. Da Silva, *Banque et crédit en Italie au XVIIe siècle*, vols. 1-2 Paris 1969.

**1.4** Monetary theory, as an explanation of the **price revolution,** predominated into the 1960s; see G. Wiebe, *Zur Geschichte der Preisrevolution des XVI. und XVII. Jahrhunderts*, Leipzig 1895 (essential at its time); see esp. E. J. Hamilton, *American Treasure and the Price Revolution in Spain, 1501-1650*, Cambridge, Mass., 1934; F. Braudel and F. C. Spooner, 'Les métaux monétaires et l'économie du XVIe siècle', in: *X Congresso Internazionale di Scienze Storiche, Roma, 4-11 settembre 1955. Relazioni*, vol. 4, Florence 1955, pp. 233-264; idem, in: *CEcHE* 4, 1966, pp. 442-456. It is only during the last two decades that, following W. Abel's lead, those who try to relate the development to manufacturing and commerce have gained ground; see esp. I. Hammarström, 'The "Price Revolution" of the Sixteenth Centrury: Some Swedish Evidence', in: *Scandinavian EcHR* 5, 1957, pp. 118-154; s.a. R. B. Outhwaite, *Inflation in Tudor and Early Stuart England*, London 1969; *The Price Revolution in Sixteenth-Century England*, ed. P. H. Ramsey, London 1971 (the articles in this volume are not all exclusively concerned with England); see also the subtle contribution by M. Morineau, in: *Histoire économique et sociale de la France* (see above section on General Histories), vol. 1, 2, pp. 867-1018. On the debate of Hamilton's position and that of his follower J. M. Keynes see esp. P. Vilar, 'Problems of the Formation of Capitalism', in: *PP* 10, 1956, pp. 15-38.

**Statistics of precious metal imports** from America are currently compiled by M. Morineau; see idem, 'Gazettes hollandaises trésors americains', in: *Anuario de historia economica y social* 2, 1969, pp. 289-361; 3, 1970, pp. 139-209, and idem, *Histoire économique et sociale du monde* (see above section on General Histories), vol. 2, pp. 80-85.

**Rising ground-rent:** E. Kerridge, 'The Movement of Rent, 1540-160', in: *EcHR* 2nd Ser., 6, 1953/54, pp. 16-34; Ch. Heimpel, *Die Entwicklung der Einnahmen und Ausgaben des Heiliggeistspitals zu Biberach an der Riss von 1500 bis 1630*, Stuttgart 1966.

**Decline of real wages:** D. Saalfeld, 'Die Wandlungen der Preis- und Lohnstruktur während des 16. Jahrhunderts in Deutschland', in: *Beiträge zu Wirtschaftswachstum und Wirtschaftsstruktur im 16. und 19. Jahrhundert*, ed. W. Fischer, Berlin 1971, pp. 9-28; E. H. Phelps Brown and Sh. V. Hopkins, 'Seven Centuries of the Prices of Consumables, compared with Builders' Wage-rates', in: *Economica NS* 23, 1956, pp. 296-314; idem, in: ibid. 24, 1957, pp. 289-306 and 26, 1959, pp. 18-37; D. Woodward, 'Wage Rates and Living Standards in Pre-industrial England', in: *PP* 91, 1981, pp. 28-46; M. Baulant, 'Le salaire des ouvriers du bâtiment à Paris de 1400 à 1726', in: *AnnESC* 26, 1971, pp. 463-483.

Reconstruction of **agricultural production** with the help of tithes: *Les fluctuations du produit de la dîme. Conjoncture décimale et domaniale de la fin du Moyen Age au XVII e siècle*, ed. J. Goy and E. Roy Ladurie, Paris 1972; E. Le Roy Ladurie and J. Goy, *Tithe and Agrarian History from the Fourteenth to the Nineteenth Century. An Essay in Comparative History*, Cambridge 1981; Bois, *Crise* (see above Introduction), pp. 111-123, 329-342; H. Neveux, *Vie et declin d'une structure économique. Les grains du Cambrésis (fin du XIVe—début du XVIIe siècle)*, Paris 1980; for Poland the estimates by J. Topolski, 'Croissance économique de la Pologne du Xe au XXe siècle', in: *Studia historiae oeconomicae* 2, 1967, pp. 3-29; see also the contributions to the relevant subject area 'Peasant, Dues, Tithes and Trends in Agricultural Production in Pre-industrial Societies', in: *Proceedings of the Seventh International Economic History Congress*, ed. M. Flinn, vol. 1, Edinburgh 1978, pp. 111-161; now complete: *Prestations paysannes, dîmes, rente foncière et mouvement de la production agricole à l'époque préindustrielle*, ed. J. Goy and E. Le Roy Ladurie, vols. 2-1, Paris 1982.

**Food crisis at beginning of 1570s:** Abel, *Massenarmut* (see above Introduction), pp. 70-98; comprehensive interpretation: D. M. Palliser, 'Tawney's Century: Brave New World or Malthusian Trap?', in: *EcHR*, 2nd Ser., 35, 1982, pp. 339-353 (in taking issue with the works by Tawney, F. J. Fisher et al., unfortunately confined to England).

**Social development:** H. Kamen, *The Iron Century. Social Change in Europe, 1550-1660*, London 1971 (good general survey); regarding the growth of the lower classes (as a result of population growth and the accumulation process) see the author's notes in: Kriedte, Medick, Schumbohm, *Industrialization* (see above Introduction), pp. 15f. with footnotes 14 and 15; on the problem of poverty see J.-P. Gutton, *La société et les pauvres. L'example de la généralité de Lyon (1534-1789)*, Paris 1971; idem, *La société et les pauvres en Europe (XVe-XVIIIe siècles)*, Paris 1974; Th. Fischer, *Städtische Armut und Armenfürsorge im 15. und 16. Jahrhundert. Sozialgeschichtliche Untersuchungen am Beispiel der Städte Basel, Freiburg i. Br. und Strassburg*, Göttingen 1979.

**Nobility:** L. Stone, *The Crisis of the Aristocracy, 1558-1641*, London 1965, abridged: Oxford 1967 (indispensable); on the gentry, apart from R. H. Tawney, 'The Rise of the Gentry, 1558-1640', in: *EcHR* 11, 1914, pp. 1-38 (the starting point of a debate which continues to this day) see the summary by G. E. Mingay, *The Gentry. The Rise and Fall of a Ruling Class*, London 1976; for Poland: A. Mączak, 'Zur Grundeigentumsstruktur in Polen im 16. bis 18. Jahrhundert', in: *JbWG* 1967, 4, pp. 11-161.

**Towns:** for England, the survey by P. Clark and P. Slack, *English Towns* (see above Introduction); of paradigmatic importance: Gascon, *Lyon* (see above section 1.3) and Bennassar, *Valladolid* (see above section 1.2).

**Peasants War:** D. W. Sabean, *Landbesitz und Gesellschaft am Vorabend des Bauernkriegs. Eine Studie der sozialen Verhältnisse im südlichen Oberschwaben in den Jahren vor 1525*, Stuttgart 1972, and P. Blickle, *Die Revolution von 1525*, München 1977.

**Status system:** L. Stone, 'Social Mobility in England, 1500-1700', in: *PP* 33, 1966, pp. 16-55.

# Chapter 2

Excellent **survey** by J. de Vries, *The Economy of Europe in an Age of Crisis*, Cambridge 1976; ditto: Kamen, *Iron Century* (see above Section 1.4). **Crisis of 1619/22:** R. Romano, 'Tra XVI e XVII secolo. Una crisi economica: 1619-1622', in: *Rivista storica italiana* 74, 1962, pp. 480-531, Engl. transl, in: *The General Crisis of the Seventeenth Century*, ed. G. Parker and L. M. Smith, London 1978, pp. 165-225; B. E. Supple, *Commercial Crisis and Change in England, 1600-1642. A Study in the Instability of a Mercantile Economy*, Cambridge 1959; Abel, *Massenarmut* (see above Introduction), pp. 130-147.

**2.1 General surveys** in Reinhard et al., *Histoire générale* (see above section on General Histories), pp. 146-196; Guillaume, Poussou, *Démographie* (see above section on General Histories), pp. 115-118, 135ff.; for Germany: G. Franz, *Der Dreissigjährige Krieg und das deutsche Volk. Untersuchungen zur Bevölkerungs- und Agrargeschichte*, Stuttgart ⁴1979; for France now most important: J. Dupâquier, *La population rurale du Bassin Parisien à l'époque de Louis XIV*, Paris 1979; for England see the pioneering study by E. A. Wrigley, 'Family Limitation in Pre-industrial England', im: *EcHR* 2nd Ser., 19, 1966, pp. 82-109, and more recently: D. Levine, *Family Formation in an Age of Nascent Capitalism*, New York 1977, pp. 103-115.

On **proto-industrial population problems** idem, op. cit., pp. 1-15, 58-87, and H. Medick, in: Kriedte, Medick, Schlumbohm, *Industrialization*, (s. above Introduction), pp. 74-93.

**2.2 General:** Abel, *Fluctuations*, (see above section on General Histories); Slicher van Bath, *Agrarian History* (see above section on General Histories), pp. 206-220, and the agrarian histories of individual countries (see above section on General Histories).

On the **development of the agricultural product** see above 1.4; see also H. -H. Wächter, *Ostpreussische Domänenvorwerke im 16. und 17. Jahrhundert*, Würzburg 1958, and J. Topolski, *Gospodarstwo wiejskie w dobrach arcybiskupstwa gnieźnieńskiego od XVI do XVIII wieku [Agriculture on the estates of the Archbishopric Gnesen from 16th to 18th Century]*, Poznan 1958 (with French synopsis).

**International commodity exchange:** J. A. Faber, 'The Decline of the Baltic Grain Trade in the Second Half of the 17th Century', in: *Acta Historiae Neerlandica* 1, 1966. pp. 108-131.

**England:** A. H. John, 'The Course of Agricultural Change, 1660-1760', in: *Essays in Agrarian History*, ed. W. E. Minchinton, vol. 1. Newton Abbot 1968, pp. 223-253; E. L. Jones, 'Agriculture and Economic Growth in England, 1660-1750: Agricultural Change,' in: *JEcH* 25, 1965, pp. 1-18; *Agriculture and Economic Growth in England, 1650-1815*, ed. E. L. Jones, London 1967 (excellent anthology, but neglects relations of production); H. J. Habakkuk, 'La disparition du paysan anglais', in: *AnnESC* 20, 1965, pp. 649-663 (indispensable).

**East-Central and Eastern Europe:** for the regions east of the River Elbe see Franz, *Dreissigjähriger Krieg* (see above 2.1), pp. 114-127 (but gives Thirty Years' War too much weight); for Poland: J. Topolski, 'La régression économique en Pologne du XVIe au XVIIIe siècle', in: *Acta Poloniae Historica* 7, 1962, pp. 28-49; Z. Cwiek, *Z dziejów wsi koronneij XVII wieku [On the history of the crown village in the 17th*

*Century]*, Warsaw 1966; for Bohemia: W. Stark, *Ursprung und Aufstieg des land-wirtschaftlichen Grossbetriebs in den Böhmischen Ländern*, Brünn 1934; for Russia: Goehrke, in: *Russland* (see above 1.2), pp. 162–170.

**2.3 On the decreasing importance of East-Central Europe:** Zs. P. Pach, 'Diminishing Share of East-Central Europe in the 17th-Century International Trade', in: *Acta Historica* 16, 1970, pp. 289–306.

**The Decline of Italy and Spain:** C. M. Cipolla, 'The Economic Decline of Italy', in: *Crisis and Change in the Venetian Economy in the 16th and 17th Centuries*, ed. B. Pullan, London 1968, pp. 127–145 (ibid. also further articles); idem; *Before the Industrial Revolution* (see above section on General Histories), pp. 236–244; J. H. Elliot, 'The Decline of Spain', in: *PP* 20, 1961, pp. 52–75; more differentiated: H. Kamen, 'The Decline of Spain: A Historical Myth?', in: *PP* 81, 1978, pp. 24–50; see also the ensuing debate in: ibid. 91, 1981, pp. 171–185.

**Central and Western Europe:** for Upper Germany see E. Schremmer, in: *Handbuch der bayerischen Geschichte* (see above 1.3), vol. 3, 1–2, pp. 504–512, 1100–1117, 1381–1386; P. Deyon, 'La production manufacturière en France au XVIIe siècle et ses problèmes', in: *XVIIe siècle* 70/71, 1966, pp. 47–63; idem., *Amiens, capitale provinciale. Etude su la société urbaine au 17e siècle*, Paris 1967; P. Goubert, *Beauvais et le Beauvaisis de 1600 à 1730*, vol. 1–2, Paris 1960; abridged version: *Cent mille provinciaux au XVIIe siècle* . . . . Paris 1968 (two studies of fundamental importance); see also A. Lottin, *Chavatte, ouvrier lillois, un contemporain de Louis XIV*, Paris 1979 (evaluation of the diary of a wool weaver).

**Proto-Industrialization:** Apart from F. F. Mendels, 'Proto-industrialization: The First Phase of the Industrialization Process', in: *JEcH* 32, 1972, pp. 241–261, and Ch. Tilly and R. Tilly, 'Agenda for European Economic History in the 1970s', in: ibid. 31, 1971, pp. 184–198, see Kriedte, Medick, Schlumbohm, *Industrialization* (see above Introduction), passim, in particular on the origins the contribution by the author, in: ibid., pp. 12–37; F. F. Mendels, 'Aux origines de la proto-industrialisation', in: *Bulletin du Centre d'histoire économique et sociale de la région lyonnaise* 2, 1978, pp. 1–21; see also the conference proceedings: 'Industrie et artisans ruraux', in: *Deuxième Conférence Internationale d'histoire économique, Aix-en-Provence, 1962*, vol. 2, Paris 1965, pp. 363–484, and *Agrarisches Nebengewerbe und Formen der Reagrarisierung im Spätmittelalter und 19./20. Jahrhundert*, ed. H. Kellenbenz, Stuttgart 1975; on the decline of Leiden, see Ch. Wilson, 'Cloth Production and International Competition in the Seventeenth Century', in: *EcHR* 2nd Ser. 13, 1960/61, pp. 209–221; for the development of the trades in the northern Netherlands and in England see, e.g., van Houtte, *Economic History* (see above section on General Histories) and Pollard and Crossley, *Wealth of Britain (see above section on General Histories)*.

**Trade with the Baltic area:** P. Jeannin, 'Les comptes du Sund comme source pour la construction d'indices généraux de l'activité économique en Europe (XVIe-XVIIIe siècle)', in: *Revue Historique* 231, 1964, pp. 55–102, 307–340 (fundamental); see also Faber, *Decline* (see above 2.2) and M. Morineau, in: *Histoire économique et sociale du monde* (see above section on General Histories), vol. 2, pp. 89–94.

**Overseas expansion:** F. Mauro, 'Towards an "Intercontinental Model": European Overseas Expansion between 1500 and 1800', in: *EcHR* 2nd Ser., 14, 1961/62, pp. 1–17 (important); see also idem, *L'expansion européenne 1600–1870* (Nouvelle Clio 27), Paris 1964; for the Atlantic economic area: D. A. Farnie, 'The Commercial Empire of the Atlantic, 1607–1783', in: *EcHR* 2nd Ser., 15, 1962/63, pp. 205/218; K. G. Davies, *The North Atlantic World in Seventeenth Century*, Minneapolis 1974 (at present the best synthesis available); for Brazil: F. Mauro, *Le Portugal et l'Atlantique au XVIIe siècle (1570-1670).* *Etude économique*, Paris 1960 (indispensable); for the Caribbean: R. Pares, *Merchants and Planters*, Cambridge 1960; R. S. Dunn, *Sugar and Slaves. The Rise of the Planter Class in the English West Indies, 1624-1713*, Chapel Hill 1972; R. B. Sheridan, *Sugar and Slavery. An Economic History of the British West Indies, 1623-1775*, Aylesbury 1974; M. Devèze, *Antilles, Guyanes, la Mer des Caraibes de 1492 a 1789*, Paris 1977, as well as the numerous works by G. Debien on the French Antilles (quoted in Devèze, op. cit., p. 377); for North America: C. P. Nettels, *The Roots of American Civilization. A History of American Colonial Life*, New York [2]1963 ([1]1938) and G. M. Walton and J. F. Shepherd, *The Economic Rise of Early America*, Cambridge 1979.

Interest in the **slave trade** has been revived since Ph.D. Curtin outlined its quantitative dimensions more sharply for the first time in his *The Atlantic Slave Trade. A Census*, Madison 1969; see e.g. the anthologies *Race and Slavery in the Western Hemisphere: Quantitative Studies*, ed. St. L. Engerman and E. D. Genovese, Princeton 1975; *La traite des noirs par l'Atlantique. Nouvelles Approches*, Paris 1976; *The Uncommon Market. Essays in the Economic History of the Atlantic Slave Trade*, ed. H. A. Germery and J. S. Hogendorn, New York 1979; different in nature, but not less stimulating was E. Williams, *Capitalism and Slavery*, London 1964 (1944), even if the later Prime Minister of Trinidad and Tobago linked slave trade and industrialization too directly. On the triangular trade: K. G. Davies, *The Royal African Company*, London 1957.

**Relations between Europe and Asia:** D. Rothermund, *Europa und Asien im Zeitalter des Merkantilismus*, Darmstadt 1978 (excellent summary); more detailed: H. Furber, *Rival Empires of Trade in the Orient, 1600-1800*, Minneapolis 1976; A. R. Disney, *Twilight of the Pepper Empire. Portuguese Trade in Southwest India in the Early Seventeenth Century*, Cambridge, Mass., 1978; on the penetration of the trading companies into Asia see N. Steensgaard, *The Asian Trade Revolution of the Seventeenth Century. The East India Companies and the Decline of the Caravan Trade*, Chicago 1974 (indispensable); on the two East India Companies and their trade with Asia see K. Glamann, *Dutch Asiatic Trade, 1620-1740*, Copenhagen 1958, and K. N. Chaudhuri, *The Trading World of Asia and the English East India Company, 1660-1760*, Cambridge 1978.

On the **trading companies** in general see E. L. J. Coornaert, in: *CEcHE* 4, 1967, pp. 223-274; see also Steensgaard, op. cit., pp. 114-153; *Companies and Trade. Essays on Overseas Trading Companies during the Ancien Régime*, ed. L. Blusse and F. Gaastra, The Hague 1981; L. Dermigny and K. Glamann, 'Le fonctionnement des compagnies des Indes', in: *Sociétés et compagnies de commerce en Orient et dans l'Océan Indien*, ed. M. Mollat, Paris 1970, pp. 443-479.

On the **export trade of the European metropoles** see Davis, *Overseas Trade* (see above 1.3); idem, 'English Foreign Trade, 1600-1700', in: *EcHR* 2nd Ser., 7, 1954/55, pp. 150-166; *The Growth of English Overseas Trade in the Seventeenth and Eighteenth Centuries*, ed. W. E. Minchinton, London 1969 (very useful anthology); J. Delumeau, 'Le commerce extérieur français au XVIIe siècle', in: *XVIIe siècle* 70/71, 1966, pp. 81-105.

On the **position of the Netherlands in the world economy of the 17th century** see Ch. Wilson, *The Dutch Republic and the Civilisation of the Seventeenth Century*, London 1968; C. R. Boxer, *The Dutch Seaborne Empire, 1600-1800*, London 1965 (good survey); see also A. -E. Sayous, 'Le rôle d'Amsterdam dans l'histoire du capitalisme commercial et financier', in: *Revue Historique* 183, 1938, pp. 242-280; V. Barbour,

*Capitalism in Amsterdam in the Seventeenth Century*, Baltimore 1950; *Dutch Capitalism and World Capitalism. Capitalisme hollandais et capitalisme mondial*, ed. M. Aymard, Cambridge 1982; on the Amsterdam "Wisselbank" see J. G. van Dillen, 'The Bank of Amsterdam', in: *History of the Principal Public Banks*, ed. J. G. van Dillen, 'The Bank of Amsterdam', in: *History of the Principal Public Banks*, ed. J. G. van Dillen, The Hague 1934, pp. 79–123; on the Stock Exchange see the introduction to N. W. Posthumus, *Inquiry into the History of Prices in Holland*, vol. 1, Leiden 1946; on the struggles with England, see esp. Ch. Wilson, *Profit and Power. A Study of England and the Dutch Wars*, London 1957; on the decline in the 18th century, idem 'The Decline of the Netherlands', in: idem, *Economic History and the Historian. Collected Essays*, London 1969, pp. 22–47 (the best survey); more detailed: J. de Vries, *De economische achteruitgang der Republiek in de achttiende eeuw*, Leiden ²1968 (1959).

**The Rise of England:** apart from the works already quoted, see R. Davis, *The Rise of the English Shipping Industry in the Seventeenth and Eighteenth Centuries*, London 1962 (important); K. G. Davies, 'Joint Stock Investment in the Late Seventeenth Century', in: *EcHR* 2nd Ser., 4, 1951/52, pp. 283–301; J. Clapham, *The Bank of England. A History*, vol. 1, Cambridge 1944; P. G. M. Dickson, *The Financial Revolution in England. A Study in the Development of Public Credit, 1688-1756*, London 1967 (fundamental); see also E. Schulin, *Handelsstaat England. Das politische Interesse der Nation am Aussenhandel vom 16. bis ins frühe 18. Jahrhundert*, Wiesbaden 1969 (analysis of the tract literature).

2.4 The starting point of the debate on the **Crisis of the 17th Century** was the important article by E. J. Hobsbawm, 'The Crisis of the Seventeenth Century', in: *Crisis in Europe, 1560-1660. Essays from Past and Present*, ed. T. Aston, London 1965, pp. 1–58 (1954); supplementary: idem, 'The Seventeenth Century in the Development of Capitalism', in: *Science and Society* 24, 1969, pp. 97–112. In this picture of the crisis, Hobsbawm failed to give sufficient weight to its demographic, agrarian, Malthusian and social aspects. It was only in the ensuing discussion that these trends were taken into account; see the anthologies *Crisis in Europe* (see above) and *General Crisis* (see above 2) and the comprehensive study by M. Hroch and J. Petráň, *17 století—krize feudální společnosti?* [The 17th Century—Crisis of Feudal Society?], Prague 1976; extended version in German: *Das 17. Jahrhundert. Krise der feudalen Gesellschaft*, Hamburg 1981. On various aspects see Abel, *Agrarkrisen* (see above section on General Histories); see also the regional studies by Goubert, Le Roy Ladurie, Jacquart (see above 2.3 and 1.2); N. Steensgaard, 'The Seventeenth-Century Crisis', in: *General Crisis* (see above 2), pp. 26–56 (stresses pressures through tax, the crisis not one of production, but if distribution), and A. Wyczański, 'W sprawie kryzysu XVII stulecia ['On the Crisis of the 17th Century'], in: *Kwartalnik Historyczny* 69, 1962, pp. 656–672 (on the burdening of the peasants with the consequences of economic recession); supplementary: idem, *Polska—rzeczą pospolitą szlachecka 1454-1764* [Poland—a republic of the nobility, 1454-1764], Warsaw 1965, pp. 199–210, 301–326. On the significance of the Thirty Years' War see H. Haan, 'Prosperität und Dreissigjähriger Krieg', in: *GG* 7, 1981, pp. 91–118.

On the **crisis of peasant society** see the French dissertations quoted above and P. Goubert, 'The French Peasantry of the Seventeenth Century: A regional Example', in: *PP* 10, 1956, pp. 55–77, and I. Gieysztorowa, 'Guerre et régression en Masovie, aux XVIe et XVIIe siècles'; in: *AnnESC* 13, 1958, pp. 651–668; on Germany the notes in: Franz, *Dreissigjähriger Krieg* (see above 2.1), pp. 107–114; for Italy, the important study by G. Delille, *Croissance d'une société rurale. Montesarchio et la vallée caudine aux XVIIe et XVIIIe siècles*, Naples 1973.

With regard to the **popular uprisings in France**, a lively debate was caused by the book of the Russian historian R. F. Porshnev, *Les soulèvements populaires en France de 1623 à 1648*, Paris 1963; see, apart from works by R. Mousnier (e.g. idem, *Fureurs paysannes. Les paysans dans les révoltes du XVIIe siècle* [France, Russia, China], Paris 1967, the regional studies, esp. Y.-M. Bercé, *Histoire des Croquants. Etude des soulevèments populaires au XVIIe siècle dans le sud-ouest de la France*, vol. 1-2, Geneva 1974; see also idem, *Croquants et nu-pieds. Les soulevèments paysans en France du XVIe au XIXe siècle*, Paris 1974 (annotated extracts from sources); *comparatiste:* C.S.L. Davies, 'Peasant Revolt in France and England: A Comparison', in: *Agricultural History Review* 21, 1973, pp. 122-134.

**"Nationalization"** and **"Oligarchization":** J. Meyer, *Noblesse et pouvoirs dans l'Europe d'ancien régime*, Paris 1974; D. J. Roorda, 'The Ruling Classes in Holland in the Seventeenth Century', in: *Britain and the Netherlands* (see above 1.2), vol. 2, Groningen 1964, pp. 109-132; and esp. Stone, *Social Mobility* (see above 1.2); see also H.-Ch. Schröder, 'Die neuere englische Geschichte im Lichte einiger Modernisierungstheoreme', in: *Studien zum Beginn der modernen Welt*, ed. R. Koselleck, Stuttgart 1977, pp. 30-65 (an excellent survey).

## Chapter 3

**3.1 Surveys** in: Reinhard et al., *Histoire générale* (see section on General Histories), pp. 197-271; Guillaume, Possou, *Démographie* (see above section on General Histories), pp. 118-121, 135ff.; J. Dupâquier, 'Les débuts de la grande aventure démographique', in: *Prospectives* 3, 1974, pp. 7-38; on England esp. D. Levine, 'Some Competing Models of Population Growth during the First Industrial Revolution', in: *JEuEcH* 7, 1978, pp. 499-516 (good survey of the state of research); on proto-industrial population see above 2.1; on the links between population growth and commercialization of agriculture in East-Central Europe see H. Harnisch, 'Bevölkerung und Wirtschaft. Über die Zusammenhänge zwischen sozialökonomischer und demographischer Entwicklung im Spätfeudalismus', in: *JbWG* 1975, pp. 57-87.

**3.2 General:** Abel, *Agrarkrisen* (see above section on General Histories), pp. 196-219; Slicher van Bath, *Agrarian History* (see above section on General Histories), pp. 221ff.; J. Blum, *The End of Old Order in Rural Europe*, Princeton 1978; for a comparative discussion of France, Central and Eastern Europe, see the review by J. de Vries in: *EcHR* 2nd Ser. 32, 1979, pp. 614f. and also the agrarian histories of individual countries (see above section on General Histories); on the development of the productive forces: M. Morineau, *Les faux-semblants d'un demarrage économique: agriculture et démographie en France au XVIIIe siècle*, Paris 1971 (contests the existence of an agricultural revolution in France, but not without underestimating the setback caused by the Revolution of 1789); R. Berthold, 'Einige Bemerkungen über den Entwicklungsstand des bäuerlichen Ackerbaus vor den Agrarreformen des 19. Jahrhunders', in: *Beiträge zur deutschen Wirtschafts- und Sozialgeschichte des 18. und 19. Jahrhunderts*, Berlin 1962, pp. 81-131; D. Saalfeld, 'Die Produktion und Intensität der Landwirtschaft in Deutschland und angrenzenden Gebieten um 1800', in: *Z. für Agrargeschichte und Agrarsoziologie* 15, 1967, pp. 137-175; **tax burdens:** F. -

W. Henning, *Dienste und Abgaben der Bauern im 18. Jahrhundert*, Stuttgart 1969; on the significance of serfdom still: R. Rosdolsky, 'The Distribution of the Agrarian Product in Feudalism', in: *JEcH* 11, 1951, pp. 247-265.

**England:** apart from the literature listed in sub-sections 1.2 and 2.2 above, see J. D. Chambers, and G. E. Mingay, *The Agricultural Revolution, 1750-1880*, London 1966; as a complementary study see the short outline by G. E. Mingay, *Enclosure and the Small Farmer in the Age of Industrial Revolution*, London 1968; J. M. Martin, 'The Small Landowner and Parliamentary Enclosure in Warwickshire', in: *EcHR* 2nd. Ser., 32, 1979, pp. 328-343; above all W. G. Hoskins, *The Midland Peasant. The Economic and Social History of a Leicestershire Village*, London 1957, ibid. pp. 247-276 on the process of enclosure (less irenical than Chambers and Mingay); among the older literature with a critical orientation: J. L. and B. Hammond, *The Village Labourer*, London 1978 (1911); for Scotland now: E. J. Hobsbawn, 'Capitalisme et agriculture: les réformateurs écossais au XVIIIe siècle', in: *AnnESC* 33, 1978, pp. 580-601.

**France:** esp. E. Le Roy Ladurie, 'Révoltes et contestations rurales en France de 1675 à 1788', in: *AnnESC* 29, 1974, pp. 6-22; R. Moore, *Social Origins* (see above 1.2), pp. 40-69; M. Block, 'La lutte pour l'individualisme agraire dans la France du XVIIIe siècle', in: *Annales d'histoire économique et sociale* 2, 1930, pp. 329-383, 511-556; H. Hinrichs, 'Die Ablösung von Eigentumsrechten. Zur Diskussion über die droits féodaux in Frankreich am Ende des Ancien Régime und in der Revolution', in: *Eigentum und Verfassung. Zur Eigentumsdiskussion im ausgehenden 18. Jahrhundert*, ed. R. Vierhaus, Göttingen 1972, pp. 112-178; see also G. van den Heuvel, *Grundprobleme der Französischen Bauernschaft 1730-1794. Soziale Differenzierung und sozio-ökonomischer Wandel vom Ancien Régime bis zur Revolution*, München 1982 (with a survey of research); for individual regions see Le Roy Ladurie, *Paysans de Languedoc* (see above 1.2); P. de Saint Jacob, *Les paysans de la Bourgogne du Nord au dernier siècle de l'ancien régime*, Paris 1960; A. Poitrineau, *La vie rurale en basse Auvergne au XVIIIe siècle*, vols. 1-2, Paris 1965.

**Germany:** see above 1.2; A. Straub, *Das badische Oberland im 18. Jahrhundert. Die Transformation einer bäuerlichen Gesellschaft vor der Industrialisierung*, Husum 1977; *Landwirtschaft und Kapitalismus. Zur Entwicklung der ökonomischen und sozialen Verhältnisse in der Magdeburger Börde vom Ausgang des 18. Jahrhunderts bis zum Ende des ersten Weltkrieges*, ed. H. -J. Rach and B. Weissel, vol. 1, Berlin 1978 (see esp. the contribution by H. Harnisch); H. -H. Müller, *Märkische Landwirtschaft vor den Agrarreformen von 1807. Entwicklungstendenzen des Ackerbaus in der zweiten Hälfte des 18. Jahrhunderts*, Potsdam 1967, as well as the supplementary articles by idem, in: *JbWG*, 1963-1966; of paradigmatic significance H. Harnisch, *Die Herrschaft Boitzenburg. Untersuchungen zur Entwicklung der sozialökonomischen Struktur ländlicher Gebiete in der Mark Brandenburg vom 14. bis zum 19. Jahrhundert*, Weimar 1968; for Silesia still unsurpassed: J. Ziekursch, *Hundert Jahre schlesischer Agrargeschichte. Vom Hubertusburger Frieden bis zum Abschluss der Bauernbefreiung*, Breslau ²1927.

**Russia:** M Confino, *Domaines et seigneurs en Russie vers la fin du XVIIIe siècle. Etude de structures agraires et de mentalités économiques*, Paris 1963. On the **beginnings of agrarian reform** H. Schissler, *Preussische Agrargesellschaft im Wandel. Wirtschaftliche, gesellschaftliche und politische Transformationsprozesse von 1763 bis 1847*, Göttingen 1978 (theory-oriented summary of latest research); H. Harnisch, 'Die agrarpolitischen Reformmassnahmen der preussischen Staatsführung in dem Jahrzehnt vor 1806/07', in: *JbWG* 3, 1977, pp. 129-153 (fundamental); K. Grünberg,

*Die Bauernbefreiung und die Auflösung des gutsherrlich-bäuerlichen Verhältnisses in Böhmen, Mähren und Schlesien*, vols. 1-2, Leipzig 1893-1894; see also R. Rozdolski, *Die grosse Steuer- und Agrarreform Josefs II. Ein Kapitel zur österreichischen Wirtschaftsgeschichte* , Warsaw 1961; E. M. Link, *The Emancipation of the Austrian Peasant, 1740-1798*, New York 1974, as well as the summary by Chr. Dipper, *Die Bauernbefreiung in Deutschland, 1790-1850*, Stuttgart 1980

**3.3 Mercantilism:** E. F. Heckscher, *Der Merkantilismus*, vols. 1-2, Jena 1932 (indispensable standard work; Engl. version: *Mercantilism*, vols. 1-2, rev. ed. London 1955); see also *Revisions in Mercantilism*, ed. D. C. Coleman, London 1969 (pb.; a collection of essential essays); esp. A. Gerschenkron, *Europe in the Russian Mirror. Four Lectures in Economic History*, Cambridge 1970, pp. 62-96; latest study: F. Blaich, *Die Epoche des Merkantilismus*, Wiesbaden 1973.

On the **development of the Atlantic economic area:** apart from the literature listed in sub-section 2.3 above, see R. Anstey, *The Atlantic Slave Trade and British Abolition*, London 1975 (Part 1); above all S. Drescher, *Econocide. British Slavery in the Era of Abolition*, Pittsburgh 1977; see also the collections: H. S. Klein, *The Middle Passage, Comparative Studies in the Atlantic Slave Trade*, Princeton 1978, and *Liverpool, the African Slave Trade, and Abolition. Essays to illustrate Current Knowledge and Research*, ed. R. Anstey and P.E.H. Hair, n.p. 1976; on the economy of the United States see D.C. North, *The Economic Growth of the United States, 1790-1860*, Englewood Cliffs 1961, Part 1; Portugal and Spain: M. Morineau, 'Or brésilien et gazettes hollandaises', in: *Revue d'histoire moderne et contemporaine* 25, 1978, pp. 3-60; V. M. Godinho, 'Le Portugal, les flottes du sucre et les flottes de l'or (1670-1770)', in: *AnnESC* 5, 1950, pp. 184-197; H.E.S. Fisher, *The Portugal Trade. A Study of Anglo-Portuguese Commerce, 1700-1770*, London 1971; R. Herr, *The Eighteenth-Century Revolution in Spain*, Princeton 1958, pp. 120-154; esp. Vilar, *Catalogne* (see above section on General Histories), vol. 3, and D. A. Brading, *Miners and Merchants in Bourbon Mexico, 1763-1810*, Cambridge 1971.

**Asia:** see the literature listed in sub-section 2.3 above; see also H. Furber, *John Company at Work. A Study of European Expansion in India in the Late Eighteenth Century*, Cambridge 1951 (indispensable); P. Nightingale, *Trade and Empire in Western India, 1784-1806*, Cambridge 1970 (important, esp. for the underlying causes of English expansionist policies); P. J. Marshall, *East Indian Fortunes. The British in Bengal in the Eighteenth Century*, Oxford 1976 (cautious in its judgment); L. Dermigny, *La Chine et l'Occident. Le commerce à Canton au XVIIIe siècle*, vols. 1-3, Paris 1964 (important, but difficult to use).

On the **foreign trade of the European metropoles:** R. Davies, 'English Trade, 1700-1774', in: *EcHR* 2nd Ser., 15, 1962/63, pp. 285-303 (fundamental); idem, *The Industrial Revolution and British Overseas Trade*, Leicester 1979; Deane and Cole, *British Economic Growth* (see above section on General Histories), pp. 41-59; P. Léon, 'Structure du commerce extérieur et évolution industrielle de la France à la fin du XVIIIe siècle', in: *Conjoncture économique* (see above Introduction), pp. 407-432 (most important); see also M. Morineau, '1750, 1787: Un changement important des structures de l'exportation française dans le monde saisi d'après les états de la balance du commerce', in: *Vom Ancien Régime zur französischen Revolution. Forschungen und Perspektiven*, ed. E. Hinrichs et al., Göttingen 1978, pp. 395-412; J. Tarrade, *Le commerce colonial de la France à la fin de l'Ancien Régime. L'évolution du régime de "L'Eclusif" de 1763 à 1789*, vols. 1-2, Paris 1972; on the re-export trade see esp. P. Butel, *Les négociants bordelais, l'Europe et les îles au XVIIIe siècle*, Paris 1974; on the rise of

Hamburg see W. Kresse, *Materialien zur Entwicklungsgeschichte der Hamburger Handelsflotte, 1765-1823,* Hamburg 1966, and H. Pohl, *Die Beziehungen Hamburgs zu Spanien und dem spanischen Amerika in der Zeit von 1740-1806,* Wiesbaden 1963. **Credit and Finance:** apart from anthologies listed in sub-section 1.3 above see J. Sperling, 'The International Payments Mechanism in the Seventeenth and Eighteenth Centuries', in: *EcHR* 2nd Ser., 14, 1961/62, pp. 446-468; for England see the essential monograph by Dickson, *Financial Revolution* (see above 2.3), as well as *Capital Formation in the Industrial Revolution,* ed. F. Crouzet, London 1972 (excellent short reader, see esp. the contributions by Crouzet and S. Pollard).

On the *development of manufacturing* general: Deane and Cole, *British Economic Growth* (see above section on General Histories), pp. 50-62; P. Léon, in: *Histoire économique et sociale de la France* (see above section on General Histories), vol. 2, pp. 217-266, 514-528; T. J. Markovitch, *Les industries lainières de Colbert à la Revolution,* Geneva 1976 (quantitative study); E. Schremmer, *Wirtschaft Bayerns* (see above Introduction); K. H. Kaufhold, *Das Gewerbe in Preussen um 1800,* Göttingen 1978 (essential synchronic study).

**Proto-Industrialization:** see literature listed in sub-section 2.3 above; on the driving forces behind proto-industrialization, see the author's contribution in: Kriedte, Medick, Schlumbohm, *Industrialization* (see above Introduction), pp. 23-37; on the proto-industrial familial economy, H. Medick, in: ibid., pp. 38-73; on production relations, J. Schlumbohm, in: ibid., pp. 34-125; on the investment strategy of the *Verleger* esp. S. D. Chapman, 'Industrial Capital before the Industrial Revolution: an Analysis of the Assets of a Thousand Textile Entrepreneurs', in: *Textile History and Economic History. Essays in Honour of Miss J. de Lacy Mann,* ed. N. B. Harte and K. G. Ponting, Manchester 1973, pp. 113-137; on the role of the towns, see P. Kriedte, 'Die Stadt im Prozess der europäischen Proto-Industrialiserung', in: *Die alte Stadt* 9, 1982, pp. 19-51; regional studies: apart from the works by Heaton and Troeltsch (see above 1.3) see A. P. Wadsworth, J.de Lacy Mann, *The Cotton Trade and Industrial Lancashire, 1600-1780,* Manchester 1931 (still the most interesting British study); R. G. Wilson, *Gentlemen Merchants. The Merchants Community in Leeds, 1700-1830,* Manchester 1971 (important for the textile industries in West Riding); P. Hudson, 'Proto-Industrialisation: the Case of the West Riding Wool Textile Industry in the 18th and early 19th Centuries', in: *History Workshop* 12, 1981, pp. 34-61; S. D. Chapman, 'The Genesis of the British Hosiery Industry', in: *Textile Industry* 3, 1972, pp. 7-50; idem, 'Enterprise and Innovation in the British Hosiery Industry, 1750-1850', in: ibid. 5, 1974, pp. 14-37; M. B. Rowlands, *Masters and Men in the West Midlands Metalware Trades before the Industrial Revolution,* Manchester 1975; D. Hey, *The Rural Metalworkers of the Sheffield Region. A Study of Rural Industry before the Industrial Revolution,* Leicester 1972; 'Aux origines de la révolution industrielle. Industrie rurale et fabriques', in: *Revue du Nord* 61, 1979, pp. 5-208; Aux origines de la révolution industrielle, Fasc. 2'. in: ibid. 63, 1981, pp. 5-251 (important collections of essays); Ph. Guignet, *Mines, manufactures et ouvriers du Valenciennois au XVIIIe siècle,* New York 1977; P. Bois, *Paysans de l'Ouest. Des structures économiques et sociales aux options politiques dépuis l'époque révolutionnaire dans la Sarthe,* Le Mans 1960 (abridged pb. edition, Paris 1971; contains important chapters on the linen industry); J. K. J. Thompson, *Clermont-de-Lodève, 1633-1798. Fluctuations in the Prosperity of a Languedocian Cloth-Making Town,* Cambridge 1982; H. Hasquin, *Une mutation. Le "Pays de Charleroi" aux XVIIe et XVIIIe siècles. Aux origines de la révolution industrielle en Belgique,* Brussels 1971; P. Lebrun, *L'industrie de la laine à Verviers pendant le XVIIIe et le début du XIXe siècle. Contribution a l'étude des* *origines de la révolution industrielle*, Liege 1948; F. F. Mendels, 'Agriculture and Peasant Industry in Eighteenth-Century Flanders', in: Kriedte, Medick, Schlumbohm, *Industrialization* (see above Introduction), pp. 161-177; H. Kisch, 'Das Erbe des Mittelalters, ein Hemmnis wirtschaftlicher Entwicklung: Aachens Tuchgewerbe vor 1790', in: *Rheinische Vierteljahrsblätter* 30, 1965, pp. 253-308; idem, 'Prussian Mercantilism and the Rise of the Krefeld Silk Industry: Variations on an Eighteenth-Century Theme' *Transactions of the American Philosophical Society* NS 58, 7, Philadelphia 1968; idem, 'From Monopoly to Laissez-faire: the Early Growth of the Wupper Valley Textile Trades', in: *JEuEcH* 1, 1972, pp. 298-407; K. H. Kaufhold, *Das Metallgewerbe der Grafschaft Mark im 18. und frühen 19. Jahrjundert*, Dortmund [1976] St. Reekers, 'Beiträge zur statistischen Darstellung der gewerblichen Wirtschaft Westfalens um 1800', Part 1-9, in: *Westfälische Forschungen* 17, 1964 pp. 83-176, 18, 1965, pp. 75-130; 19, 1966, pp. 27-78; 20, 1967, pp. 58-108; 21, 1968, pp. 98-161; 23, 1971, pp. 75-106; 25, 1973, pp. 59-167; 26, 1974, pp. 60-83; 29, 1978/79, pp. 24-118; J. Schlumbohm, 'Der saisonale Rhythmus der Leinenproduktion im Osnabrücker Land während des späten 18. und der esten Halfte des 19. Jahrhunderts', in: *Archiv für Sozialgeschichte* 19, 1979, pp. 263-298; A. Kunze, 'Vom Bauerndorf zum Weberdorf. Zur sozialen und wirtschaftlichen Struktur der Waldhufendörfer der südlichen Oberlausitz im 16., 17. und 18. Jahrhundert', in: *Oberlausitzer Forschungen. Beiträge zur Landesgeschichte*, ed. M. Reuther, Leipzig 1961, pp. 165-192, 350; B. Schöne, *Kultur und Lebensweise der Lausitzer Bandweber (1750-1850)*, Berlin 1977; Kisch, *Textile Industries* (see above 1.3); A. Klima, 'The Role of Domestic Industry in Bohemia in the Eighteenth Century', in: *EcHR* 2nd Ser., 27, 1974, pp. 48-56; M. Kulczykowski, *Andrychowski ośrodek płócienniczy w XVIII i XIX wieku[The Centre of the Linen Trade in Andrychów in the 18th and 19th Centuries]*, Wroclaw 1973, synopis in French in: *AnnESC* 24, 1969, pp. 61-69; V. K. Jacunskij, 'Formation en Russie de la grande industrie textile sur la base de la production rurale', in: *Deuxième Conférence* (see above 2.3), vol. 2, pp. 365-376; R. Braun, *Industrialisierung und Volksleben. Veränderungen der Lebensformen unter Einwirkung der textilindustriellen Heimarbeit in einem ländlichen Industriegebiet (Zürcher Oberland) vor 1800*, Göttingen ²1979 (essential reading for the world of the small manufacturers).

On the **Manufacturer** mainly in East-Central and Eastern Europe on which research was focused up to the 1960s, see, e.g., H. Krüger, *Zur Geschichte der Manufakturen und der Manufakturarbeiter in Preussen. Die mittleren Provinzen in der zweiten Hälfte des 18. Jahrhunderts*, Berlin 1958; R. Forberger, *Die Manufaktur in Sachsen vom Ende des 16. bis zum Anfang des 19. Jahrhunderts*, Berlin 1958; Schremmer, *Wirtschaft Bayerns* (see above Introduction), pp. 501-572; A. Klima, *Manufacturní obdobív Cechach [The Period of Manufacturers in Bohemia]*, Prague 1955; W. Kula, *Szkice o manufakturach w Polsce XVIII wieku [Sketches of the Manufactures in Poland in the 18th Century]*, Warsaw 1956.

On the **silk mills** see C. Poni, 'Archéologie de la fabrique: La diffusion des moulins à soie "alla bolognese" dans les Etats vénitiens du XVIe au XVIIIe siècle', in: *AnnESC* 27, 1972, pp. 1475-1496 and idem, 'All'origine del sistema di fabrica: Technologia e organizzazione produttiva dei mulini da seta nell'Italia settentrionale (sec. XVII-XVIII)', in: *Rivista Storica Italiana* 88, 1976, pp. 444-497.

On **textile printing** see esp. P. Caspard, 'L'accumulation du capital dans l'indiennage au XVIIIème siècle', in: *Revue du Nord* 61, 1979, pp. 115-124; idem, *La Fabrique-Neuve de Cortaillod, 1752-1854. Entreprise et profit pendant la révolution industrielle*, Paris 1979; idem, 'Die Fabrik auf dem Dorfe', in: *Wahrnehmungsformen und Protestverhalten. Studien zur Lage der Unterschichten im 18. und 19.*

*Jahrhundert*, ed. D. Puls, Frankfurt 1979, pp. 105-142; S. Chassagne, *La manufacture de toiles imprimées de Tournemine-lès-Angers (1752-1820). Etude d'une entreprise et d'une industrie au XVIIIe siècle*, Paris 1971; idem, *Oberkampf. Un entrepreneur capitaliste au siècle des lumières*, Paris 1980; now above all S. D. Chapman and S. Chassagne, *European Textile Printers in the Eighteenth Century: A Study of Peel and Oberkampf*, London 1981.

On the **beginning of the industrialization process in England** see P. Mantoux, *The Industrial Revolution in the Eighteenth Century. An Outline of the Beginnings of the Modern Factory System in England*, London 1961 (transl. from the French, 1906, 1928; still the best work in many respects, with an eye trained by Marxism and an extensive bibliographical appendix); D. S. Landes, *The Unbound Prometheus. Technological Change and Industrial Development in Western Europe from 1750 to the Present*, Cambridge 1969, esp. chapter 2 (the most important recent work); see also T. S. Ashton, *The Industrial Revolution, 1760-1830*, Oxford 1969; Ph. Deane, *The First Industrial Revolution*, Cambridge ²1979; P. Mathias, *The First Industrial Nation. An Economic History of Britain, 1700-1914*, London 1969; idem, *The Transformation of England. Essays in the Economic and Social History of England in the Eighteenth Century*, London 1979; other important studies: F. Crouzet, 'Angleterre et France au XVIIIe siècle. Essai d'analyse comparée de deux croissances économiques',in: *AnnESC* 21, 1966, pp. 254-291 (Engl. transl. in: *The Causes of the Industrial Revolution in England*, ed. R. M. Hartwell, London 1967, pp. 139-174); M. Lévy-Leboyer, 'Les processus d'industrialisation: le cas de l'Angleterre et de la France', in: *Revue Historique* 239, 1968, pp. 281-298; see also this author's contribution in: Kriedte, Medick, Schlumbohm, *Industrialization* (see above Introduction), pp. 136-145. On the leading sectors of the industrialization process: S. D. Chapman, *The Cotton Industry in the Industrial Revolution*, London 1972; M. M. Edwards, *The Growth of the British Cotton Trade, 1780-1815*, Manchester 1967; Th. S. Ashton, *Iron and Steel in the Industrial Revolution*, Manchester ⁴1968 (1924); Ch. K. Hyde, *Technological Change and the British Iron Industry, 1700-1870*, Princeton 1977.

*On the* **home market/foreign market question:** Hobsbawm, *Industry* (see above section on General Histories), pp. 42-54; D. C. Eversley, 'The Home Market and Economic Growth in England, 1750-1780', in: *Land, Labour and Population. Essays presented to J. D. Chambers*, London 1967, pp. 206-259, as well as P. Bairoch, 'Commerce international et genèse de la révolution industrielle anglaise', in: *AnnESC* 28, 1973, pp. 540-571; on the development of the English home market town now above all J. Thirsk, *Economic Policy and Projects. The Development of a Consumer Society in Early Modern England*, Oxford 1978; on the connection between import of Indian cotton, textile printing and industrialization see P. Leuillot, 'L'influence du commerce oriental sur l'économie occidentale', in: *Sociétés et compagnies* (see above 2.3), pp. 611-629.

**3.4 General:** Abel, *Fluctuations* (see above section on General Histories); Vilar, *Or* (see above 1.3), pp. 313ff.

**Ground-rent and wages:** Labrousse, *Esquisse* (see above Introduction), vol. 2, pp. 369-618; idem, in: *Histoire économique et sociale de la France*, vol. 2, pp. 473-497; E. W. Gilboy, *Wages in Eighteenth Century England*, Cambridge, Mass., 1934, as well as *The Standard of Living in Britain in the Industrial Revolution*, ed. A. J. Taylor, London 1975 (esp. the first two contributions); Henning, *Dienste* (see above 3.2), pp. 166-168; D. Saalfeld, 'Lebensstandard in Deutschland. Einkommensverhältnisse städtischer Populationen in der Übergangsperiode zum Industriezeitalter', in:

*Wirtschaftliche und soziale Strukturen im säkularen Wandel. Festschrift für W. Abel zum 70. Geburtstag*, vol. 2, Hannover 1974, pp. 417–443. On the continued **growth of the lower classes** see above 1.4; on individual towns see esp. M. Garden, *Lyon et les Lyonnais au XVIIIe siècle*, Paris 1970, abridged pb. edition: Paris 1975; J. -C. Perrot, *Genèse d'une ville moderne. Caen au XVIIIe siècle*, Paris 1975; D. Roche, *Le peuple de Paris. Essai sur la culture populaire au XVIIIe siècle*, Paris 1981; more particularly on the problem of poverty see J. Kaplow, *The Names of Kings. The Parisian Labouring Poor in the Eighteenth Century*, New York 1972, and above all O. H. Hufton, *The Poor of Eighteenth-Century France, 1750–1789*, Oxford 1974.

On the **world of the small manufacturers:** Schöne, *Kultur and Lebensweise* (see above 3.3); Braun, *Industrialisierung und Volksleben* (see above 3.3); H. Medick, in: Kriedte, Medick, Schlumbohm, *Industrialization* (see above Introduction), pp. 64–73; A. Griessinger, *Das symbolische Kapital der Ehre. Streikbewegungen und Kollektives Bewusstsein deutscher Handwerksgesellen im 18. Jahrhundert*, Frankfurt 1981. On the **problem of work-discipline and time:** E. P. Thompson, 'Time, Work-discipline, and Industrial Capitalism' in: *PP* 38, 1967, pp. 56–97.

On the **"moral economy of the crowd" and its forms of expression:** E. P. Thompson, 'The Moral Economy of the English Crowd in the Eighteenth Century', in: *PP* 50, 1971, pp. 76–136; see also L. A. Tilly, 'The Food Riot as a Form of Political Conflict in France', in: *Journal of Interdisciplinary History* 2, 1971/72, pp. 23–57. **Riots in the artisanal sector:** E. J. Hobsbawm, 'The Machine Breakers', in: *PP* 1952, pp. 57–70; see also W. J. Shelton, *English Hunger and Industrial Disorders. A Study of Social Conflict during the First Decade of George III's Reign*, London 1973.

On the **bourgeoisie of the Ancien Régime:** important general observations by R. Robin, *La société française en 1789: Semur-en-Auxois*, Paris 1970, pp. 15–54; see also M. Vovelle and D. Roche, 'Bourgeois, rentiers, propriétaires. Eléments pour la définition d'une catégorie sociale à la fin du XVIIIe siècle', in: *Actes du 84e congrès national des sociétés savantes. Section d'histoire moderne et contemporaine*, Paris 1960, pp. 419–452 (a comparison of Paris with le Marais and Chartres); A. Daumard and F. Furet, *Structures et relations sociales à Paris au milieu du XVIIIe siècle*, Paris 1961; emphasizing the dynamic aspect more strongly: M. Vovelle, 'L'Elite et le mensonge des mots', in: *AnnESC* 29, 1974, pp. 49–72; on England apart from the literature listed in sub-section 2.4 above, see H. Perkin, *The Origins of Modern English Society, 1780–1880*, London 1969, esp. chapter 2; on Central Europe see, e.g. F. G. Dreyfus, *Sociétés et mentalités à Mayence dans la seconde moitié du XVIIIe siècle*, Paris 1968; general analysis; R. Braun, 'Zur Einwirkung sozio-kultureller Umweltbedingungen auf das Unternehmerpotential und das Unternehmerverhalten', in: *Wirtschafts- und sozialgeschichtliche Probleme der frühen Industrialisierung*, ed. W. Fischer, Berlin 1968, pp. 247–284.

# Conclusion

On the **physical product** in England and France, see J. Marczewski, *Introduction à l'histoire quantitative*, Geneva 1965, pp. 86–109; on Central Europe see F. -W. Henning, 'Die Wirtschaftsstruktur mitteleuropäischer Gebiete an der Wende zum 19. Jahrhundert unter besonderer Berücksichtigung des gewerblichen Bereichs', in: *Beiträge zu Wirtschaftswachstum* (see above 1.4), pp. 101–167. For the following see also this author's contribution in: Kriedte, Medick, Schlumbohm, *Industrialization* (see above Introduction), pp. 135ff. as well as the notes for the introduction; on the role of the non-European world, see P. O'Brien, 'European Economic Development: The Contribution of the Periphery ', in: *EcHR* 2nd Ser., 35, 1982, pp. 1-18; on the significance of the French Revolution, see Moore, *Social Origins* (s.1.2), pp. 70ff.; E. Labrousse, 'The Evolution of the French Peasant Society from the Eighteenth Century to the Present', in: *French Society and Culture since the Old Regime*, ed. E. M. Acomb and M. L. Brown, New York 1966, pp. 44-66, and V. Hunecke, Antikapitalistische Strömungen in der Französischen Revolution. Neuere Kontroversen der Forschung', in: *GG* 4, 1978, pp. 291-323; on the crisis during the first half of the 19th century, see Abel, *Fluctuations* (see above section on General Histories); idem, *Massenarmut* (see above Introduction), pp. 302-396; this author, in: Kriedte, Medick, Schlumbohm, *Industrialization* (see above Introduction).

# Sources

## 1. Tables

**Table 1:** *The Fontana Economic History of Europe*, ed. C. E. Cipolla, vol. 2, London 1974, p. 33; ibid. vol. 3, 1973, p. 29; C. McEvedy and R. Jones, *Atlas of World Population History*, Harmondsworth 1978, pp. 41-114; *An Introduction to the Sources of European Economic History, 1500-1800*, vol. 1: *Western Europe*, ed. Ch. Wilson and G. Parker, London 1977; *European Demography and Economic Growth*, ed. W. R. Lee, London 1979, as well as the literature for individual countries.

**Table 2:** E. A. Wrigley, in: *Daedalus* 97, 2, 1968, pp. 559, 570, 574; D. Levine, *Family Formation in an Age of Nascent Capitalism*, New York 1977, pp. 123, 125; L. Henry, *Anciennes familles genevoises*, Paris 1956, pp. 55, 153, 156; T. H. Hollingsworth, *The Demography of the English Peerage*, London 1964, pp. 11, 56f., 66.

**Table 3:** B. H. Slicher van Bath, in: *Acta Historiae Neerlandica* 2, 1967, p. 95, here taken from the revised edition in: *The Cambridge Economic History of Europe*, vol. 5, ed. E. E. Rich and C. H. Wilson, Cambridge 1977, p. 81.

**Table 4:** W. G. Hoskins, *Provincial England*, London 1963, pp. 162f.

**Table 5:** J. Jacquart, *La crise rurale en Ile-de-France, 1550-1670*, Paris 1974, p. 106.

**Table 6:** A. Wyczański, *Studia nad folwarkiem szlacheckim w Polsce w latach 1500-1655*, Warsaw 1976, pp. 84, 104, 108, 109, 113; M. Kamler, *Folwark szlachecki w Wielkopolsce w latach 1580-1655*, Warsaw 1976, pp. 14f., 21, 162.

**Table 7:** H. van der Wee, *The Growth of the Antwerp Market and the European Economy*, vol. 1, Louvain 1963, p. 523.

**Table 8:** J. D. Gould, in: *EcHR* 2nd Ser., 24, 1971, p. 251 (at £6 sh13 4d. per shortcloth).

**Table 9:** *Tabeller over skibsfart og varetransport gennem Øresund, 1497-1660*, ed. N. E. Bang, vol. 2A, Copenhagen 1922, pp. 139-197; N. Steensgaard, *The Asian Trade Revolution of the Seventeenth Century*, Chicago 1974, pp. 155, 168; E. J. Hamilton, *American Treasure and the Price Revolution in Spain, 1501-1650*, Cambridge, Mass., 1934, p. 42; M. Morineau, in: *Histoire économique et sociale du monde*, ed. P. Léon, vol. 2, Paris 1978, p. 83; N. W. Posthumus, *Inquiry into the History of Prices in Holland*, vol. 2, Leiden 1964, pp. 768, 774, and H. H. Mauruschat, *Gewürze, Zucker und Salz im vorindustriellen Europa*, PhD. thesis (Economics) Göttingen 1975, appendix ibid., Table 3 and 6.

**Table 10:** R. Ehrenberg, *Das Zeitalter der Fugger*, vol. 1. Jena ³1922, pp. 146, 148, 394.

**Table 11:** E. Kerridge, in: *EcHR* 2nd Ser., 6, 1953/54, p. 28.

**Table 12:** K. Blaschke, *Bevölkerungsgeschichte von Sachsen bis zur industriellen Revolution*, Weimar 1967, pp. 190f.

**Table 13:** M. Spufford, *Contrasting Communities*, Cambridge 1974, pp. 167f.

**Table 14:** L. Stone, *The Crisis of the Aristocracy, 1558-1641*, London 1965, pp. 762, 764.

**Table 15:** G. E. Mingay, *The Gentry*, London 1976, p. 59 (following J. P. Cooper and F. M. L. Thompson).

**Table 16:** See Table 1.

**Table 17:** Levine, *Family Formation* (see Table 2), pp. 113, 97, 61; H. Charbonneau, *Tourouvre-au-Perche aux XVIIe et XVIIIe siècles*, Paris 1970, p. 73; M. Lachiver, *La population de Meulan du XVIIe au XIXe siècle*, Paris 1969, p. 139; A. E. Imhof, in: *Historische Demographie als Sozialgeschichte. Giessen und Umgebung vom 17. zum 19. Jahrhundert*, vol. 1, Darmstadt 1975, p. 315; Henry, *Familles* (see Table 2), p. 55; Hollingsworth, *Demography* (see Table 2), p. 11.

**Table 18:** J. D. Chambers, *The Vale of Trent*, Cambridge 1957, p. 20.

**Table 19:** H. K. Roessingk, *Inlandse tabak*, Wageningen 1976, p. 340.

**Table 20:** A. Wyczański, *Studia nad gospodarką starostwa korczyńskiego, 1500-1660*, Warsaw 1964, pp. 217, 221.

**Table 21:** N. W. Posthumus, *De geschiedenis van de leidsche lakenindustrie*, vols. 2-3, s-Gravenhage 1939, pp. 930f., 941, 1098.

**Table 22:** Ph.D. Curtin, *The Atlantic Slave Trade*, Madison 1969, p. 268; the figures for 1761/1810 corrected according to S. Drescher, *Econocide*, Pittsburgh 1977, p. 28, and R. Anstey, in: *EcHR* 2nd Ser., 30, 1977, p. 267.

**Table 23:** K. G. Davies, *The Royal African Company*, London 1957, pp. 350-363; the imports evaluated according to Davies, ibid., pp. 180f. (2.1), 364 (2.2; more detailed now D. Galenson, in: *EcHR* 2nd Ser., 32, 1979, pp. 241-249) and wholesale prices in Amsterdam (2.3).

**Table 24:** K. Glamann, *Dutch Asiatic Trade, 1620-1740*, Copenhagen 1958, pp. 13f.

**Table 25:** K. N. Chaudhuri, *The Trading World of Asia and the English East India Company, 1660-1760*, Cambridge 1978, pp. 507-549.

**Table 26:** R. Davis, in: *EcHR* 2nd Ser., 7, 1954/55, pp. 164f.

**Table 27:** E. Boody Schumpeter, *English Overseas Trade Statistics, 1697 to 1808*, Oxford 1960, pp. 15-18.

**Table 28:** M. Morineau, in: *Histoire économique et sociale et sociale de la France*, ed. F. Braudel and E. Labrousse, vols. 1, 2, Paris 1977, pp. 979f.

**Table 29:** A. Nowak, *Początki kryzysu sił wytwórczych na wsi wielkopolskiej w końcu XVI i pierwszej połowie XVII wieku*, Warsaw 1975, p. 218.

**Table 30:** G. King, *Two Tracts*, ed. G. E. Barnett, Cambridge, Mass., 1936, p. 31.

**Table 31:** See Table 1.

**Table 32:** Levine, *Family Formation* (see Table 2), pp. 74, 92.

**Table 33:** G. E. Mingay, in: *EcHR* 2nd Ser., 14, 1961/62, p. 481.

**Table 34:** H. Harnisch, *Die Herrschaft Boitzenburg*, Weimar 1968, pp. 168f.

**Table 35:** I. D. Koval'čenko, *Russkoe krest'yanstvo v pervoir polovine XIX v.*, Moskow 1967, pp. 62f.

**Table 36:** D. Richardson, in: *Liverpool, the African Slave Trade, and Abolition*, ed. R. Anstey and P. E. H. Hair, n.d. 1976, p. 78.

**Table 37:** L. Dermigny, *La Chine et l'Occident*, vol. 2, Paris 1964, p. 691.

**Table 38:** R. Davis, in: *EcHR* 2nd Ser., 15, 1962/63, pp. 300-303.

**Table 39:** R. Davis, op. cit., p. 292.

**Table 40:** P. Léon, in: *Conjoncture économique, structures sociales. Hommage à E. Labrousse*, Paris 1974, pp. 423-426.

**Table 41:** J. Hartmann, *Die kurmainzischen Ämter des mittleren und oberen Eichsfeldes*, Ph.D. thesis Halle 1961 (ts),pp. 160, 201; H. Godehardt, in: *Eichsfelder Heimathefte* 1970, p. 65.

**Table 42:** Ch. Engrand, in: *Revue du Nord* 61, 1979, pp. 62-68.

**Table 43:** E. Barkhausen, *Die Tuchindustrie in Montjoie, ihr Aufstieg und Niedergang*, Aachen 1925, p. 71.

**Table 44:** R. Heck, *Studia nad położeniem ekonomicznym lundności wiejskiej na Śląsku w XVI w.*, Wrocław 1959, p. 58; B. Kaczmarski, in: *Atlas historyczny Polski. Śląsk w końcu XVIII wieku*, ed. J. Janczak and T. Ładogórski, vols. 1, 2, Wrocław 1976, p. 59.

**Table 45:** A. Daumard and F. Furet, *Structures et relations sociales à Paris au milieu du XVIIIe siècle*, Paris 1961, pp. 18f.

## 2. Graphs

**Fig. 1:** W. Abel, *Agricultural Fluctuations in Europe from the Thirteenth to 'the Twentieth Centuries*, London 1980, pp. 360f.

**Fig. 2:** M. Lachiver, *Histoire de Meulan et de sa région par les textes*, Meulan 1965, p. 186; J. Dupâquier et al., *Mercuriales du Pays de France et du Vexin Français (1640-1792)*, Paris 1968, pp. 123-132.

**Fig. 3:** A. Lottin, *Chavatte, ouvrier lillois, un contemporain de Louis XIV*, Paris 1979, pp. 108, 121.

**Fig. 4:** *Tabeller* (see Table 9), vol. 2A, Copenhagen 1922, pp. 3-541; M. Bogucka, *Handel zagraniczny Gdańska w pierwszej połowie XVII wieku*, Wrocław 1970, p. 38, n. 32; Cz. Biernat, *Statystyka obrotu towarowego Gdańska w latach, 1651-1815*, Warsaw 1962, pp. 286f.; J. Pelc, *Ceny w Gdańsku w XVI i XVII wieku*, Lvóv 1937, p. 117.

**Fig. 5:** H. Wiese, in: idem and J. Bölts, *Rinderhandel und Rinderhaltung in nordwesteuropäischen Küstengebieten vom 15. bis zum 19. Jahrhundert*, Stuttgart 1966, pp. 61f.

**Fig. 6:** E. M. Carus-Wilson and O. Coleman, *England's Export Trade, 1275-1547*, Oxford 1963, pp. 112-119; J. D. Gould, *The Great Debasement*, Oxford 1970, pp. 120, 136; F. J. Fisher, in: *EcHR* 10, 1940, p. 96 and ibid., 2nd Ser., 3, 1950/51, p. 153; B. E. Supple, *Commercial Crisis and Change in England, 1600-1642*, Cambridge 1959, pp. 28, 258. The statistical basis for the period after 1606 is poor.

**Fig. 7:** E. Westermann, *Das Eislebener Garkupfer und seine Bedeutung für den europäischen Kupfermarkt, 1460-1560*, Köln 1971, pp. 255, 302, 319f.; J. Vlachovič, in: *Schwerpunkte der Kupferproduktion und des Kupferhandels in Europa, 1500-1650*, ed. H. Kellenbenz, Köln 1977, pp. 171, 408f.; see also R. Hildebrandt, in: ibid., p. 193. The decline of production in Schwaz was partly compensated for by the output in Röhrer Bühel and Radmer-on-Hasel. Whereas in 1501/10 ca. 95% of the copper produced in the Alpine region originated in Schwaz, it was only about 30% in 1611/20.

**Fig. 8:** H. and P. Chaunu, *Séville et l'Atlantique (1504-1650)*, vol. 6, 1, Paris 1956, p. 337 (the tonnage unweighted following M. Morineau's criticism).

**Fig. 9:** P. Bowden, in: *The Agrarian History of England and Wales*, ed. J. Thirsk, vol. 4, Cambridge 1967, p. 862.

**Fig. 10:** Hamilton, *American Treasure* (see Table 9), p. 34 (up to 1580); M. Morineau (see Table 9), p. 83 (from 1581; idem, in: *Revue d'histoire moderne et contemporaine* 25, 1978, p. 43 (for Brazil from 1701; maxima).

**Fig. 11:** E. H. Phelps Brown and Sh. V. Hopkins, in: *Economica* NS 23, 1956, pp. 312f. and ibid., 26, 1959, pp. 35f.

**Fig. 12:** B. Veyrassat-Herren, in: *Les fluctuations du produit de la dîme*, ed. J. Goy and E. Le Roy Ladurie, Paris 1972, pp. 99-101; A. Silbert, in: ibid., pp. 151f.; J. Goy and A.-L. Head-König, in: ibid., pp. 266-271.

**Fig. 13:** *Tabeller* (see Table 9), vol. 2A, Copenhagen 1922; *Tabeller over skibsfart og varetransport gennem Øresund, 1661-1783, og gennem Storebaelt, 1701-1748*, ed. N. E. Bang and K. Korst, vols. 2, 1-2, 2, 2, Copenhagen 1939-1953; F. Snapper,

*Oorlogsinvloeden op de overzeese handel van Holland 1551-1719*, Amsterdam 1959, pp. 312-315; Abel, *Fluctuations* (see Fig. 1), pp. 306f.

**Fig. 14:** Posthumus, *Geschiedenis* (see Table 21), vol. 2-3, pp. 129, 930f.; P. Deyon and A. Lottin, in: *Revue du Nord* 49, 1967, pp. 30-33; D. Sella, in: *AnnESC* 12, 1957, pp. 30f.

**Fig. 15:** Curtin, *Slave Trade* (see Table 22), pp. 116, 119, 216, 234; Drescher, *Econocide* (see Table 22), pp. 27f., 31; Anstey (see Table 22), p. 267.

**Fig. 16:** N. Steensgaard, in: *Scandinavian EcHR* 18, 1970, p. 9.

**Fig. 17:** P. Jeannin, in: *Revue Historique* 231, 1964, p. 333 with note 2, p. 332.

**Fig. 18:** Levine, *Family Formation* (see Table 2), p. 63.

**Fig. 19:** *British Sessional Papers. House of Commons 1836*, vol. 8, 2, p. 501; B. R. Mitchell in collaboration with Ph. Deane, *Abstract of British Historical Statistics*, Cambridge 1962, pp. 486-488.

**Fig. 20:** Boody Schumpeter, *Trade Statistics* (see Table 27), pp. 17f.; Morineau, (see Fig. 10). p. 43.

**Fig. 21:** Dermigny, *Chine* (see Table 37), vol. 2, pp. 521-524.

**Fig. 22:** Mitchell and Deane, *Abstract* (see Fig. 19), pp. 279-281.

**Fig. 23:** A. Kunze, in: *Oberlausitzer Forschungen*, ed. M. Reuther, Leipzig 1961, p. 187.

**Fig. 24:** *Schlesische Provinzialblätter* 31, 1800, pp. 9-12.

**Fig. 25:** P. Caspard, *La Fabrique-Neuve de Cortaillod, 1752-1854*, Paris 1979, pp. 186f., 195.

**Fig. 26:** Mitchell and Deane, *Abstract* (see Fig. 19), pp. 177f., 294.

**Fig. 27:** F. -K. Riemann, *Ackerbau und Viehhaltung im vorindustriellen Deutschland*, Kitzingen 1953, pp. 171, 175.

**Fig. 28:** E. W. Gilboy, in: *The Review of Economic Statistics* 18, 1936, p. 140.

# Index

Aachen, 39, 135, 139
Abel, W., 26, 52
Agricultural crisis, 11, 52ff., 65ff., 94
Agricultural prices, 4f., 27, 65, 92, 109, 137, 161
Agricultural revolution, 105ff.
Amiens, 12, 74
Amsterdam, 41, 45, 53, 77f., 86ff., 127ff.
Antwerp, 27, 32, 35, 41, 44, 46, 53, 89
Aristocracy, 56ff., 99f., 154
Arkwright, R., 142f., 152
Asiento, 81
Aubin, H., 39
Augsburg, 32, 35, 38, 51, 58, 74, 147

Balibar, E., 2
Banking, 46ff., 87ff., 128ff.
Bank of England, 90, 129
Bank of San Carlos (Madrid), 129
Bank of Scotland, 129
Bath, Slicher van, 26
Bloch, M., 23
Bodin, Jean, 18
Bohemia, 62, 70
Bois, G., 15, 53
Bourdieu, P., 151
Bourgeoisie, 154f.
Brandenburg (Mark), 28, 61, 69, 105, 112
Braudel, F., 46, 48, 59
Braun, R., 151
Bridgwater, Duke of, 115

Caisse d'Escompte, 129
Calw, 34, 36
Cambrésis, 53
Capitalist world-system, 1, 42ff., 71f., 82, 117f., 121ff.
Casa da India, 84
Chambers, J.D., 19
Charles V, 25, 47
Chaunu, P., 19

Chayanov, A.V., 2, 137
Child, J., 89
Chippenham, 55f.
Classes, see *social structure*
Coleman, D.C., 34
Colonialism, 13, 43ff., 79, 89, 95, 123ff., 145
Columbus, Chr., 42
Colyton, 20, 63f., 103
Compagnie des Indes, 85
Consbruch, 12
Cort, H., 143
Cortaillod, 140f.
Crompton, 143

Danzig, 27ff., 53, 57, 67
Darby, A., 143
Deane, Ph, 71
Defoe, D., 87, 154
Demographic change, 3f., 6ff., 19f., 53ff., 61ff., 73, 91, 101ff., 136, 146ff.
Dobb, M., 91, 138

East India Company, Dutch: 83f., 85ff., 121f.; English: 45, 83ff., 121ff.
Ehrenberg, R., 47
Enclosure, 22ff., 98, 106f., 111
Engels, F., 27
Estado da India, 44, 79

Factory system, 140ff., 152, 161
Feudal lords, 2ff., 10, 12, 19, 24, 26, 51, 59, 69, 97f., 110, 114, 146, 157
Feudal mode of production, 1ff., 8, 15f., 74f., 159, 161
Feudal obligations, 2, 16f., 92, 146; see also *serfdom*
Flanders, 35f., 66, 132
Florence, 40, 72
Forster, G., 135
Frankfurt, 8, 129, 149, 155

Frederick II (the Great), 115
Fronde, 74, 94
Fugger, 32f., 38, 47, 59

Gascon, R., 60
Geneva, 19, 20, 129
Genoa, 45ff., 72, 88
Genovesi, A., 9
Gentry, 56, 99f.
Giro- und Lehnbanco (Berlin), 129
Godelier, M., 142
Grain exports, 27ff., 40f., 53, 67, 114
Greer, L. de, 88
Guest, R., 142
Guicciardini, F., 25
Guilds, 9, 12, 14

Hamburg, 45, 53, 127, 149, 155
Hammond, J.L., 111
Hargreaves, J., 142
Hill, Chr., 89
Hobsbawm, E.J., 13, 75, 95f., 142, 145, 153
Hoffmann, W., 13
Hondschoote, 34, 74
Hudson Bay Company, 85, 89
Hüpeden, C.L.P., 136
Hurepoix, 24, 92

Industrial capitalism, 90, 115ff., 130f.,
    144, 154, 161
Industrial revolution, 16, 96, 142ff., 158,
    160
Inflation, 48ff., 94, 145f.
Iron production, 36, 78, 132, 141f.

John, A.H., 130

Kaufsystem, 36, 78, 116, 138
King, G., 77, 99f.
Kisch, H., 35
Koppelwirtschaft, 26, 108f., 113
Kula, W., 16, 57

Labrousse, E., 11, 106, 147
Land development, 21, 105f.
Landlords, see *feudal lords*
Languedoc, 24, 55, 62, 66, 92
Law, J., 129
Leicestershire, 23f., 57f., 104
Leiden, 34, 72, 76, 90, 131

Léon, P., 129
Le Roy Ladurie, E., 7, 55, 92, 111
Levant Company, 45
Liège, 39, 66, 135
Lille, 32, 34, 72, 74, 135
Live-stock farming, 14, 22, 24f., 30, 68, 96
London, 35, 45f., 77f., 86f., 90, 128ff.
Louis XIV, 74
Lyons, 46, 57f., 152

Malestroit, de, 18
Malthus, Th., 19, 53, 63, 92
Mansfeld, 37ff.
Marriage, 19f., 63f., 103f.
Manufaktur (manufacture), 116f., 139ff.,
    151ff.
Marx, K., 40, 52, 90, 131
Masovia, 62, 98
Merchant capitalism, 1, 9f., 13, 47f., 71f.,
    85ff., 95, 118, 123ff., 131, 138, 142, 148,
    153f., 159
Merrington, D., 10
Mesta, 25, 66
Meulan, 5, 63
Mevius, D., 69
Mining, 7, 32, 36ff., 43, 77f., 96, 115, 119,
    132
Modzelewski, K., 7
Moore, B., 160
Moravia, 70
More, Th., 22
Morineau, M., 127

Navigation Acts, 89
Neusohl, 37f.
Newcomen, Th., 144
Nuremberg, 32, 35, 39, 74
Nutritional standards, 52, 94, 146ff.

Open fields, 22, 68
Orelli, S. von, 151

Pares, R., 80
Paris, 8, 155
Peasant uprisings, 98
Philip II, 47
Pinto, I. de, 130
Po Valley, 21
Population, see *demographic change*
Postlethwayt, M., 118

Price revolution, 18, 23f., 48ff.
Proto-industrialisation, 13, 70ff., 90, 95, 98, 104ff., 117, 133ff., 142f., 154, 160f.
Purchasing system, see *Kaufsystem*
Putter-out, see *Verleger*

Quesnay, F., 10

Rattenberg, 37
Ravensberg, 12
Reconquista, 43
Re-exports, 86ff., 12ff., 144
Re-feudalization, 69, 75
Rent, 6, 24, 58f., 92, 111
Röhrer Bühel, 37
Romano, R., 25, 61
Royal African Company, 82, 85, 89, 148ff.
Rural industry, 12ff., 58, 64f., 96, 110, 133ff., 151ff.
Russell, J.C., 18
Russia Company, 45

Savery, Th., 144
Saxony, 30, 54f., 57, 61, 103, 128, 132f., 149, 152
Scheibler, J.H. & Sons, 139f.
Schroetter, F.L. von, 112
Schwaz, 37, 39
Self-exploitation, 2, 137
Senckenberg, J.C., 155
Serfdom, 2, 27f., 58f., 68f., 112f.
Shipping, 40, 67, 78, 86f., 117f., 120f., 127
Silesia, 13
Slavery, 17, 80ff., 118f., 145
Small-holders, 54ff., 74f., 100, 110f., 149ff.
Social structure, 55ff., 69, 99f., 154ff., 160
Sombart, W., 139
Spooner, F., 48
St. Malo, 13
Starvation, 4f., 20, 53f., 102f., 148ff.
State and taxation, 6, 15f., 58f., 73, 92f., 97ff., 115f., 156, 160
Steensgard, N., 85
Stone, L., 59
Stratification, see *social structure*
Szlachta, 29, 57

Taufers, 37
Terra Ferma, 20, 25
Textile manufacture, 12, 14, 23, 32ff., 72f., 76f., 90f., 95, 131ff., 139, 144f., 151f.; exports, 33ff., 84ff., 122, 144
Thompson, E.P., 153
Thornton, Th., 52
Thünen Circles, 26, 31, 108f.
Tilly, Ch. and R., 64
Topolski, J., 30
Trade, Asian: 44f., 78, 83f., 121ff.; Baltic: 27ff., 45, 70f., 78; Mediterranean: 32f., 71, 95; Trans-Atlantic: 42, 71, 73, 79f., 82, 118ff.
Treaty of Methuen, 117

Up-and-down husbandry, 22, 26
Urban craftsman, 8ff., 32, 39, 58, 74, 76, 90ff., 159

Verleger, 36, 95, 135ff., 142, 148, 153, 156
Vienna, 30, 52
Vilar, P., 5, 42f.
Village community, 2, 19, 75, 114
Vorwerk, 17, 27f., 30f., 70, 75, 93f., 98, 104, 111ff., 146, 159

Wages, 51f., 94f., 97, 146f.
Wage labour, 28, 39, 54, 58, 94, 110, 112, 151f., 158
Wallerstein, I., 121, 160
Wars, 20, 31; 58 (Peasants' War of 1525); 63, 89 (Anglo-Dutch); 94, 117 (Spanish War of Succession); 117 Austrian War of Succession); 117 (Seven Years' War); 126 (American War of Independence)
Watt, J., 144
Wee, H. van der, 44, 88
Weber, M., 9, 46, 158
Wilkinson, J., 143
Wilson, Ch., 128
Wisselbank, 88, 129
Wolf, J., 103
Wyczanski, A., 28

Zimmern Chronicle, 21
Zöllner, F., 138